DISCOVERING The AMERICAN PAST

A Look at the Evidence

SECOND EDITION

Volume I: To 1877

William Bruce Wheeler

University of Tennessee

Susan D. Becker

University of Tennessee

HOUGHTON MIFFLIN COMPANY   Boston

Dallas   Geneva, Illinois   Palo Alto   Princeton, New Jersey

Acknowledgments

CHAPTER ONE

Source 1: From *Journal of First Voyage to America, by Christopher Columbus* (New Canaan, CT: Albert Boni and Charles Boni, 1924), pp. 24–29. Reprinted by permission.

Source 3: From Hernando Cortés, *Five Letters, 1519–1526,* trans. J. Bayard Morris (New York: W. W. Norton), pp. 21–25, 56–57.

Source 4: From *The Complete Works of Captain John Smith,* edited by Philip L. Barbour, Vol. I. Copyright 1986, pp. 160–175. Reprinted by permission of University of North Carolina Press.

Source 5: German woodcut, 1509. The British Library.

Source 6: Adoration of the Magi. Cathedral of Viseu, Viseu, Museu de Grao Vasco, Portugal.

Source 7: German woodcut, 1517–1518. Stuttgart, Graphisone Sammlung, Stratsgalerie, Stuttgart.

Acknowledgments continue following page 306.

Cover photograph courtesy of I.N. Phelps Stokes Collection; Miriam & Ira D. Wallach Division of Art, Prints & Photographs; The New York Public Library; Astor, Lenox and Tilden Foundations.

Printed in the U.S.A.
Library of Congress Catalog Card Number: 89-080971
ISBN: 0-395-43298-7

ABCDEFGHIJ-B-9543210/89

CONTENTS

CHAPTER SIX

The Clash of Political Philosophies:
The Debate over Universal Suffrage
in New York (1821)   112

CHAPTER SEVEN

Away from Home:
The Working Girls of Lowell   146

CHAPTER EIGHT

The "Peculiar Institution": Slaves Tell Their Own Story

CHAPTER NINE

War and Manifest Destiny: A Problem in Causation

PREFACE

The response of students and teachers to the first edition of *Discovering the American Past: A Look at the Evidence* (1986) has been extremely gratifying, thus warranting a second edition of the book. That response has confirmed our suspicion that students have a strong desire to learn about United States history *and* will put forth considerable effort to do so, provided that the nation's history is presented in a way that they find both challenging and stimulating. Students appear to enjoy "doing history" rather than simply being told about it. In other words, students respond to the challenge to be *active learners,* and not merely passive vessels into which information is poured.

We began this book with an urgent desire to tap the already existing interest students have in the past and a firm belief that the study of American history can contribute to an understanding of the contemporary world. It does this in two important ways: (1) it can put the present in perspective by giving us an appreciation of the trends, forces, and people who served to shape contemporary American life, and (2) it can teach us the skills we need in order to examine and analyze our present environment and culture. Our goals in this book, then, are to interest students in historical issues and to help them develop and sharpen the crucial skills that people need to live in today's society.

Those of us who are historians find ourselves surrounded by a wealth of primary evidence that can be used to reconstruct American history. This evidence ranges from the more traditional sources such as letters, newspapers, public documents, speeches, and oral reminiscences to the less traditional sources such as photographs, buildings, statistics, film scripts, and cartoons. Moreover, as historians we know how exciting it can be to sort and analyze this evidence, arrange it in various ways, formulate a hypothesis, and arrive at a probable explanation for at least a part of our collective past.

In *Discovering the American Past,* we have tried to present a series of historical issues and events so as to engage students' interest in a wide variety of different types of primary evidence. We have also tried to provide a good mixture of types of historical situations and a balance among political, social, diplomatic, intellectual, and cultural history. In addition, each type of historical evidence is combined with an introduction to the appropriate methodology in an effort to teach students a variety of historical skills. As much as possible, we have tried "to let the evidence speak for itself" and have avoided leading students to one particular interpretation or another. In this book, then, we have created a kind of historical sampler that we believe will help students learn the methods and skills historians use, as well as help them learn historical content. This approach is effective in many different classroom situations including seminars, small classes, and large lecture classes with discussion sections.

Each chapter is divided into six parts: The Problem, Background, The Method, The Evidence, Questions to Consider, and Epilogue. We have made a major alteration in the format of the book for this edition. "The Problem" section this time begins with an anecdote and then states the central questions students must answer. Then, a "Background" section has been added, to help students understand the historical context of the problem. The format of the remaining sections is the same as in the first edition. The section called "The Method" gives students suggestions for studying and analyzing the evidence. "The Evidence" section is the heart of the chapter, providing a variety of primary source material on a particular historical event or issue. The section called "Questions to Consider" focuses students' attention on specific evidence and on linkages among different evidence material. The "Epilogue" section gives the aftermath or the historical outcome of the evidence—what happened to the people involved, who won the election, the results of a debate, and so on.

In response to student and faculty reactions to the first edition, we have made many changes in content. Exactly one-third (seven of twenty-one) of the chapters are new, either replacing those that students and faculty found less stimulating or, in some cases, adding chapters to fill certain gaps in the first edition. Volume I begins with a new chapter on Europeans' first encounters with American Indians. Chapter 6 is also new, on debates about universal male suffrage at the New York State constitutional convention in 1821. In Volume II, we have added new chapters on American imperialism (Chapter 4), the Progressives and child labor regulation (Chapter 6), the decision to drop the atomic bomb (Chapter 8), the second red scare and the 1947 hearings of the House Committee on Un-American Activities (Chapter 9), and politics and television during the presidential election of 1988 (Chapter 11). In addition to these new chapters, all the chapters from the first edition have been rethought, discussed, revised, and tested in classrooms.

An Instructor's Manual suggests ways that might be useful in guiding students through the evidence, questions students often ask, and a variety of ways in which the students' learning may be evaluated.

Finally, we would like to thank the many people who have helped us in our effort. Our colleagues at the University of Tennessee have been extremely supportive—offering suggestions, reading chapter drafts, and testing the new chapters in their own classes. We would like to thank especially Cathy Matson, Paul Bergeron, John R. Finger, Michael J. McDonald, Charles W. Johnson, and Jonathan Utley. Connie Lester offered invaluable assistance on the Instructor's Manual. Helping to prepare the manuscript were Cynthia Ogle, Jill Finger, Tracy Phelps, and Lisa Medlin. During the spring of 1989, Bruce Wheeler was a Brown Visiting Professor at the University of the South. While there, people who assisted him in preparing the manuscript included Sondra Bridges, Minnie Childers, Jim Jones, and Cathy Young. Finally, colleagues at other institutions who reviewed chapter drafts made significant contributions to this edition, and we would like to thank them for their generosity, both in time and in helpful ideas and suggestions. These reviewers were:

Kathleen Berkeley
University of North Carolina Wilmington
Nancy H. Bowen
Del Mar College
Carolle Carter
Menlo College
John C. Chalberg
Normandale Community College

George Q. Flynn
Texas Technological University
Carl J. Guarneri
St. Mary's College of California
Thomas Hietala
Grinnell College
John V. Jezierski
Saginaw Valley State College
Charles McCormick
Fairmont State College
Clay McShane
Northeastern University
James Matray
New Mexico State University
John K. Nelson
University of North Carolina, Chapel Hill
Gregory Schmidt
Winona State University
Jason H. Silverman
Winthrop College
Daniel Blake Smith
University of Kentucky
Deborah White
Rutgers University
John Scott Wilson
University of South Carolina

As with the first edition, we dedicate this book to our colleagues at our own university and elsewhere who seek to offer a challenging and stimulating academic experience to their students, and to those students themselves, who make those efforts worthwhile.

A STRANGE NEW WORLD:
THE EUROPEANS' FIRST ENCOUNTERS
WITH AMERICAN INDIANS

THE PROBLEM

In 1492, Christopher Columbus became the first European who met American Indians and recorded his observations. In the next few years, Europeans became increasingly fascinated with the New World and its inhabitants. Explorers' accounts were published and widely circulated, as were artistic renderings of the Indians by European artists, some of whom had never traveled to the New World or met a single Indian.

From explorers' accounts and artistic renderings, Europeans and early colonists gained their first—and sometimes only—impressions of these newly found people. More important, the images that early explorers and artists conveyed fostered perceptions about America's original inhabitants

that made subsequent Indian—white relations confusing, difficult, and ultimately disharmonious. The European hunger for land may have made the tragedies that followed almost inevitable, yet Europeans' early perceptions of Indians were an important factor in how explorers and early colonists dealt with Indian peoples and, in the end, subdued them.

In this chapter you will be examining and analyzing selected explorers' accounts and artistic interpretations of American Indians. You will be trying to determine *not* what American Indians were *really* like, only what Europeans *perceived* them as being. To find out what the diverse peoples collectively known as Indians were really like, most European explorers

CHAPTER 1

A STRANGE NEW
WORLD: THE
EUROPEANS'
FIRST
ENCOUNTERS
WITH AMERICAN
INDIANS

and artists would offer poor evidence indeed. Better able to answer that question would be archaeologists, cultural anthropologists, and cultural geographers. In this chapter, however, we will be dealing less with reality than what Europeans perceived that reality to have been, principally because those perceptions strongly influenced how Europeans and early colonists dealt with Indian peoples. For that purpose, evidence from European explorers and artists can provide excellent clues.

BACKGROUND

By the time Europeans first encountered the various peoples they collectively called Indians, the American Indians had inhabited the Western Hemisphere for approximately 20,000 to 40,000 years.[1] Although there is considerable disagreement about when these people first appeared in the Americas, it is reasonable to assume that they first migrated to the Western Hemisphere sometime in the middle of the Pleistocene Age. During that period (roughly from 75000 to 8000 B.C.), huge glaciers covered a large portion of North America, the ice cap extending southward to the approximate present border of the United States and Canada. These glaciers, which in some places were more than 9,000 feet thick, interrupted the water cycle because moisture falling as rain or snow was caught by the glaciers and frozen and was thus prevented from draining back into the seas or evaporating into the atmosphere.

This process lowered ocean levels 250 to 300 feet, exposing a natural land bridge spanning the Bering Strait (between present-day Alaska and the Soviet Union)[2] across which people from Asia could easily migrate, probably in search of game. It is almost certain that various peoples from Asia did exactly that and then followed an ice-free corridor along the base of the Rocky Mountains southward into the more temperate areas of the American Southwest (that, because of the glaciers, were wetter, cooler, and contained large lakes and forests) and then either eastward into other areas of North America or even farther southward into Central and South America. These migrations took thousands of years, and some Indian peoples were still moving when Europeans first encountered them.

About 8000 B.C., the glacial cap began to retreat fairly rapidly, raising ocean levels to approximately their

1. Other estimates run as high as 70,000 years. Whatever the case, it is almost certain that Indians were not native to the Western Hemisphere because no subhuman remains have ever been found.

2. Presently the Bering Strait is only 180 feet deep. Thus a lowering of ocean levels 250 to 300 feet would have exposed a considerable land bridge between Asia and North America.

present-day levels and cutting off further migration from Asia, thus isolating America's first human inhabitants from other peoples for thousands of years. This isolation was almost surely the cause of the inhabitants' extraordinarily high susceptibility to the diseases that Europeans later brought with them, such as measles, tuberculosis, and smallpox, to which the peoples of other continents had built up natural resistance. The glacial retreat also caused large portions of the American Southwest to became hot and arid, thus scattering Indian peoples in almost all directions. Nevertheless, for thousands of years a strong oral tradition enabled Indians to preserve stories of their origins and subsequent isolation. Almost all Indian peoples retained accounts of a long migration from the west and a flood.

The original inhabitants of the Western Hemisphere obtained their food principally by hunting and gathering, killing mammoths, huge bison, deer, elk, antelope, camels, horses, and other game with stone weapons and picking wild fruits and grasses. Beginning about 5000 B.C., however, Indians in present-day Mexico began practicing agriculture. By the time Europeans arrived, most Indians were domesticating plants and raising crops, although their levels of agricultural sophistication were extremely diverse.

The development of agriculture (which occurred about the same time in Europe and the Americas) profoundly affected Indian life. Those peoples who adopted agriculture abandoned their nomadic ways and lived in settled villages (some of the Central American ones became magnificent cities). This more sedentary life permitted them to erect permanent housing, create and preserve pottery and art, and establish more complex political and social institutions. Agriculture also led to a sexual division of labor, with women planting, raising, and harvesting crops and men hunting to supplement their villages' diets with game. With more and better food, most likely Indian populations grew more rapidly, thus furthering the need for more complex political and social structures. The development of agriculture also affected these peoples' religious beliefs and ceremonies, increasing the homage to sun and rain gods who could bring forth good harvests. Contact with other Indian peoples led to trading, a practice with which Indians were quite familiar by the time of European intrusion.

Those Indian cultures that made the transition from food gathering to food producing often attained an impressive degree of economic, political, social, and technological sophistication. In Central America, the Mayas of present-day Mexico and Guatemala built great cities, fashioned elaborate gold and silver jewelry, devised a form of writing, were proficient in mathematics and astronomy, and constructed a calendar that could predict solar eclipses and was more accurate than any system in use in Europe at the time. The conquerors of the Mayas, the Aztecs, built on the achievements of their predecessors, extending their political and economic power chiefly by subjugating other Indian peoples. By the time Europeans first appeared in Mexico in 1519, the Aztecs had constructed the magnificent city of Tenochtilan (the site of present-day Mexico

CHAPTER 1

A STRANGE NEW
WORLD: THE
EUROPEANS'
FIRST
ENCOUNTERS
WITH AMERICAN
INDIANS

City), which rivaled European cities in both size and splendor.

It is important to remember, however, that Indian life was marked by enormous diversity, far more so than life in Europe. Although no Indian peoples had developed the wheel or domesticated large animals for food and labor, some Indian cultures had reached a level of sophistication that from our twentieth-century perspective compared favorably with those of Europe, although other Indian cultures were considerably less technologically advanced. Scattered throughout the hemisphere, the Indian people spoke a variety of languages (about three hundred in North America alone); had developed a wide variety of political, religious, and social structures; and were widely diverse as to family structure, burial practices, appreciation of the creative arts, the role of women, and the capacity to make war. Europeans tended to see all Indians as similar, but in fact, diversity among Indian peoples was more the rule.

The Indians of eastern North America probably were among the least developed of the Indian peoples. Among the last to migrate to the lands they collectively claimed, they were also among the last to develop agricultural techniques, which were still comparatively crude at the time of the Europeans' arrival. Yet even here diversity was the rule. In the Ohio and Tennessee river valleys, Indians (collectively known as Mound Builders) combined farming and food gathering, constructing

impressive cities and burial mounds. In the Northeast, the Seneca practiced a form of shifting agriculture that best fit the lives of a seminomadic people. Most eastern Indians, however, relied principally on food gathering rather than cultivation and on hunting for deer (for food, clothing, bowstrings, and weapon tips) and bear (for moccasins, winter robes, cooking oil, and bed coverings). Some had developed authoritarian political and social structures (such as the Powhatan Confederacy in Virginia), although most eastern Indians belonged to less complex political systems of clans and tribes. Yet, whatever eastern Indian people the explorers first encountered, they were, as historian Gary Nash noted, "far from the forest primitives that Europeans pictured." In many ways different from Europeans, American Indian peoples nevertheless had developed economic, political, social, diplomatic, and ideological systems that met their diverse needs.

Yet, as you will see, Europeans who met Indian peoples in North and Central America went far beyond merely describing them as different. Indeed, these Europeans created images of Indians that became important factors in how Europeans chose to deal with Indians. It is these images you will be examining and analyzing in this chapter, with a view to answering two central questions: 1. How did Europeans perceive Indians? 2. How did those perceptions influence their subsequent behavior toward American Indian peoples?

THE METHOD

You will be working with two distinct *types* of evidence: (1) selections from the accounts of four European explorers (Christopher Columbus, Amerigo Vespucci, Hernando Cortés, and John Smith), and (2) representations of Indians by European artists, some of whom never saw an Indian. Some of these artists undoubtedly used their active imaginations to construct their images of American Indians, and others relied on explorers' accounts or word-of-mouth reports from those who had seen the Indians the explorers had brought to Europe.

You must deal with these two types of evidence differently. The explorers were trying to describe American Indians to people who had never seen them. After you read each explorer's account, think of some *adjectives* that that explorer might use to describe Indians. How do those adjectives present a collective *image* of Indians? How do the stories each explorer tells reinforce that image? As you read each account, make a list of those adjectives and then combine them to form a collective image. Be willing also to read between the lines. Sometimes an explorer may be simply trying to explain a specific incident or practice of the Indians, yet, intentionally or unintentionally, that explorer is creating an image of Indians in the minds of the readers.

The second type of evidence, artistic representations, seems quite different from the written accounts. Yet if you think of art as words made into pictures, you will see that you can approach this type of evidence as you approached the explorers' accounts. Study each picture carefully, looking especially for how Indians are portrayed. First, how are they portrayed physically? Second, how is their nature or character portrayed in their behavior in the work of art? Again, you can create a list of adjectives and deduce a collective image from the list.

One important thing you will recognize is that there was not one single image of the American Indian. As you examine the evidence and your lists of adjectives, you will see that Indians were portrayed quite differently. How many different images did the explorers and artists create? How important are these differences? As you analyze the evidence in this chapter, keep the two central questions in mind.

CHAPTER 1

A STRANGE NEW
WORLD: THE
EUROPEANS'
FIRST
ENCOUNTERS
WITH AMERICAN
INDIANS

THE EVIDENCE

Source 1 from *Journal of First Voyage to America, by Christopher Columbus* (New York: Albert Boni and Charles Boni, 1924), pp. 24–29.

1. Christopher Columbus (1492).[3]

As I saw that they were very friendly to us, and perceived that they could be much more easily converted to our holy faith by gentle means than by force, I presented them with some red caps, and strings of beads to wear upon the neck, and many other trifles of small value, wherewith they were much delighted, and became wonderfully attached to us. Afterwards they came swimming to the boats, bringing parrots, balls of cotton thread, javelins and many other things which they exchanged for articles we gave them, such as glass beads, and hawk's bells; which trade was carried on with the utmost good will. But they seemed on the whole to me, to be a very poor people. They all go completely naked, even the women, though I saw but one girl. All whom I saw were young, not above thirty years of age, well made, with fine shapes and faces; their hair short, and coarse like that of a horse's tail, combed toward the forehead, except a small portion which they suffer to hang down behind, and never cut. Some paint themselves with black, which makes them appear like those of the Canaries, neither black nor white; others with white, others with red, and others with such colours as they can find. Some paint the face, and some the whole body; others only the eyes, and others the nose. Weapons they have none, nor are acquainted with them, for I showed them swords which they grasped by the blades, and cut themselves through ignorance. They have no iron, their javelins being without it, and nothing more than sticks, though some have fish-bones or other things at the ends. They are all of a good size and stature, and handsomely formed. I saw some with scars of wounds upon their bodies, and demanded by signs the cause of them; they answered me in the same way, that there came people from other islands in the neighbourhood who endeavoured to make prisoners of them, and they defended themselves. I thought then, and still believe, that these were from the continent. It appears to me, that the people are ingenious, and would be good servants; and I am of opinion that they would very readily become Christians, as they appear to have no religion. They very quickly learn such words as are spoken to them. If it

3. Although there is some dispute, the Indians Columbus described in this selection probably were Arawaks.

please our Lord, I intend at my return to carry home six of them to your Highnesses, that they may learn our language. . . .

At daybreak great multitudes of men came to the shore, all young and of fine shapes, very handsome; their hair not curled but straight and coarse like horse-hair, and all with foreheads and heads much broader than any people I had hitherto seen; their eyes were large and very beautiful. . . .

They were straight-limbed without exception, and not with prominent bellies but handsomely shaped. They came to the ship in canoes, made of a single trunk of a tree, wrought in a wonderful manner considering the country; some of them large enough to contain forty or forty-five men, others of different sizes down to those fitted to hold but a single person. They rowed with an oar like a baker's peel, and wonderfully swift. . . .

Seeing some of them with little bits of this metal hanging at their noses, I gathered from them by signs that by going southward or steering round the island in that direction, there would be found a king who possessed large vessels of gold, and in great quantities. I endeavoured to procure them to lead the way thither, but found they were unacquainted with the route. . . .

The natives are an inoffensive people, and so desirous to possess any thing they saw with us, that they kept swimming off to the ships with whatever they could find, and readily bartered for any article we saw fit to give them in return, even such as broken platters and fragments of glass. . . .

I do not . . . see the necessity of fortifying the place, as the people here are simple in war-like matters, as your Highnesses will see by those seven which I have ordered to be taken and carried to Spain in order to learn our language and return, unless your Highnesses should choose to have them all transported to Castile, or held captive in the island. I could conquer the whole of them with fifty men, and govern them as I pleased. . . .

Source 2 from *The Letters of Amerigo Vespucci,* trans. Clements R. Markham (London: The Hakluyt Society, 1894), pp. 6–21.

2. Amerigo Vespucci (1497–1498).[4]

What we knew of their life and customs was that they all go naked, as well the men as the women, without covering anything, no otherwise than as they come out of their mothers' wombs. They are of medium stature, and

4. The Indians described in this selection were probably coastal Indians of Central America, but a particular Indian people cannot be determined with precision.

CHAPTER 1

A STRANGE NEW
WORLD: THE
EUROPEANS'
FIRST
ENCOUNTERS
WITH AMERICAN
INDIANS

very well proportioned. The colour of their skins inclines to red, like the skin of a lion, and I believe that, if they were properly clothed, they would be white like ourselves. They have no hair whatever on their bodies, but they have very long black hair, especially the women, which beautifies them. They have not very beautiful faces, because they have long eyelids, which make them look like Tartars. They do not allow any hairs to grow on their eyebrows, nor eyelashes, nor in any other part except on the head, where it is rough and dishevelled. They are very agile in their persons, both in walking and running, as well the men as the women; and think nothing of running a league or two, as we often witnessed; and in this they have a very great advantage over us Christians. They swim wonderfully well, and the women better than the men; for we have found and seen them many times two leagues at sea, without any help whatever in swimming.

Their arms are bows and arrows, well made, except that they have no iron, nor any other kind of hard metal. Instead of iron they use teeth of animals or of fish, or a bit of wood well burnt at the point. They are sure shots, and where they aim they hit. In some places the women use these bows. They have other weapons like lances, hardened by fire, and clubs with the knobs very well carved. They wage war among themselves with people who do not speak their language, carrying it on with great cruelty, giving no quarter, if not inflicting greater punishment. . . .

They have no leader, nor do they march in any order, no one being captain. The cause of their wars is not the desire of rule nor to extend the limits of their dominions, but owing to some ancient feud that has arisen among them in former times. When asked why they made war, they have no other answer than that it is to avenge the death of their ancestors and their fathers. They have neither king nor lord, nor do they obey anyone, but live in freedom. Having moved themselves to wage war, when the enemy have killed or captured any of them, the oldest relation arises and goes preaching through the streets and calling upon his countrymen to come with him to avenge the death of his relation, and thus he moves them by compassion. They do not bring men to justice, nor punish a criminal. Neither the mother nor the father chastise their children, and it is wonderful that we never saw a quarrel among them. They show themselves simple in their talk, and are very sharp and cunning in securing their ends. They speak little, and in a low voice. . . .

Their mode of life is very barbarous, for they have no regular time for their meals, but they eat at any time that they have the wish, as often at night as in the day—indeed, they eat at all hours. They take their food on the ground, without napkin or any other cloth, eating out of earthen pots which they make, or out of half calabashes. They sleep in certain very large nets made of cotton, and suspended in the air. . . .

They are a people of cleanly habits as regards their bodies, and are constantly washing themselves. When they empty the stomach they do everything so as not to be seen, and in this they are clean and decent; but in making water they are dirty and without shame, for while talking with us they do such things without turning round, and without any shame. They do not practise matrimony among them, each man taking as many women as he likes, and when he is tired of a woman he repudiates her without either injury to himself or shame to the woman, for in this matter the woman has the same liberty as the man. They are not very jealous, but lascivious beyond measure, the women much more so than the men. I do not further refer to their contrivances for satisfying their inordinate desires, so that I may not offend against modesty. They are very prolific in bearing children, and in their pregnancy they are not excused any work whatever. The parturition is so easy, and accompanied by so little pain, that they are up and about the next day. They go to some river to wash, and presently are quite well, appearing on the water like fish. If they are angry with their husbands they easily cause abortion with certain poisonous herbs or roots, and destroy the child. Many infants perish in this way. . . .

They eat little flesh, unless it be human flesh, and your Magnificence must know that they are so inhuman as to transgress regarding this most bestial custom. For they eat all their enemies that they kill or take, as well females as males, with so much barbarity that it is a brutal thing to mention, how much more to see it, as has happened to me an infinite number of times. They were astonished at us when we told them that we did not eat our enemies. . . .

At a distance of three leagues from the beach we came to a village of few houses and many inhabitants, there not being more than nine habitations. Here we were received with so many barbarous ceremonies that the pen will not suffice to write them down. There were songs, dances, tears mingled with rejoicings, and plenty of food. We remained here for the night. Here they offered their wives to us, and we were unable to defend ourselves from them. We remained all night and half the next day. . . .

Next day we saw a great number of the people on shore, still with signs of war, sounding horns and various other instruments used by them for defiance, and all plumed and painted, so that it was a very strange thing to behold them. All the ships, therefore, consulted together, and it was concluded that these people desired hostility with us. It was then decided that we should do all in our power to make friends with them, and if they rejected

CHAPTER 1

A STRANGE NEW
WORLD: THE
EUROPEANS'
FIRST
ENCOUNTERS
WITH AMERICAN
INDIANS

our friendship we should treat them as enemies, and that we should make slaves of as many as we could take. Being armed as well as our means admitted, we returned to the shore. They did not oppose our landing, I believe from fear of the guns. Forty of our men landed in four detachments, each with a captain, and attacked them. After a long battle, many of them being killed, the rest were put to flight. We followed in pursuit until we came to a village, having taken nearly 250 prisoners. We burnt the village and returned to the ships with these 250 prisoners, leaving many killed and wounded. On our side no more than *one was killed, and twenty-two were wounded,* who all recovered. God be thanked! . . .

Source 3 from Hernando Cortés, *Five Letters, 1519–1526,* trans. J. Bayard Morris (New York: W. W. Norton), pp. 21–25, 56–57.

3. Hernando Cortés (1519).[5]

To our mind it is probable that this land contains as many riches as that from which Solomon is said to have obtained the gold for the temple: but so little time has passed since our landing that we have been unable to explore the country further than some five leagues inland and some ten or a dozen leagues along the coast on either side of the place where we first landed; from the sea much more may be seen and more we certainly saw while skirting the coast in our ships.

The natives who inhabit the island of Cozumel and the land of Yucatán from its northern point to where we are now settled, are of middle height, and well-proportioned, except that in our district they disfigure their faces in various ways, some piercing the ears and introducing large and extremely ugly ornaments, others the lower part of the nose and upper lip in which they insert large circular stones having the appearance of mirrors, others still piercing the thick underlip right through to the teeth and hanging therefrom round stones or pieces of gold so heavy that they drag the lip down, giving an extraordinarily repulsive appearance. They wear as clothes a kind of highly coloured shawl, the men wear breech clouts, and on the top half of the body cloaks finely worked and painted after the fashion of Moorish draperies. The common women wear highly coloured robes reaching from the waist to the feet and others which cover only the breast, all the

5. Cortés encountered numerous Indian peoples on his march to Tenochtilan. Those described here are the Cozumels (a Mayan-related group), the Aztecs, and the Tlaxcalas (Cortés spelled it Tlascalans), who helped him against the Aztecs.

rest of the body being uncovered; but the women of high rank wear bodices of fine cotton, very loose fitting, cut and embroidered after the vestment worn by our bishops and abbots. Their food is composed of maize and such cereals as are to be found on the other Islands, *potuoyuca* almost exactly similar to that eaten in Cuba, except that they roast it instead of making it into bread; in addition they have whatever they can obtain by fishing or hunting; and they also breed large numbers of hens similar to those of the mainland which are as big as peacocks. There are a few large towns very passably laid out. The houses in those parts which can obtain stone are of rough masonry and mortar, the rooms being low and small, very much after the Moorish fashion. Where no stone can be got they build their houses of baked bricks, covering them over with plaster and the roofs with a rough kind of thatch. . . .

In addition they have their mosques, temples and walks, all of very fair size, and in them are the idols which they worship whether of stone, clay or wood, the which they honour and obey in such a manner and with such ceremonies that many sheets of paper would not suffice to give your Majesties a minute and true account of them. These private mosques where they exist are the largest, finest and most elaborately built buildings of any that there are in the town, and as such they keep them very much bedecked with strings of feathers, gaily painted cloths and all manner of finery. And always on the day before they are to begin some important enterprise they burn incense in these temples, and sometimes even sacrifice their own persons, some cutting out their tongues, others their ears, still others slicing their bodies with knives in order to offer to their idols the blood which flows from their wounds; sometimes sprinkling the whole of the temple with blood and throwing it up in the air, and many other fashions of sacrifice they use, so that no important task is undertaken without previous sacrifice having been made. One very horrible and abominable custom they have which should certainly be punished and which we have seen in no other part, and that is that whenever they wish to beg anything of their idols, in order that their petition may find more acceptance, they take large numbers of boys and girls and even of grown men and women and tear out their heart and bowels while still alive, burning them in the presence of those idols, and offering the smoke of such burning as a pleasant sacrifice. Some of us have actually seen this done and they say that it is the most terrible and frightful thing that they have ever seen. Yet the Indians perform this ceremony so frequently that, as we are informed and have in part seen from our own scanty experience since we have been in this land, there is no year passes in which they do not thus kill and sacrifice fifty souls in every such temple, and the practice is general from the island of Cozumel to the region in which

CHAPTER 1

A STRANGE NEW
WORLD: THE
EUROPEANS'
FIRST
ENCOUNTERS
WITH AMERICAN
INDIANS

we have now settled. Your Majesties can therefore be certain that since the land is large and they seem to have a large number of temples there can be no year (so far as we have been able up to the present to ascertain) in which they have not sacrificed in this manner some three or four thousand souls. Your Majesties may therefore perceive whether it is not their duty to prevent such loss and evil, and certainly it will be pleasing to God if by means of and under the protection of your royal Majesties these peoples are introduced into and instructed in the holy Catholic Faith, and the devotion, trust and hope which they now have in their idols turned so as to repose in the divine power of the true God; for it is certain that if they should serve God with that same faith, fervour and diligence they would work many miracles. And we believe that not without cause has God been pleased to allow this land to be discovered in the name of your royal Majesties, that your Majesties may reap great merit and reward from Him in sending the Gospel to these barbarian people who thus by your Majesties' hands will be received into the true faith; for from what we know of them we believe that by the aid of interpreters who should plainly declare to them the truths of the Holy Faith and the error in which they are, many, perhaps all of them, would very quickly depart from their evil ways and would come to true knowledge, for they live more equably and reasonably than any other of the tribes which we have hitherto come across. . . .

During the three days I was there they provided us with very indifferent food which grew worse each day, and the nobles and chief men of the city hardly ever came to speak with me. And being somewhat perplexed by this I learnt through the agency of my interpreter, a native Indian girl who came with me from Putunchan (a great river of which I informed your Majesty in my first letter), that a girl of the city had told her that a large force of Muteczuma's[6] men had assembled nearby, and that the citizens themselves, having removed their wives, and children and clothes, intended to attack us suddenly and leave not one of us alive. The native girl had added that if [we] wanted to escape [we] had better go with her, and she would look after [us]. On hearing this I took one of the natives of the city secretly aside without any perceiving it and interrogated him: whereupon he confirmed all that the native girl and the Tlascalans had told me. On the strength of such evidence and the signs of preparation that I perceived, I determined to surprise rather than be surprised, and sending for some nobles of the city I told them that I wished to speak with them and assembled them all in a certain room; and meantime I ordered that our men should be on the alert and that

6. More familiar to us as Montezuma.

at the sound of a musket shot they should fall upon a large number of Indians who were either close to or actually inside our quarters. So it was
done; for having got the nobles into the room I left them, leapt on my horse
and ordered the musket to be fired, and upon which we fell upon the Indians
in such fashion that within two hours more than three thousand of them lay
dead. . . .

Source 4 from Philip L. Barbour, ed., *The Complete Works of Captain John Smith*
(Chapel Hill: Published for The Institute of Early American History and Culture
by the University of North Carolina Press, 1986), Vol. I, pp. 160–175.

*[The authors have modernized the spelling, and, in a few instances, a modern syn-
onym has been substituted for a word no longer in use.]*

4. John Smith (1607).[7]

Their hair is generally black, but few have any beards. The men wear half
their heads shaven, the other half long; for barbers they use their women,
who with 2 shells will grate away the hair. . . . They are very strong, of an
able body and full of agility, able to endure to lie in the woods under a tree
by the fire, in the worst of winter, or in the weeds and grass in ambush in
the summer. They are inconstant in every thing. . . . Crafty, timorous, quick
of apprehension and very ingenuous. Some are of disposition fearful, some
bold, most wary, all Savage. Generally covetous of copper, beads, and such-
like trash. They are soon moved to anger, and so malicious, and they seldom
forget an injury. They seldom steal one from another, lest their conjurers
should reveal it, and so they be pursued and punished. . . . Their women are
careful not to be suspected of dishonesty without the leave of their husbands. Each household knoweth their own lands and gardens, and most live
of their own labors. For their apparel, they are some time covered with the
skins of wild beasts, which in winter are dressed with the hair, but in summer without . . . But the women are always covered about their middles with
a skin and very modest to be seen bare. They adorn themselves most with
copper beads and paintings. Their women some have their legs, hands,
breasts and face cunningly tattooed with diverse works, as beasts, serpents,

7. The Indians Smith dealt with in Virginia were members of the Powhatan Confederacy, a
coalition of several tribes. It should be noted that Smith was part of a colonization effort by
the Virginia Company, and was not just an explorer.

CHAPTER 1

A STRANGE NEW
WORLD: THE
EUROPEANS'
FIRST
ENCOUNTERS
WITH AMERICAN
INDIANS

artificially wrought into their flesh with black spots. In each ear commonly they have 3 great holes, whereat they hang chains bracelets or copper. Some of their men wear in these holes a small green and yellow colored snake, nearly half a yard in length, which crawling and lapping herself about his neck often times familiarly would kiss his lips. . . .

Their buildings and habitations are for the most part by the rivers or not far from some fresh spring. Their houses are built . . . of small young saplings bowed and tied, and so close covered with mats, or the barks of trees very handsomely, that notwithstanding either wind, rain or weather, they are as warm as stoves, but very smoky, yet at the top of the house there is a hole made for the smoke to go into right over the fire. . . .

Their women (they say) are easily delivered of child, yet do they love children very dearly. To make them hardy, in the coldest mornings they wash them in the rivers and by painting and ointments so tan their skins that after a year or two, no weather will hurt them.

The men spend their times in fishing, hunting, wars and such menlike exercises, scorning to be seen in any woman-like exercise, which is the cause that the women be very painful and the men often idle. The women and children do the rest of the work. . . .

For their music they use a thick cane, on which they pipe as on a Recorder. For their wars they have a great deep platter of wood. They cover the mouth thereof with a skin, at each corner they tie a walnut, which meeting on the backside near the bottom, with a small rope they tie them together till it be taut and still, that they may beat upon it as upon a drum. But their chief instruments are rattles made of small gourds or pumpkin shells. . . . These mingled with their voices sometimes 20 or 30 together, make such a terrible noise as would rather frighten than delight any man. . . .

There is yet in Virginia no place discovered to be so Savage in which Savages have not a religion. . . . All things that were able to do them hurt beyond their prevention they adore with their kind of divine worship. . . . But their chief God they worship is the Devil. Him they call Oke and serve him more of fear than love. They say they have conference with him, and fashion themselves as near to his shape as they can imagine. . . . It could not be perceived that they keep any day as more holy than another. But only in some great distress of want, fear of enemies, times of triumph and gathering together their fruits, the whole country of men, women and children come together in solemnities. The manner of their devotion is sometimes to make a great fire, in the house or fields, and all to sing and dance about it with rattles and shouts together, 4 or 5 hours. . . .

Although the country people be very barbarous, yet have they amongst them such government, as that their Magistrates for good commanding, and their people for due subjection, and obeying, excel many places that would be counted very civil. The form of their Commonwealth is a monarchical government, as one Emperor rules over many kings or governors. Their chief ruler is called Powhatan. . . . What he commandeth they dare not disobey in the least thing. It is strange to see with what great fear and adoration all these people do obey this Powhatan. For at his feet they present whatsoever he commandeth, and at the least frown of his brow, their greatest spirits will tremble with fear. And no marvel, for he is very terrible and tyrannical in punishing such as offend him. For example, he caused certain malefactors to be bound hand and foot, then having of many fires gathered great store of burning coals, they make these coals round in the form of a cockpit, and in the midst they cast the offenders to broil to death. Sometimes he causeth the heads of them that offend him to be laid upon an alter or sacrificing stone, and one with clubs beets out their brains. When he would punish any notorious enemy or malefactor, he causeth him to be tied to a tree, and with mussel shells or reeds, the executioner cutteth off his joints one after another, ever casting what they cut off into the fire; then doth he proceed with shells and reeds to strip the skin from his head and face; then do they rip his belly and so burn him with the tree and all. . . .

CHAPTER 1

A STRANGE NEW
WORLD: THE
EUROPEANS'
FIRST
ENCOUNTERS
WITH AMERICAN
INDIANS

Sources 5 through 10 from Hugh Honor, *The European Vision of America*
(Cleveland: Cleveland Museum of Art, 1975), plates 3, 4, 5, 8, 64, 65.

5. German Woodcut, 1509.

6. *Adoration of the Magi,* Portuguese Oil on Panel, 1505.

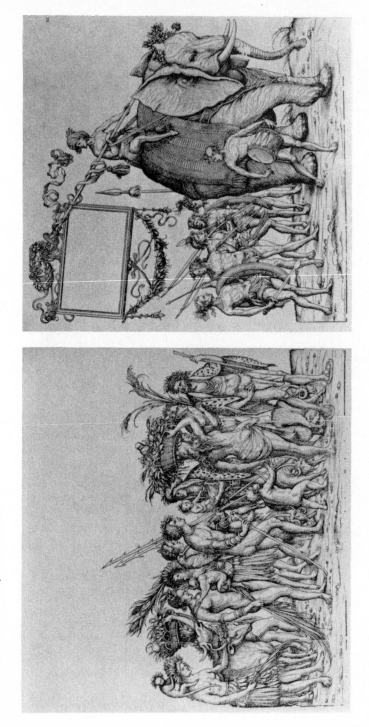

7. German Woodcut, 1517–1518.

8. Portuguese Oil on Panel, 1550.

9. German Engraving, 1590.

CHAPTER 1

A STRANGE NEW
WORLD: THE
EUROPEANS'
FIRST
ENCOUNTERS
WITH AMERICAN
INDIANS ·

10. German Engraving, 1591.

Sources 11 and 12 from Stefan Lorant, ed., *The New World: The First Pictures of America* (New York: Duell, Sloan & Pearce, 1946), pp. 51 and 119.

11. German Engraving, 1591.

12. German Engraving, 1591.

Sources 13 and 14 from Honor, *The European Vision of America*, plates 85, 91.

13. French Engraving, 1575.

CHAPTER 1

A STRANGE NEW
WORLD: THE
EUROPEANS'
FIRST
ENCOUNTERS
WITH AMERICAN
INDIANS

14. French Engraving, 1579–1600.

AMERICA.

Sources 15 and 16 from Paul Hulton, *America 1585: The Complete Drawings of John White* (Chapel Hill: University of North Carolina Press, 1984), pp. 70–71.

15. English Watercolor, 1585.

CHAPTER 1

A STRANGE NEW
WORLD: THE
EUROPEANS'
FIRST
ENCOUNTERS
WITH AMERICAN
INDIANS

16. English Watercolor, 1585.

QUESTIONS TO CONSIDER

As you read each explorer's account (Sources 1 through 4), it helps to look for five factors:

1. Physical appearance (bodies, hair, clothing, jewelry, etc.). This description can provide important clues about each explorer's attitudes about the Indians he confronted.
2. Nature or character (childlike, bellicose, cunning, honest, intellectual, lazy, etc.). Be sure to note the examples each explorer used to provide his analysis of the Indians' nature or character.
3. Political, social, religious practices (behavior of women, ceremonies, eating habits, government, etc.). Descriptions of these practices can provide excellent insight into the explorer's general perception of the Indians he encountered. Be especially sensitive to the explorer's use of descriptive adjectives.
4. Overall impressions of the Indians. In other words, what was each explorer's collective image or impression?
5. What did each explorer think should be done with the Indians?

Keep in mind that each explorer encountered a different Indian people. Even so, you will be able to compare each explorer's account with those of the other explorers, especially with regard to points 2 and 4.

Once you have analyzed each explorer's account using points one through four, you should be able to explain how, based on his overall impression of the Indians he encountered, each explorer thought the Indians should be dealt with (point 5). Sometimes the explorer, through words or actions, will come right out and tell you, but in other cases you will have to use a little imagination (Columbus and Cortés are fairly obvious, whereas Vespucci and Smith are not). For Vespucci and Smith, ask yourself the following question: If this is my collective perception of Indians, how should those people be dealt with?

You can also handle the artistic representations (Sources 5 through 16) in this manner, using the five points when looking at each rendering of an Indian. Each artist tried to convey his notion of the Indians' nature or character. Some of these impressions are obvious, but others are less so. Think, however, of the art as words made into pictures. How are the Indians portrayed? What are they doing? How are they dealing with Europeans? On the basis of these artistic representations, decide how the various artists believed Indians should be dealt with. For example, the Indian women in Source 5 are in the process of doing something. What is it? On the basis of these actions, what would you say is the artist's perception of Indians? Moreover, how would that perception affect the artist's—and viewers'—opinion of how Indians should be dealt with? Follow these steps for all the artistic representations.

Finally, put together the two types of evidence. How many different perceptions of American Indians are there? How might each perception affect the ways European and early colonists dealt with American Indians?

[25]

CHAPTER 1

A STRANGE NEW
WORLD: THE
EUROPEANS'
FIRST
ENCOUNTERS
WITH AMERICAN
INDIANS

EPILOGUE

The American Indian peoples were terribly vulnerable to Europeans. Whether warlike or peaceful, Indians rapidly succumbed to the numerous diseases that Europeans brought with them. Smallpox was especially devastating. It has been estimated that millions of Indians in North, Central, and South America fell victim to this disease, against which they had no resistance. Whole villages were wiped out and whole nations decimated as (in the words of one Roman Catholic priest) "they died in heaps."

In addition, Indians were no match for European military technology and modes of warfare. Although many Indian peoples were skillful and courageous warriors, their weaponry was no equal to the European broadsword, pike, musket, or cannon. Moreover, battles between Indian peoples could best be described as skirmishes, in which few lives were lost and several prisoners taken. The Indians could not imagine wholesale slaughtering of their enemies, a practice some Europeans found acceptable as a means of acquiring gold and land. By no means passive peoples in what ultimately would become a contest for a hemisphere, Indians nevertheless lacked the military technology and tactics to hold Europeans permanently at bay.

Nor were the Indians themselves united against their European intruders. All the explorers and early settlers were able to pit one Indian people against another, thus dividing the opposition and in the end conquering

them all. In this practice Cortés was particularly adept; he found a number of villages ready to revolt against Montezuma and used those schisms to his advantage. Brief attempts at Indian unity against European intruders generally proved temporary and therefore unsuccessful.

As Europeans had misperceptions of the peoples they encountered, so did some Indians misperceive Europeans. Initially, some Central American Indians, including the mighty Aztecs, thought Cortés's party were the "white gods" from the east; Cortés's actions quickly disabused them of this notion. Indians of the Powhatan Confederacy in Virginia thought the Europeans were indolent because initially they could not grow their own food. This image too was soon shattered. In sum, Indian perceptions of Europeans often worked against any notions that they were a threat—until it was too late.

Finally, once Europeans had established footholds in the New World, the Indians undercut their own position. After they came to recognize the value of European manufactured goods (iron pots, firearms, etc.), the Indians increasingly engaged in wholesale hunting and trapping of animals with the skins and furs for which Europe lusted. Thus, not only did the Indians lose their economic and cultural independence, they also nearly eliminated certain animal species that had sustained them for so long. An ecological disaster was in the making, driven by the European view of the environment as something to exploit, a view to which the Indians gradually succumbed.

Therefore, for a number of reasons, Indians were extremely vulnerable to the European "invasion" of the Americas. A key factor in that vulnerability, however, was the European images of Indian peoples. Whether they viewed them as innocent, naive children or as treacherous, dangerous savages, in the end most Europeans considered Indians their inferiors. By placing this badge of inferiority on Indian peoples, most Europeans then could justify a number of ways Indians could be dealt with (avoidance, conquest, "civilizing," trading, removal, extermination). Ultimately for the Indian peoples, all methods proved disastrous. Although different European peoples (Spanish, French, English) often treated American Indians differently, in the end the results were the same.

CHAPTER TWO

THE THREAT
OF ANNE HUTCHINSON

THE PROBLEM

In the cold, early spring of 1638, Anne Hutchinson and her children left Massachusetts to join her husband and their many friends who had moved to an island in Narragansett Bay. Just a year before, in 1637, Hutchinson and her family had been highly respected, prominent members of a Puritan church in Boston. But then she was put on trial and sentenced to banishment from the Massachusetts Bay colony and excommunication from her church—next to death, the two worst punishments that could befall a Puritan in the New World.

What had Anne Hutchinson done? Why was she such a threat to the Massachusetts Bay colony? You will be reading the transcript of her trial in 1637 to find the answers to these questions.

BACKGROUND

The English men and women who came to the New World in the seventeenth and early eighteenth centuries did so for a variety of reasons. Many who arrived at Jamestown colony were motivated by the promise of wealth; at one point, Virginians grew tobacco in the streets and even threatened their own existence by favoring tobacco (a crop they could sell) over food crops. In contrast, the majority of the early settlers of Pennsylvania were Friends (Quakers) in search of religious freedom. In short, the American colonies represented for thousands of English men and women a chance to make significant changes in their lives.

Such was the case with the Puritans who settled and dominated the colony of Massachusetts Bay, founded in 1630. Although technically still members of the Church of England, the Puritans were convinced that many of that church's beliefs and practices were wrong and that the Church of England needed to be thoroughly purified (hence their name). Puritans were convinced that the Church of England, which had broken away from the Roman Catholic church and the pope during the reign of Henry VIII, was still encumbered with unnecessary ceremony, rituals, and hierarchy—things they called "popery." Popery, the Puritans believed, actually obstructed the ties between God and human beings, and therefore should be eliminated.

The Puritans were more Calvinist than many of their English contemporaries, and they did not believe that human salvation could be earned by individual effort (such as going to church, leading a good life, or helping one's neighbors). The Puritans called this type of salvation a "covenant of works," a notion they believed was simply wrong. Instead, they insisted that salvation came only as a free gift from God (a "covenant of grace"), and those few who received it were the true "saints." Of course, God expected everyone to lead a good life—those who were not yet saved would be preparing for the possibility of God's grace, while those who were already saints would naturally live according to God's laws. Some ministers, like John Cotton,

de-emphasized the idea of preparation, and believed that God's grace could be granted instantaneously to anyone. All Puritans, however, agreed that only saints should be full members of the Church.

Believing it impossible to effect their reforms in England, many Puritans sought "voluntary banishment," as one of them called it, to the New World. Fired by the sense that God was using them to revolutionize human history, more than one thousand men, women, and children arrived during the first decades of the founding of New England to form their model community based on the laws of God and following His commandments. "We shall be as a city upon a hill," exulted Puritan leader and colonial governor John Winthrop, "the eyes of all people are upon us."

Probably the best protection the Puritans had against the harsh New England environment was their sense of community and mission. Seeing themselves as the modern version of the ancient Israelites, Puritans believed that God had made a covenant (contract) with the Puritans of New England. As Winthrop explained, "Thus stands the cause between God and us: we are entered into covenant with Him. . . . The God of Israel is among us." Puritans believed the covenant stipulated that the entire community must follow God's laws as interpreted by Puritan leaders. If they did, God would reward them; if not, the community would be punished. Therefore community solidarity was essential, and individual desires and thoughts had to be subjugated to those of the community itself.

Thus, although Puritans sought religious freedom for themselves, they were not really willing to grant it to others. Dissent and discord, they reasoned, would lead to the breakdown of community cohesion, the inevitable violation of the covenant, and the punishment of the community in the same way God had punished the ancient Israelites when *they* had broken their covenant. Non-Puritans who migrated to the Massachusetts Bay colony were required to attend the Puritan church, although they could not become members and hence could not vote in either church or civil elections. Those who refused to abide by these rules were banished from the colony. Moreover, those Puritans who were not saints also had to obey these regulations and similarly could not be church members and could not vote. Thus there was a hierarchy of authority in Massachusetts that controlled both the colony's church and the government. To become a saint, one had to be examined by a committee and demonstrate to that committee's satisfaction that he or she had experienced a personal revelation from God and that the Holy Spirit resided in him or her. There was no agreement among the ministers about the exact nature of this revelation. For most, it simply meant that individuals would recognize the Holy Spirit moving within them. Other ministers urged their congregations to seek out (and not fear) more direct revelations. This was far more controversial, as you will see in Anne Hutchinson's trial.

In fact, there was a good deal of dissension in Massachusetts Bay colony. Religious squabbles were not uncommon, often arising between saints over biblical interpretation, the theological correctness of one minister or another, or the behavior of certain fellow colonists. Indeed, to a limited extent, Puritans actually welcomed these disputes because they seemed to demonstrate that religion was still a vital part of the colonists' lives. As John Winthrop said, "The business of religion is the business of the Puritans." Participants of weeknight gatherings at various church members' homes often engaged in these religious debates, and they were tolerated by both the ministers and the colony's civil leaders as long as the squabbles did not get out of control.

By the mid-1630s, however, one of the disputes had grown to such an extent that it threatened both the religious and secular unity of the colony. Some Puritans in both England and Massachusetts Bay had begun to espouse an extreme version of the covenant of grace: they believed that, having been assured of salvation, an individual was virtually freed from the manmade laws of both church and state, taking his or her commands only from God, who communicated His wishes to the saints. Called Antinomians (from *Anti,* "against," and *nomos,* "law"), these Puritan extremists attacked what one of them called the "deadness" of religious services and charged that several ministers were preaching the covenant of works. This charge was extremely offensive to these ministers who did not at all believe they were teaching salvation through good behavior, but rather preparation for the possibility of God's grace. Carried to its logical extension, of course, Antinomianism threatened to overthrow the authority of the ministers and even the power of the colonial government itself. Growing in numbers and intensity, the Antinomians in 1636 were able to elect one of their followers to replace Winthrop as colonial governor, although Winthrop managed to return to the office the next year.

Into this highly charged atmosphere stepped Anne Hutchinson, age forty-three, who had arrived in Massachusetts Bay in 1634 and soon became embroiled in the Antinomian controversy, or, as other Puritans called it, the "Antinomian heresy." The daughter of a clergyman who had been imprisoned twice for his religious unorthodoxy, Anne had married prosperous businessman William Hutchinson in 1612, when she was twenty-one years old. Before arriving in Massachusetts Bay, she had given birth to fourteen children, eleven of whom were alive in 1634.

Anne Hutchinson's many duties at home, however, did not prevent her from remaining very active in the church. Extremely interested in religion and theological questions, she was particularly influenced by John Cotton, a Puritan minister who had been forced to flee from England to Massachusetts Bay in 1633 because of his religious ideas. Upon arrival in the colony, Cotton said he was shocked by the extent to which colonists had been "lulled into security" by their growing belief that they could earn salvation through good works. Attacking this in sermons and in letters to other clergymen, Cotton helped fuel the Antinomian cause as well as Anne Hutchinson's religious ardor.

At first the Hutchinsons were seen as welcome additions to the community, largely because of William's prosperity and Anne's expertise in herbal medicines, nursing the sick, and midwifery. Soon, however, Anne Hutchinson began to drift into religious issues. She began to hold weeknight meetings in her home, at first to expand upon the previous Sunday's sermons and later to expound her own religious notions—ideas very close to those of the Antinomians. In November 1637, Anne's brother-in-law (John Wheelwright, another Puritan minister), was banished from the colony because of his radical sermons, and Anne was brought to trial before the General Court of Massachusetts Bay. With Governor Winthrop presiding, the court met to decide the fate of Mrs. Hutchinson. Privately, Winthrop called Anne Hutchinson a person of "nimble wit and active spirit and a very voluble [fluent] tongue." Winthrop himself, however, believed that women should be submissive and supportive like his wife and sister, and there was ample support for his position in the Bible.[1] No matter what he thought of Anne Hutchinson's abilities, publicly the governor was determined to be rid of her.

Why were Winthrop and other orthodox Puritans so opposed to Hutchinson? What crime had she committed? Some of Wheelwright's followers had been punished for having signed a petition supporting him, but Anne

1. Genesis 1:28–3:24; the First Letter of Paul to the Corinthians 11:1–16; the Letter of Paul to the Ephesians, Chapters 5 and 6, all verses.

Hutchinson had not signed the petition. Many other Puritans had held religious discussions in their homes, and more than a few had opposed the views of their ministers. Technically, Anne Hutchinson had broken no law. Why, then, was she considered such a threat that she was brought to trial and ultimately banished from the colony?

THE METHOD

For two days Anne Hutchinson stood before the General Court, presided over by the unsympathetic Governor John Winthrop. Fortunately, a fairly complete transcript of the proceedings has been preserved. In that transcript are the clues that you as the historian-detective will need to answer the question. Although spelling and punctuation have been modernized in most cases, the portions of the transcript you are about to read are reproduced verbatim. At first, some of the seventeenth-century phraseology might seem a bit strange. As are most spoken languages, English is constantly changing—think of how much English has changed since Chaucer's day. Yet if you read slowly and carefully, the transcript should give you no problem.

Before you begin studying the transcript, keep in mind two additional instructions:

1. Be careful not to lose sight of the central question: why was Anne Hutchinson such a threat to Massachusetts Bay colony? The transcript raises several other questions, some of them so interesting that they might pull you off the main track. As you read through the transcript, make a list of the various ways you think Anne might have threatened Massachusetts Bay.

2. Be willing to read between the lines. As you read each statement, ask yourself what is being said. Then try to deduce what is actually meant by what is being said. Sometimes people say exactly what they mean, but often they do not. They might intentionally or unintentionally disguise the real meaning of what they are saying, but the real meaning can usually be found. In conversation with a person face to face, voice inflection, body language, and other visual clues often provide the real meaning to what is being said. In this case, where personal observation is impossible, you must use both logic and imagination to read between the lines.

Source 1 from an excerpt of the examination from Thomas Hutchinson (Anne's great-grandson), *The History of the Colony and Province of Massachusetts-Bay*, Vol. II, ed. Lawrence Shaw Mayo (Cambridge, Mass.: Harvard University Press, 1936), pp. 366–391.

1. The Examination of Mrs. Anne Hutchinson at the Court at Newton, November 1637.[2]

CHARACTERS

Mrs. Anne Hutchinson, the accused

General Court, consisting of the governor, deputy governor, assistants, and deputies

Governor, John Winthrop, chair of the court

Deputy Governor, Thomas Dudley

Assistants, Mr. Bradstreet, Mr. Nowel, Mr. Endicott, Mr. Harlakenden, Mr. Stoughton

Deputies, Mr. Coggeshall, Mr. Bartholomew, Mr. Jennison, Mr. Coddington, Mr. Colborn

Clergymen and Ruling Elders:

  Mr. Peters, minister in Salem

  Mr. Leveret, a ruling elder in a Boston church

  Mr. Cotton, minister in Boston

  Mr. Wilson, minister in Boston, who supposedly made notes of a previous meeting between Anne Hutchinson, Cotton, and the other ministers

  Mr. Sims, minister in Charlestown

MR. WINTHROP, GOVERNOR. Mrs. Hutchinson, you are called here as one of those that have troubled the peace of the commonwealth and the churches here; you are known to be a woman that hath had a great share in the promoting and divulging of those opinions that are causes of this trouble, and to be nearly joined not only in affinity and affection with some of those the court had taken notice of and passed censure upon, but you have spoken divers things as we have been informed very prejudicial to the honour of the churches and ministers thereof, and you

2. Normally the trial would have been held in Boston, but Anne Hutchinson had numerous supporters in that city, so the proceedings were moved to the small town of Newton, where she had few allies.

have maintained a meeting and an assembly in your house that hath been condemned by the general assembly as a thing not tolerable nor comely in the sight of God nor fitting for your sex, and notwithstanding that was cried down you have continued the same. Therefore we have thought good to send for you to understand how things are, that if you be in an erroneous way we may reduce you that so you may become a profitable member here among us. Otherwise if you be obstinate in your course that then the court may take such course that you may trouble us no further. Therefore I would intreat you to express whether you do assent and hold in practice to those opinions and factions that have been handled in court already, that is to say, whether you do not justify Mr. Wheelwright's sermon and the petition.

MRS. HUTCHINSON. I am called here to answer before you but I hear no things laid to my charge.

GOV. I have told you some already and more I can tell you.

MRS. H. Name one, Sir.

GOV. Have I not named some already?

MRS. H. What have I said or done?

[Here, in a portion of the transcript not reproduced, Winthrop accused Hutchinson of harboring and giving comfort to a faction that was dangerous to the colony.]

MRS. H. Must not I then entertain the saints because I must keep my conscience?

GOV. Say that one brother should commit felony or treason and come to his brother's house. If he knows him guilty and conceals him he is guilty of the same. It is his conscience to entertain him, but if his conscience comes into act in giving countenance and entertainment to him that hath broken the law he is guilty too. So if you do countenance those that are transgressors of the law you are in the same fact.

MRS. H. What law do they transgress?

GOV. The law of God and of the state.

MRS. H. In what particular?

GOV. Why in this among the rest, whereas the Lord doth say honour thy father and thy mother.[3]

MRS. H. Ey, Sir, in the Lord.

GOV. This honour you have broke in giving countenance to them.

3. Exodus 20:12. Anne Hutchinson's natural father was in England and her natural mother was dead. To what, then, was Winthrop referring?

MRS. H. In entertaining those did I entertain them against any act (for there is the thing) or what God hath appointed?

GOV. You knew that Mr. Wheelwright did preach this sermon and those that countenance him in this do break a law?

MRS. H. What law have I broken?

GOV. Why the fifth commandment.[4]

MRS. H. I deny that for he [Wheelwright] saith in the Lord.

GOV. You have joined with them in the faction.

MRS. H. In what faction have I joined with them?

GOV. In presenting the petition.

MRS. H. Suppose I had set my hand to the petition. What then?

GOV. You saw that case tried before.

MRS. H. But I had not my hand to the petition.

GOV. You have councelled them.

MRS. H. Wherein?

GOV. Why in entertaining them.

MRS. H. What breach of law is that, Sir?

GOV. Why dishonouring of parents.

MRS. H. But put the case, Sir, that I do fear the Lord and my parents. May not I entertain them that fear the Lord because my parents will not give me leave?

GOV. If they be the fathers of the commonwealth, and they of another religion, if you entertain them then you dishonour your parents and are justly punishable.

MRS. H. If I entertain them, as they have dishonoured their parents I do.

GOV. No but you by countenancing them above others put honor upon them.

MRS. H. I may put honor upon them as the children of God and as they do honor the Lord.

GOV. We do not mean to discourse with those of your sex but only this: you do adhere unto them and do endeavor to set forward this faction and so you do dishonour us.

MRS. H. I do acknowledge no such thing. Neither do I think that I ever put any dishonour upon you.

GOV. Why do you keep such a meeting at your house as you do every week upon a set day? . . .

MRS. H. It is lawful for me so to do, as it is all your practices, and can you find a warrant for yourself and condemn me for the same thing? The

4. "Honour thy father and thy mother: that thy days may be long upon the land which the Lord thy God giveth thee." Exodus 20:12.

ground of my taking it up was, when I first came to this land because I did not go to such meetings as those were, it was presently reported that I did not allow of such meetings but held them unlawful and therefore in that regard they said I was proud and did despise all ordinances. Upon that a friend came unto me and told me of it and I to prevent such aspersions took it up, but it was in practice before I came. Therefore I was not the first.

GOV. For this, that you appeal to our practice you need no confutation. If your meeting had answered to the former it had not been offensive, but I will say that there was no meeting of women alone, but your meeting is of another sort for there are sometimes men among you.

MRS. H. There was never any man with us.

GOV. Well, admit there was no man at your meeting and that you was sorry for it, there is no warrant for your doings, and by what warrant do you continue such a course?

MRS. H. I conceive there lies a clear rule in Titus that the elder women should instruct the younger and then I must have a time wherein I must do it.

GOV. All this I grant you, I grant you a time for it, but what is this to the purpose that you Mrs. Hutchinson must call a company together from their callings to come to be taught of you?

MRS. H. Will it please you to answer me this and to give me a rule for then I will willingly submit to any truth. If any come to my house to be instructed in the ways of God what rule have I to put them away?

GOV. But suppose that a hundred men come unto you to be instructed. Will you forbear to instruct them?

MRS. H. As far as I conceive I cross a rule in it.

GOV. Very well and do you not so here?

MRS. H. No, Sir, for my ground is they are men.

GOV. Men and women all is one for that, but suppose that a man should come and say, "Mrs. Hutchinson, I hear that you are a woman that God hath given his grace unto and you have knowledge in the word of God. I pray instruct me a little." Ought you not to instruct this man?

MRS. H. I think I may. Do you think it is not lawful for me to teach women and why do you call me to teach the court?

GOV. We do not call you to teach the court but to lay open yourself.

[In this portion of the transcript not reproduced, Anne Hutchinson and Governor Winthrop continued to wrangle over specifically what law she had broken.]

GOV. Your course is not to be suffered for. Besides that we find such a course as this to be greatly prejudicial to the state. Besides the occasion that it is to seduce many honest persons that are called to those meetings and your opinions being known to be different from the word of God may seduce many simple souls that resort unto you. Besides that the occasion which hath come of late hath come from none but such as have frequented your meetings, so that now they are flown off from magistrates and ministers and since they have come to you. And besides that it will not well stand with the commonwealth that families should be neglected for so many neighbours and dames and so much time spent. We see no rule of God for this. We see not that any should have authority to set up any other exercises besides what authority hath already set up and so what hurt comes of this you will be guilty of and we for suffering you.

MRS. H. Sir, I do not believe that to be so.

GOV. Well, we see how it is. We must therefore put it away from you or restrain you from maintaining this course.

MRS. H. If you have a rule for it from God's word you may.

GOV. We are judges, and not you ours and we must compel you to it.

[Here followed a discussion of whether or not men as well as women attended Anne Hutchinson's meetings. In response to one question, Hutchinson denied that women ever taught at men's meetings.]

DEPUTY GOVERNOR. I would go a little higher with Mrs. Hutchinson. About three years ago we were all in peace. Mrs. Hutchinson from that time she came hath made a disturbance, and some that came over with her in the ship did inform me what she was as soon as she was landed. I being then in place dealt with the pastor and teacher of Boston and desired them to enquire of her, and then I was satisfied that she held nothing different from us. But within half a year after, she had vented divers of her strange opinions and had made parties in the country, and a length it comes that Mr. Cotton and Mr. Vane[5] were of her judgment, but Mr. Cotton had cleared himself that he was not of that mind. But now it appears by this woman's meeting that Mrs. Hutchinson hath so forestalled the minds of many by their resort to her meeting that now she hath a potent party in the country. Now if all these things have endangered us as from that foundation and if she in particular hath

5. Henry Vane, an ally of the Antinomians, was elected governor of Massachusetts Bay colony in 1636 and lost that office to Winthrop in 1637.

disparaged all our ministers in the land that they have preached a covenant of works,[6] and only Mr. Cotton a covenant of grace,[7] why this is
not to be suffered, and therefore being driven to the foundation and it
being found that Mrs. Hutchinson is she that hath depraved all the
ministers and hath been the cause of what is falled out, why we must
take away the foundation and the building will fall.

MRS. H. I pray, Sir, prove it that I said they preached nothing but a covenant
of works.

DEP. GOV. Nothing but a covenant of works. Why a Jesuit[8] may preach truth
sometimes.

MRS. H. Did I ever say they preached a covenant of works then?

DEP. GOV. If they do not preach a covenant of grace clearly, then they preach
a covenant of works.

MRS. H. No, Sir. One may preach a covenant of grace more clearly than another, so I said.

DEP. GOV. We are not upon that now but upon position.

MRS. H. Prove this then Sir that you say I said.

DEP. GOV. When they do preach a covenant of works do they preach truth?

MRS. H. Yes, Sir. But when they preach a covenant of works for salvation,
that is not truth.

DEP. GOV. I do but ask you this: when the ministers do preach a covenant of
works do they preach a way of salvation?

MRS. H. I did not come hither to answer to questions of that sort.

DEP. GOV. Because you will deny the thing.

MRS. H. Ey, but that is to be proved first.

DEP. GOV. I will make it plain that you did say that the ministers did preach
a covenant of works.

MRS. H. I deny that.

DEP. GOV. And that you said they were not able ministers of the New Testament, but Mr. Cotton only.

MRS. H. If ever I spake that I proved it by God's word.

COURT. Very well, very well.

MRS. H. If one shall come unto me in private, and desire me seriously to tell
then what I thought of such an one, I must either speak false or true in
my answer.

6. For an explanation of the covenant of works, see the "Background" section.
7. For an explanation of the covenant of grace, see the "Background" section.
8. The Society of Jesus (Jesuits) was a Roman Catholic order that placed special emphasis
on missionary work and combating Protestantism. The Jesuits were particularly detested
by many Protestants, including the Puritans.

[In this lengthy section, Hutchinson was accused of having gone to a meeting of ministers and accusing them all—except John Cotton—of preaching a covenant of works rather than a covenant of grace. The accusation, if proven, would have been an extremely serious one. Several of the ministers testified that Hutchinson had made this accusation.]

DEP. GOV. I called these witnesses and you deny them. You see they have proved this and you deny this, but it is clear. You said they preached a covenant of works and that they were not able ministers of the New Testament; now there are two other things that you did affirm which were that the scriptures in the letter of them held forth nothing but a covenant of works and likewise that those that were under a covenant of works cannot be saved.

MRS. H. Prove that I said so.

GOV. Did you say so?

MRS. H. No, Sir. It is your conclusion.

DEP. GOV. What do I do charging of you if you deny what is so fully proved?

GOV. Here are six undeniable ministers who say it is true and yet you deny that you did say that they did preach a covenant of works and that they were not able ministers of the gospel, and it appears plainly that you have spoken it, and whereas you say that it was drawn from you in a way of friendship, you did profess then that it was out of conscience that you spake and said, "The fear of man is a snare. Wherefore shall I be afraid, I will speak plainly and freely."

MRS. H. That I absolutely deny, for the first question was thus answered by me to them: They thought that I did conceive there was a difference between them and Mr. Cotton. At the first I was somewhat reserved. Then said Mr. Peters, "I pray answer the question directly as fully and as plainly as you desire we should tell you our minds. Mrs. Hutchinson we come for plain dealing and telling you our hearts." Then I said I would deal as plainly as I could, and whereas they say I said they were under a covenant of works and in the state of the apostles why these two speeches cross one another. I might say they might preach a covenant of works as did the apostles, but to preach a covenant of works and to be under a covenant of works is another business.

DEP. GOV. There have been six witnesses to prove this and yet you deny it.

MRS. H. I deny that these were the first words that were spoken.

GOV. You make the case worse, for you clearly shew that the ground of your opening your mind was not to satisfy them but to satisfy your own conscience.

[There was a brief argument here about what Hutchinson actually said at the gathering of ministers, after which the Court adjourned for the day.]

The next morning

GOV. We proceeded the last night as far as we could in hearing of this cause of Mrs. Hutchinson. There were divers things laid to her charge: her ordinary meetings about religious exercises, her speeches in derogation of the ministers among us, and the weakening of the hands and hearts of the people towards them. Here was sufficient proof made of that which she was accused of in that point concerning the ministers and their ministry, as that they did preach a covenant of works when others did preach a covenant of grace, and that they were not able ministers of the New Testament, and that they had not the seal of the spirit, and this was spoken not as was pretended out of private conference, but out of conscience and warrant from scripture alleged the fear of man is a snare and seeing God had given her a calling to it she would freely speak. Some other speeches she used, as that the letter of the scripture held forth a covenant of works, and this is offered to be proved by probable grounds. If there be any thing else that the court hath to say they may speak.

[At this point a lengthy argument erupted when Hutchinson demanded that the ministers who testified against her be recalled as witnesses, put under oath, and repeat their accusations. One member of the Court said that "the ministers are so well known unto us, that we need not take an oath of them."]

GOV. I see no necessity of an oath in this thing seeing it is true and the substance of the matter confirmed by divers. Yet that all may be satisfied, if the elders will take an oath they shall have it given them. . . .

MRS. H. I will prove by what Mr. Wilson hath written[9] that they [the ministers] never heard me say such a thing.

MR. SIMS. We desire to have the paper and have it read.

MR. HARLAKENDEN. I am persuaded that is the truth that the elders do say and therefore I do not see it necessary how to call them to oath.

GOV. We cannot charge any thing of untruth upon them.

MR. HARLAKENDEN. Besides, Mrs. Hutchinson doth say that they are not able ministers of the New Testament.

9. Wilson had taken notes at the meeting between Mrs. Hutchinson and the ministers. Hutchinson claimed that these notes would exonerate her. They were never produced and are now lost.

MRS. H. They need not swear to that.

DEP. GOV. Will you confess it then?

MRS. H. I will not deny it or say it.

DEP. GOV. You must do one.

[More on the oath followed.]

DEP. GOV. Let her witnesses be called.

GOV. Who be they?

MRS. H. Mr. Leveret and our teacher and Mr. Coggeshall.

GOV. Mr. Coggeshall was not present.

MR. COGGESHALL. Yes, but I was. Only I desired to be silent till I should be called.

GOV. Will you, Mr. Coggeshall, say that she did not say so?

MR. COGGESHALL. Yes, I dare say that she did not say all that which they lay against her.

MR. PETERS. How dare you look into the court to say such a word?

MR. COGGESHALL. Mr. Peters takes upon him to forbid me. I shall be silent.

MR. STOUGHTON. Ey, but she intended this that they say.

GOV. Well, Mr. Leveret, what were the words? I pray, speak.

MR. LEVERET. To my best remembrance when the elders did send for her, Mr. Peters did with much vehemency and intreaty urge her to tell what difference there was between Mr. Cotton and them, and upon his urging of her she said, "The fear of man is a snare, but they that trust upon the Lord shall be safe." And being asked wherein the difference was, she answered that they did not preach a covenant of grace so clearly as Mr. Cotton did, and she gave this reason of it: because that as the apostles were for a time without the spirit so until they had received the witness of the spirit they could not preach a covenant of grace so clearly.

[Here Hutchinson admitted that she might have said privately that the ministers were not able ministers of the New Testament.]

GOV. Mr. Cotton, the court desires that you declare what you do remember of the conference which was at the time and is now in question.

MR. COTTON. I did not think I should be called to bear witness in this cause and therefore did not labour to call to remembrance what was done; but the greatest passage that took impression upon me was to this purpose. The elders spake that they had heard that she had spoken some condemning words of their ministry, and among other things they did first pray her to answer wherein she thought their ministry did differ from mine. How the comparison sprang I am ignorant, but sorry I was that any comparison should be between me and my brethren and uncomfortable it was. She told them to this purpose that they did not hold forth a covenant of grace as I did. . . . I told her I was very sorry that she put comparisons between my ministry and theirs, for she had said more than I could myself, and rather I had that she had put us in fellowship with them and not have made the discrepancy. She said she found the difference. . . . And I must say that I did not find her saying they were under a covenant of works, not that she said they did preach a covenant of works.

[Here John Cotton tried to defend Hutchinson, mostly by saying he did not remember most of the events in question.]

MRS. H. If you please to give me leave I shall give you the ground of what I know to be true. Being much troubled to see the falseness of the constitution of the Church of England, I had like to have turned Separatist. Whereupon I kept a day of solemn humiliation and pondering of the thing, the scripture was brought unto me—he that denies Jesus Christ to be come in the flesh is antichrist. This I considered of and in considering found that the papists[10] did not deny him to come in the flesh, nor we did not deny him. Who then was antichrist? Was the Turk antichrist only? The Lord knows that I could not open scripture; he must by his prophetical office open it unto me. So after that being unsatisfied in the thing, the Lord was pleased to bring this scripture out of the Hebrews. He that denies the testament denies the testator, and in this did open unto me and give me to see that those which did not teach the new covenant had the spirit of antichrist, and upon this he did discover the ministry unto me, and ever since, I bless the Lord. He hath let me see which was the clear ministry and which the wrong. Since that time I confess I have been more choice and he hath left me to distinguish between the voice of my beloved and the voice of Moses, the voice of John Baptist and the voice of antichrist, for all those voices are spoken of in scripture. Now if you do condemn me for speaking what in my conscience I know to be truth I must commit myself unto the Lord.

MR. NOWELL. How do you know that that was the spirit?

MRS. H. How did Abraham know that it was God that bid him offer his son, being a breach of the sixth commandment?

DEP. GOV. By an immediate voice.

MRS. H. So to me by an immediate revelation.

10. "Papists" is a Protestant term for Roman Catholics, referring to the papacy.

DEP. GOV. How! an immediate revelation.

MRS. H. By the voice of his spirit to my soul. . . .

[In spite of the general shock that greeted her claim that she had experienced an immediate revelation from God, Hutchinson went on to state that God had compelled her to take the course she had taken and that God had said to her, as He had to Daniel of the Old Testament, that "though I should meet with affliction, yet I am the same God that delivered Daniel out of the lion's den, I will also deliver thee."]

MRS. H. You have power over my body but the Lord Jesus hath power over my body and soul, and assure yourselves thus much: you go on in this course you begin you will bring a curse upon you and your posterity, and the mouth of the Lord hath spoken it.

DEP. GOV. What is the scripture she brings?

MR. STOUGHTON. Behold I turn away from you.

MRS. H. But now having seen him which is invisible I fear not what man can do unto me.

GOV. Daniel was delivered by miracle. Do you think to be deliver'd so too?

MRS. H. I do here speak it before the court. I took that the Lord should deliver me by his providence.

MR. HARLAKENDEN. I may read scripture and the most glorious hypocrite may read them and yet go down to hell.

MRS. H. It may be so.

[Anne Hutchinson's "revelations" were discussed among the stunned Court.]

MR. BARTHOLOMEW. I speak as a member of the court. I fear that her revelations will deceive.

[More on revelations followed.]

DEP. GOV. I desire Mr. Cotton to tell us whether you do approve of Mrs. Hutchinson's revelations as she hath laid them down.

MR. COTTON. I know not whether I do understand her, but this I say: If she doth expect a deliverance in a way of providence, then I cannot deny it.

DEP. GOV. No, sir. We did not speak of that.

MR. COTTON. If it be by way of miracle then I would suspect it.

DEP. GOV. Do you believe that her revelations are true?

MR. COTTON. That she may have some special providence of God to help her is a thing that I cannot bear witness against.

DEP. GOV. Good Sir, I do ask whether this revelation be of God or no?

MR. COTTON. I should desire to know whether the sentence of the court will bring her to any calamity, and then I would know of her whether she expects to be delivered from that calamity by a miracle or a providence of God.

MRS. H. By a providence of God I say I expect to be delivered from some calamity that shall come to me.

[Revelations were further discussed.]

DEP. GOV. These disturbances that have come among the Germans have been all grounded upon revelations, and so they that have vented them have stirred up their hearers to take up arms against their prince and to cut the throats of one another, and these have been the fruits of them, and whether the devil may inspire the same into their hearts here I know not, for I am fully persuaded that Mrs. Hutchinson is deluded by the devil, because the spirit of God speaks truth in all his servants.

GOV. I am persuaded that the revelation she brings forth is delusion.

[All the court but some two or three ministers cried out, "We all believe it—we all believe it." Hutchinson was found guilty. Coddington made a lame attempt to defend Hutchinson but was silenced by Governor Winthrop.]

GOV. The court hath already declared themselves satisfied concerning the things you hear, and concerning the troublesomeness of her spirit and the danger of her course amongst us, which is not to be suffered. Therefore if it be the mind of the court that Mrs. Hutchinson for these things that appear before us is unfit for our society, and if it be the mind of the court that she shall be banished out of our liberties and imprisoned till she be sent away, let them hold up their hands.

[All but three did so.]

GOV. Those that are contrary minded hold up yours.

[Only Mr. Coddington and Mr. Colborn did so.]

MR. JENNISON. I cannot hold up my hand one way or the other, and I shall give my reason if the court require it.

GOV. Mrs. Hutchinson, the sentence of the court you hear is that you are banished from out of our jurisdiction as being a woman not fit for our society, and are to be imprisoned till the court shall send you away.

MRS. H. I desire to know wherefore I am banished?

GOV. Say no more. The court knows wherefore and is satisfied.

QUESTIONS TO CONSIDER

Now that you have examined the evidence, at least one point is very clear: the political and religious authorities of Massachusetts Bay were determined to get rid of Anne Hutchinson, whether or not she actually had broken any law. They tried to bait her, force admissions of guilt from her, confuse her, browbeat her. Essentially, they had already decided on the verdict before the trial began. So we know that Anne Hutchinson was a threat—and a serious one—to the colony.

And yet the colony had dealt quite differently with Roger Williams, a Puritan minister banished in 1635 because of his extreme religious beliefs. Williams was given every chance to mend his ways, Governor Winthrop remained his friend throughout Williams's appearances before the General Court, and it was only with great reluctance that the Court finally decided to send him out into the "wilderness."

Why, then, was Anne Hutchinson such a threat, and why was her trial such an ordeal? Obviously, she did pose a religious threat. As you look back through the evidence, try to clarify the exact points of difficulty between Hutchinson and the ministers. What was the basis of the argument over covenants of grace and works? What was Hutchinson supposed to have said? Under what circumstances had she allegedly said this? To whom? What was the role of her own minister, John Cotton, in the trial?

One must remember that Anne Hutchinson's trial took place in the midst of the divisive Antinomian controversy. What threat did the Antinomians pose to Massachusetts Bay and Puritanism? Was Anne Hutchinson an Antinomian? How would you prove whether or not she was?

Hutchinson's place or role in the community also seems to have come into question during the trial. What do the questions about the meetings she held in her home reveal? Look beyond what the governor and members of the Court are actually saying. Try to imagine what they might have been thinking. How might Hutchinson's meetings have eventually posed a threat to the larger community?

Finally, look through the transcript one more time. It provides some clues, often subtle ones, about the relationships between men and women in colonial Massachusetts. Puritan law and customs gave women approximately equal status with men, and of course women could join the church, just as men could. But in every society there are unspoken assumptions about how men and women should behave. Can you find any evidence that Anne Hutchinson violated these assumptions? If so, what did she do? Again, why would this be dangerous?

In conclusion, try to put together all you know from the evidence to answer the central question: why was Anne Hutchinson such a threat to Massachusetts Bay colony?

EPILOGUE

Even after their banishment, misfortune continued to plague the Hutchinson family. After moving to Narragansett Bay, Hutchinson once again became pregnant. However, by then she was more than forty-five years old and had begun her menopause. The fetus did not develop naturally and was aborted into a hydatidiform mole (resembling a cluster of grapes), which was expelled with considerable pain and difficulty. Many believed that the "birth" of this "monster baby" was proof of Anne Hutchinson's religious heresy.

In 1642, Hutchinson's husband died, and she moved with her six youngest children to the Dutch colony of New Netherland in what is now the Bronx borough of New York City. The next year she and all but one of her children were killed by Indians.

Ten years after Anne Hutchinson was banished from Massachusetts Bay, John Winthrop died. Winthrop believed to the end of his life that he had had no choice other than to expel Hutchinson and her family. However, even Winthrop's most sympathetic biographer, historian Edmund S. Morgan, describes the Hutchinson trial and its aftermath as "the least attractive episode" in Winthrop's long public career.

Massachusetts Bay continued to try to maintain community cohesion for years after Anne Hutchinson and her family were expelled. But as the colony grew and prospered, change ultimately did come. New generations were born that seemed unable to embrace the original zeal of the colony's founders.

New towns were formed, which increased the colony's size and made uniformity more difficult. Growth and prosperity also seemed to bring an increased interest in individual wealth and a corresponding decline in religious fervor. Reports of sleeping during sermons, fewer conversions of young people, blasphemous language, and growing attention to physical pleasures were numerous, as were reports of election disputes, intrachurch squabbling, and community bickering.

To those who remembered the old ways of Massachusetts Bay, such straying from the true path was more than unfortunate. The Puritans believed that as the ancient Israelites had been punished by God when they broke their covenant, so they would have to pay for their indiscretions. As one Puritan minister said, "In the time of their prosperity, see how the Jews turn their backs and shake off the authority of the Lord." The comparison was lost on almost no one.

Jeremiads—stories that predicted disasters because of the decline in religious zeal and public morality—were especially popular in the 1660s. The minister and physician Michael Wigglesworth's poem "The Day of Doom" (specifically written for the general public) was "read to pieces," according to historian Perry Miller. Wigglesworth's more sophisticated but heartfelt poem "God's Controversy with New England" was equally popular among more educated readers. Hence it is not surprising that by the late 1680s (more than forty years after

Anne Hutchinson's death) a wave of religious hysteria swept across Massachusetts Bay colony. Convinced that they had broken their covenant with God, many Puritans grimly awaited their punishment, spending long hours in churches listening to sermons. When in 1692 a few young girls in Salem Village began accusing some of their neighbors of being possessed by Satan, many were convinced that the day of punishment finally had arrived. Before that incident had run its course, twenty people had been killed, nineteen of them by hanging, and many more temporarily imprisoned. Although the Puritans' congregational church remained the official established church of Massachusetts until 1822, the original community cohesion had been altered long before that.

RHYTHMS OF COLONIAL LIFE:
THE STATISTICS OF
COLONIAL MASSACHUSETTS BAY

An important benefit of studying history is the ability to measure both change over time and people's reactions or adjustments to those changes. Today's world is changing with incredible speed. Recently you probably drove a fuel-injected automobile along an interstate highway while listening to an FM stereo radio station or a cassette tape, exited from the highway for a fast-food snack, continued home and prepared a full meal in a microwave oven, and then watched a film or a previously taped television program on your videocassette recorder or worked with your personal computer. These are all activities that no American could have engaged in thirty years ago. Indeed, we live in a society that expects change, generally welcomes it, and tries to plan for it.

Centuries ago, change took place at a considerably slower pace. Yet change did occur in colonial America, sometimes with what for the colonists must have seemed like startling speed. Colonial Massachusetts Bay was such a society. A child born in that colony in 1650, whether male or female, experienced a profoundly different life from that of a child born in 1750. In some ways, the differences in those two children's lives were dramatic and unwelcome.

What were the differences in the lives of the people of Massachusetts Bay between 1650 and 1750? How can we account for those differences? How might those differences have affected those people's thoughts, attitudes, feelings, and behavior? In this chapter you will be using statistics to measure change over time in colonial Massachusetts Bay and how men, women, and children reacted to and attempted to adapt to those changes. Then, using your historical imagination, you will explain how those changes and adaptations might have affected the emotions and actions of those colonists.

More specifically, by the 1760s and early 1770s, an increasing number of Massachusetts Bay colonists were willing to protest and ultimately take up arms against Great Britain. Do the changes in the lives of the people of Massachusetts Bay help explain why these colonists made those momentous decisions?

BACKGROUND

The years between the settlement of the colonies and the American Revolution are critical ones in American history. In those years, which in some colonies stretched to more than a century,[1] stability was gradually achieved, economic bases were laid, political institutions were established, social structures and institutions evolved, and intellectual and cultural life eventually thrived. As the population increased and as older settlements matured, new towns and settlements were founded on the edge of the receding wilderness, thus repeating the process of settlement, stability, growth, and maturation. And, although most colonists were still tied to England by bonds of language, economics, government, and affection, over the years those bonds gradually

loosened until the colonists, many without fully realizing it, had become something distinctly different than simply Englishmen and women who happened to reside in another land. In some ways, then, the American Revolution was the political realization of earlier economic, social, cultural, and political trends and events in colonial life.

These trends and events occurred, with some variations, in all the colonies, especially the Massachusetts Bay colony. Founded in 1630 by Puritans from England, Massachusetts Bay grew rapidly, aided in its first decade by 15,000 to 20,000 immigrants from England, and after that by natural increase.[2] By 1700, Massachusetts Bay's population had risen to almost 56,000 and by 1750, to approximately 188,000 making it one of Great Britain's most populous North American possessions.

1. The following colonies had been in existence for a century or more when the American Revolution broke out in 1775: Virginia, Massachusetts Bay, Rhode Island, Connecticut, Maryland, New York, and New Jersey. Settlements of Europeans also existed in New Hampshire and Delaware areas more than a century before the Revolution, although they did not formally become colonies until later.

2. The outbreak of the English civil war in 1642 drastically reduced emigration from England to Massachusetts Bay, largely because Puritans in England believed it was important to stay and fight against Charles I. In 1649, when Charles I was deposed and beheaded, a Puritan commonwealth was established in England, which lasted until 1660.

CHAPTER 3

RHYTHMS OF
COLONIAL LIFE:
THE STATISTICS
OF COLONIAL
MASSA-
CHUSETTS BAY

This rapid population growth forced the government of Massachusetts Bay (called the General Court, which included the governor, the deputy governor, the executive council of assistants, and the representatives, all elected annually by the freemen[3]) to organize new towns. Within the first year of settlement, the five original towns of Massachusetts Bay were laid out—Dorchester, Roxbury, Watertown, Newtown (now Cambridge), Charlestown, and Boston, all on the Charles River. By the time Middlesex County (west of Boston) was organized in 1643, there were eight towns in that county alone, and by 1700, there were twenty-two.

The organization of towns was an important way for Puritan leaders to keep control of the rapidly growing population. Unlike settlers in the middle and southern colonies, colonists in Massachusetts Bay could not simply travel to an uninhabited area, select a parcel of land, and receive individual title to the land from the colonial governor. Instead, a group of men who wanted to establish a town had to apply to the General Court for a land grant for the entire town. Leaders of the prospective new town were then selected, and the single church was organized. Having received the grant from the General Court, the new town's leaders apportioned the available land among the male heads of households who were church members, holding in common some land for grazing and other uses (hence the "town common"). In this way the Pu-

ritan leadership retained its own control of the fast-growing population, ensured Puritan economic and religious domination, and guaranteed that large numbers of dissenters—men and women who might divert the colony from its "holy mission" in the wilderness—would not be attracted to Massachusetts Bay.

Economically, Massachusetts Bay prospered from the very beginning, witnessing no "starving time" as did Virginia. Yet of all the major colonies, Massachusetts Bay fit the least well into England's mercantilist system, whereby colonies supplied raw materials to the mother country and in turn purchased the mother country's manufactured products. Because comparatively rocky soil and a short growing season kept crop yields low and agricultural surpluses meager, many people in Massachusetts Bay had to seek other ways of making a living. Many men petitioned the General Court to organize new towns on the frontier; others turned to either the sea as fishermen, traders, shippers, and seamen or native manufacturing enterprises such as iron product manufacturing, rum distilling, shipbuilding, and ropemaking. Except for fishing, none of these activities fit into England's mercantile plans for her empire, and some undertakings were prohibited outright by the Navigation Acts (1660, 1663, and later, which set up the mercantile system), which most citizens of Massachusetts Bay ignored.

The restoration of the English monarchy in 1660 in the person of Charles II greatly concerned the Massachusetts Bay colonists. It was no secret that Charles II loathed Puritanism. Equally serious, the new monarch

3. A freeman was an adult male who was accepted by his town (hence a landowner) and was a member of the Puritan congregational church.

made it clear that the Navigation Acts were to be enforced. After more than twenty years of wrangling among the colony, the king, and the Lords of Trade, in 1684 the Massachusetts Bay charter was revoked; in 1685, the colony was included in a grand scheme to reorganize the northern colonies into the Dominion of New England, with one royal governor and no elected assembly.[4] The dominion's governor, the undiplomatic Sir Edmund Andros, further alienated Massachusetts Bay colonists by levying taxes on them without consultation or consent, enforcing the Navigation Acts, favoring religious toleration in Massachusetts Bay, and calling their land titles into question. As a result, Massachusetts Bay colonists were only too glad to use the confusion and instability accompanying England's Glorious Revolution of 1688 to stage a bloodless coup that deposed Andros and returned the colony to its original form of government, an act that the mother country ultimately approved. Thus from almost the very beginning, the colonists of Massachusetts Bay were politically aware and jealously guarded their representative government.

Not only were the Massachusetts Bay colonists' political ideas sharpened and refined decades before the American Revolution; their other ways of thinking were also greatly affected. Two important intellectual movements in Europe, the Enlightenment and the Great Awakening, had an enormous impact in America. The Enlighten-

ment was grounded in the belief that human reason could discover the natural laws that governed the universe, nature, and human affairs; human reason and scientific observation would reveal those natural laws to human beings. Although the Enlightenment's greatest impact was on the well-educated and therefore the wealthier, even the "common" people were affected by it. The Great Awakening was a religious revival that swept through the colonies in the 1740s and 1750s. Touched off by English preacher George Whitefield, the Great Awakening emphasized humanity's utter sinfulness and need for salvation. In hundreds of emotional revival meetings, complete with shouting, moaning, and physical gyrations, thousands were converted. Because the Great Awakening undermined the traditional churches and their leaders, most clergymen (called "Old Lights") opposed the movement, but to little avail.

On the surface, the Enlightenment and the Great Awakening seemed to have nothing in common. The Enlightenment emphasized human reason, whereas the Great Awakening appealed more to emotion than to reason. Both movements, however, contained a strong streak of individualism: the Enlightenment emphasized the potential of the human mind, and the Great Awakening concentrated on the individual soul. Each movement in its own way increased the colonists' sense of themselves as individuals who possessed both individual rights and individual futures. The colonists who once huddled together for protection and mutual assistance in tiny settlements had, by the mid-eighteenth century, grown, changed, and matured, as had the settlements they had built.

4. The Dominion of New England included the colonies of New Jersey, New York, Connecticut, Rhode Island, Plymouth, and Massachusetts Bay, which included lands that later became New Hampshire and Maine.

CHAPTER 3

RHYTHMS OF
COLONIAL LIFE:
THE STATISTICS
OF COLONIAL
MASSA-
CHUSETTS BAY

They harbored new attitudes about themselves, their society, their individual futures, and, almost inevitably, their government. Hence the life and thought of a Massachusetts Bay colonist (or, indeed, any colonist) born in 1750 was profoundly different from that of one born in 1650.

When most people think of the colonial period in America, they invariably think of the colonial leaders, men and women who held the economic, social, and political reins of the society. But these leaders—the John Winthrops and Anne Hutchinsons, the Jonathan Edwardses and Benjamin Franklins, the William Penns and Nathaniel Bacons—represent only a tiny fraction of the men and women who lived in the colonies between 1607 and 1775. And yet, to understand the processes of growth, change, and maturation more fully, it is necessary for us to study the lives of the "ordinary" men, women, and children as well as those of their economic, social, and political "betters." How did the processes of growth, change, and maturation affect small farmers and artisans, their spouses,

sons, and daughters? How did the situations of these people change over time? How did they react to those changes? Indeed, if we can learn more about the lives of all Americans, not just those of the prominent colonists, we will be able to better understand the extent to which growth, change, and maturation helped affect the coming of the American Revolution.

It is considerably easier to collect information about the leading colonial figures than the "average" men and women. Few of the farmers, artisans, or laborers left diaries or letters to provide clues to their thoughts and behavior; fewer made speeches or participated in decision making; fewer still talked with leaders like Washington and Jefferson, so their thoughts and actions were much less likely to be recorded for us by others. In some ways, then, a curtain has been drawn across a large part of American colonial history, obscuring the lives, thoughts, and feelings of the vast majority of the colonists. Sometimes even their names have been lost.

THE METHOD

How can we hope to reconstruct the lives, thoughts, and feelings of people who left no letters, diaries, sermons, speeches, or votes for us to analyze? Recently, historians have become more imaginative in using the relatively limited records at their disposal to examine the lives of ordinary men, women, and children who lived during the colonial period. Almost every per-

son, even the poorest, left some record that she or he existed. That person's name may appear in any of a number of records, including church records stating when she or he was baptized, marriage records, property-holding records, civil- or criminal-court records, military records, tax records, and death or cemetery records. It is in these records that the lives of the ordinary men,

Table 1

Type of Record	Questions
Census	Is the population growing or shrinking or stationary? Is the ratio of males to females roughly equal?[5] Does that ratio change over time?
Marriage	At what age are women marrying? Is that age changing over time?
Wills, probate	How are estates divided? Is that method changing over time? Based on real estate and personal property listed, is the collective standard of living rising, falling, or stationary? Based on dates of death, is the population living longer?
Land, tax	What percentage of the adult male population owns land? Is that percentage changing over time? Is the land evenly distributed among the adult male population?

women, and children of colonial America can be examined. An increasing number of historians have been carefully scrutinizing those records to recreate the lives and attitudes of those who left no other evidence.

How is this done? Most historians interested in the lives of the ordinary colonists rely heavily on statistics. Instead of trying to uncover all the records relating to one person or family (which might not be representative of the whole population), these historians use statistics to create *collective biographies,* that is, biographies of population *groups* (farmers in Andover, Massachusetts, for example) rather than biographies of certain individuals. The historians collect all (or a sample of all) the birth, death, and marriage records of a community and look at all (or

a sample of all) the wills, probate records,[6] tax and landholding records, and census returns. These historians are forming an aggregate or collective picture of a community and how that community has changed over time. Are women marrying later? What percentage of women remain unmarried? Are women having fewer children than they were in another time? Are inheritance patterns (the methods of dividing estates among heirs) changing over time? Are farms increasing or decreasing in size? To the historian, each statistical summary of records (each set of statistics or *aggregate* picture) contains information that increases understanding of the community being studied.

After the statistics are compiled, what does the historian do next? Each set of statistics is examined separately to see what changes are occurring over time. Table 1 shows the types of questions historians ask of several different types of records.

5. Because males and females are born in roughly equal numbers, an unequal ratio of males to females (called a sex ratio) must be explained by events such as wars, out-migration, in-migration, or differing mortality rates for males and females.

6. Probate records are public records of processed wills.

CHAPTER 3

RHYTHMS OF
COLONIAL LIFE:
THE STATISTICS
OF COLONIAL
MASSA-
CHUSETTS BAY

Having examined each set of statistics, the historian places the sets in some logical order, which may vary depending on the available evidence, the central questions the historian is attempting to answer, and the historian's own preferences. Some historians prefer a "birth-to-death" ordering, actually beginning with age-at-marriage statistics for females and moving chronologically through the collective life of the community's population. Others prefer to isolate the demographic statistical sets (birth, marriage, migration, and death) from the economic sets (such as landholding and division of estates).

Up to this point the historian has (1) collected the statistics and arranged them into sets, (2) examined each set and measured tendencies or changes over time, and (3) arranged the sets in some logical order. Now the historian must begin asking "why" for each set. For example:

1. Why does the method of dividing estates change over time?
2. Why are women marrying later?
3. Why are premarital pregnancies increasing?

In many cases, the answer to each question (and other "why" questions) is in one of the other statistical sets. That may cause the historian to alter his or her ordering of the sets to make the story more clear.

The historian is actually linking the sets to one another to form a chain. When two sets have been linked (because one set answers the "why" question of another set), the historian repeats the process until all the sets have been linked to form one chain of evidence. At that point the historian

can summarize the tendencies that have been discovered and, if desired, can connect those trends or tendencies with other events occurring in the period, such as the American Revolution.

One example of how historians link statistical sets together to answer the question why is sufficient. Source 1 in the Evidence section shows that the white population growth in Massachusetts Bay was extremely rapid between 1660 and 1770 (the growth rate actually approximates those of many non-Western developing nations today). How can we account for this rapid growth? Look at Source 4, which deals with the survival rate of children born in the town of Andover between 1640 and 1759. Note that between 1640 and 1699, the survival rate was very high (in Sweden between 1751 and 1799, 50 percent of the children born did not reach the age of fifteen). Also examine Source 16, the average number of births per marriage in Andover. Note that between 1655 and 1704, the average number of births per marriage was very high, between 5.3 and 7.6. Thus we can conclude that the population grew so rapidly in Massachusetts Bay between 1660 and 1700 because women gave birth to large numbers of children *and* a high percentage of those children survived. By following this process, you will be able to link together all the statistical sets.

In this chapter you will be using the statistics provided to identify important trends affecting the men, women, and children of Massachusetts Bay in the century preceding the American Revolution. Use the process described above:

1. Examine each statistical set, especially for a change over time.
2. Ask why that change took place.
3. Find the answer in another set, thereby establishing a linkage.
4. Repeat the process until all the sets have been linked together.
5. Then ask the central questions: What important trends affected the men, women, and children of colonial Massachusetts Bay in the century preceding the American Revolution? How were people likely to think and feel about those trends? Finally, how might those trends have contributed to the decision of Massachusetts Bay colonists to revolt against Great Britain?

As you will see, most of the statistical sets deal with Concord and Andover, two older towns in the Massachusetts Bay colony (see the following map). These two towns were chosen because historians Robert Gross and Philip Greven collected much statistical information about Concord and Andover, respectively; we have arranged the data in tabular form. Evidence suggests that these two towns are fairly representative of other towns in the eastern part of the colony. Concord, a farm town founded in 1635, was the first town in Massachusetts Bay established away from the Charles River. The area was rich in furs, and settlers initially were able to trap the furs (especially beaver) for income. Andover was organized in 1646, the original settlers mainly from other towns in the colony. In Andover, the people lived in the village and walked out to farm their land, which was organized in the open-field system (landowners owned several strips of land in large open fields and worked the fields in common). In Concord, many settlers lived outside the village and near the fields, building clusters of houses along the Concord River (which was spanned by the soon-to-be-famous Concord Bridge).

As you examine the statistical sets from these two towns, note that the dates for the sets do not always match. Understand both *what* you are examining and *when* that particular factor is being measured. For example, the statistical set on premarital conceptions in Andover records that phenomenon from 1655 to 1729, whereas the same phenomenon in Concord is measured from 1740 to 1744 (see Source 17). Assuming that this trend is similar in both towns, how would you use those two sets of statistics?

At first the statistics appear cold and impersonal and seem to tell us little that is worth knowing. But we cannot just skip this problem and get on to the political events leading up to the American Revolution (such as the Boston Massacre) and the important battles of the Revolution. It is crucial to remember that some of the men and boys who were on the streets of Boston on the evening of March 5, 1770, are counted in these statistics. And some of the men who participated in the Battles of Lexington and Concord also appear in these statistics. Are there any links between what the statistics represent and the subsequent behaviors of these people?

The eastern part of Massachusetts Bay Colony, 1755. Reproduced from Thomas Jefferys' "A Map of the Most Inhabited part of New England, Containing the Provinces of Massachusetts Bay, and New Hampshire, with the Colonies of Conecticut and Rhode Island. November 29, 1755"; in Jefferys' *A General Topography of North America and the West Indies* (London, 1768); courtesy of the Map Division, The New York Public Library, Astor, Lenox and Tilden Foundations.

Source 1 reprinted from U.S. Bureau of the Census, *Historical Statistics of the United States, Colonial Times to 1957* (Washington, D.C.: U.S. Government Printing Office, 1960), p. 756.

1. Growth of White Population, Massachusetts Bay, 1660–1770.

Year	Total Population	Average Annual Growth Rate (%)
1660	20,082	---
1670	30,000	4.9
1680	39,752	3.3
1690	49,504	2.5
1700	55,941	1.3
1710	62,390	1.2
1720	91,008	4.6
1730	114,116	2.6
1740	151,613	3.3
1750	188,000	2.4
1760	222,600	1.8
1770	235,308	5.7

Source 2 data from Philip J. Greven, Jr., *Four Generations: Population, Land, and Family in Colonial Andover, Massachusetts* (Ithaca, N.Y.: Cornell University Press, 1970), p. 179.

2. Growth of White Population, Town of Andover, 1680–1776.

Year	Population	Average Annual Growth Rate (%)
1680	435	---
1685	600	7.6
1695	710	1.8
1705	945	3.3
1715	1,050	1.1
1725	1,305	2.4
1735	1,630	2.5
1745	1,845	1.3
1755	2,135	1.6
1764	2,442	1.6
1776	2,953	1.8

CHAPTER 3

RHYTHMS OF
COLONIAL LIFE:
THE STATISTICS
OF COLONIAL
MASSA-
CHUSETTS BAY

Source 3 data from Robert A. Gross, *The Minutemen and Their World* (New York: Hill and Wang, 1976), p. 15.

3. Growth of Population, Town of Concord, 1679–1750.

Year	Population	Average Annual Growth Rate (%)
1679	480	---
1706	920	3.3
1710	c. 1,000	2.2
1725	c. 1,500	3.3
1750	c. 2,000	1.3

Sources 4 through 6 data from Greven, *Four Generations: Population, Land, and Family in Colonial Andover, Massachusetts,* pp. 191, 189, 177. Source 6 data also from Gross, *The Minutemen and Their World,* p. 209.

4. Children Born Between 1640 and 1759 Who Lived to at Least Age 10, Andover.

Years	Rate
1640–1669	917 per 1,000
1670–1699	855 per 1,000
1700–1729	805 per 1,000
1730–1759	695 per 1,000

5. Children Who Died Before Reaching Age 20, Andover, 1670–1759.

Years	Number	Mortality Rate[7]
1670–1699	87	225 per 1,000
1700–1729	206	381 per 1,000
1730–1759	142	534 per 1,000

7. The mortality rate is the ratio of the number of deaths per thousand people. It is used to compare the deaths in two or more populations of unequal size, like Andover and Boston.

6. Population Density, Concord and Andover.

Year	Concord	Andover
1706	14.7 per square mile	
1754	44.2 per square mile	
1764		41 per square mile
1776		50 per square mile

Source 7 data from James A. Henretta, *The Evolution of American Society, 1700–1815: An Interdisciplinary Approach,* 1st ed. (Lexington, Mass.: D. C. Heath, 1973), p. 15.

7. Average New England Farm Size.

1650s: 200–300 acres (3–6% cultivated)
1750s: under 100 acres (10–15% cultivated)

Sources 8 through 10 data from Gross, *The Minutemen and Their World,* pp. 210, 215, 214.

8. Average Landholding, Concord.

Year	Amount of Land
1663	259 acres
1749	56 acres

9. Crop Yields per Acre, Concord.

Year	Grain	Hay
1749	13.2 bushels	0.82 ton
1771	12.2 bushels	0.71 ton

CHAPTER 3

RHYTHMS OF
COLONIAL LIFE:
THE STATISTICS
OF COLONIAL
MASSA-
CHUSETTS BAY

10. Amount of Land Necessary to Pasture One Cow, Concord.

Year	Average
1749	1.4
1771	2.2

Source 11 data from Henretta, *The Evolution of American Society, 1700–1815,* p. 19.

11. Average Period of Fallow,[8] New England Farms.

1650: field left fallow between 7 and 15 years
1770: field left fallow between 1 and 2 years

Source 12 data from Greven, *Four Generations: Population, Land, and Family in Colonial Andover, Massachusetts,* p. 216.

12. Abbot Family, Andover, Massachusetts.

1650: George Abbot was only adult male Abbot
1750: 25 adult male Abbots in Andover

Source 13 data from Henretta, *The Evolution of American Society,* 1st ed., pp. 29–30.

13. Division of Estates, Andover, Massachusetts.

First generation: 95% of all estates divided among all male heirs
Second generation: 75% of all estates divided among all male heirs
Third generation: 58% of all estates divided among all male heirs
Fourth generation (came to maturity after 1750): under 50% of all estates
divided among all male heirs

8. Fallow land is plowed and tilled but left unseeded during a growing season. Land is left fallow to replenish the soil's nutrients. Colonial farmers as a rule did not use fertilizer.

Source 14 from Gross, *The Minutemen and Their World,* p. 216.

14. Insolvent Estates, Concord.

Years	Total Estates	Number of Insolvent Estates
1740–1760	19	1
1760–1774	30	11

Sources 15 through 17 data from Greven, *Four Generations: Population, Land, and Family in Colonial Andover, Massachusetts,* pp. 33, 23, 105, 183, 113. Source 17 data also from Gross, *The Minutemen and Their World,* p. 217.

15. Average Age at Marriage for Females, Andover, 1650–1724.

Year	Age
1650–1654	18.0
1660–1664	18.8
1670–1674	20.4
1680–1684	21.6
1690–1694	21.6
1700-1704	21.0
1710–1714	24.0
1720–1724	23.9

16. Average Births per Marriage, Andover, 1655–1764.

Year	Births
1655–1664	5.8
1665–1674	5.3
1675–1684	5.7
1685–1694	6.0
1695–1704	7.6
1705–1714	7.5
1715–1724	5.7
1725–1734	4.8
1735–1744	4.1
1745–1754	4.0
1755–1764	3.9

CHAPTER 3

RHYTHMS OF
COLONIAL LIFE:
THE STATISTICS
OF COLONIAL
MASSA-
CHUSETTS BAY

17. Percentage of Premarital Conceptions,[9] Andover and Concord.

Years	Andover	Concord
1655–1674	0.0	
1675–1699	7.0	
1700–1739	11.3	
1740–1749		19
1750–1759		26
1760–1774		41

Source 18 data from Gary B. Nash, "Urban Wealth and Poverty in Pre-Revolutionary America," *Journal of Interdisciplinary History,* 6 (Spring 1976), 545–584.

18. Percentage of Group Migration[10] into Boston, 1747–1771.

Group	1747	1759	1771
Single men	3.0	8.5	23.4
Single women	4.0	16.8	20.0
Widows and widowers	7.9	8.9	4.4
Married couples	33.6	27.4	27.5
Children	51.5	38.4	24.7
	100.0%	100.0%	100.0%

Source 19 data from Gross, *The Minutemen and Their World,* p. 218.

19. Sex Ratio, Concord, 1765.

88 males to 100 females

9. *Premarital conceptions* refers to first-born children who are born less than nine months from the date of marriage.
10. *Migration* refers to internal migration, not immigration from Europe.

Sources 20 through 22 data from Nash, "Urban Wealth and Poverty in Pre-Revolutionary America," 545–584.

20. Distribution of Wealth by Percentage[11] in Boston, 1687 and 1771.

Wealth Distribution	1687	1771
Wealth possessed by the richest 5% of the people	30.2	48.7
Wealth possessed by the next wealthiest 5% of the people	16.1	14.7
Wealth possessed by the next wealthiest 30% of the people	39.8	27.4
Wealth possessed by the next wealthiest 30% of the people	11.3	9.1
Wealth possessed by the poorest 30% of the people	2.6	0.1

21. Taxables[12] in Boston, 1728–1771.

Year	Population	Taxables
1728	12,650	c. 3,000
1733	15,100	c. 3,500
1735	16,000	3,637
1738	16,700	3,395
1740	16,800	3,043
1741	16,750	2,972
1745	16,250	2,660
1750	15,800	c. 2,400
1752	15,700	2,789
1756	15,650	c. 2,500
1771	15,500	2,588

22. Poor Relief in Boston, 1700–1775.

Years	Population	Average Annual Expenditure in Pounds	Expenditure in Pounds per 1,000 Pop.
1700–1710	7,500	£ 173	£23
1711–1720	9,830	181	18
1721–1730	11,840	273	23
1731–1740	15,850	498	31
1741–1750	16,240	806	50
1751–1760	15,660	1,204	77
1761–1770	15,520	1,909	123
1771–1775	15,500	2,478	156

11. See Questions to Consider for assistance in reading this source.
12. *Taxables* refers to the number of people who owned a sufficient amount of property (real estate and buildings) to be taxed.

CHAPTER 3

RHYTHMS OF
COLONIAL LIFE:
THE STATISTICS
OF COLONIAL
MASSA-
CHUSETTS BAY

QUESTIONS TO CONSIDER

When using statistics, one must first look at each set individually. For each set, ask the following questions:

1. What does this set of statistics measure?
2. How does what is being measured change over time?
3. Why does that change take place? As noted, the answer to this question can be found in another set or sets. When you connect one set to another, statisticians say that you have made a "linkage."

A helpful way of examining the statistical sets is to think of three children born in Massachusetts Bay—one in 1650, a second in 1700, and the third in 1750. As you look at the statistical evidence, ask yourself how the lives of these three children (male or female) were different. What factors account for those differences?

Begin by examining Sources 1 through 3, which deal with population increase in Massachusetts Bay as a whole, in Andover, and in Concord. How does population growth change over time? How can Sources 4, 5, 15, and 16 help you answer the "why" question for population growth?

Because immigration to Massachusetts Bay from Europe declined drastically in the 1640s and did not resume significantly until the early 1700s, population increases in the period in between can be explained only by migration from other colonies (which was negligible) or by natural increase. How did natural increase change over time (Sources 16, 4, and 5)? How would you

explain this change? To answer that question, you will have to use your historical imagination as well as *all* the rest of the sources. For example, how might you explain the dramatic increase in child mortality, as seen in Source 5?

We can see that one result of population growth in Andover and Concord was a rise in population density. What were the *results* of that increase in population density? Begin by examining Sources 6 through 11. How did farming change over time? Why was this so (see earlier sources plus Source 12, on the Abbot family)? How did those changes affect the division of estates (Source 13) and the number of insolvent estates (Source 14), and why? Did economic changes have any effect on the female life cycle? Consider the following demographic changes: the average age at marriage for Andover females (Source 15); the number of births per marriage (Source 16); and the significant increase in premarital conceptions (Source 17).

At this point, it helps to pause and take stock of what you have learned. What was the relationship between population growth and farming? Between changes in farming and social conditions? Would you say that the lifestyle of Massachusetts Bay colonists was improving, declining, or stationary during the first century of the colony's history? How would you prove your answer?

As noted at the beginning of this chapter, one important factor that historians study is the ability of people to adapt to changes in their environments or circumstances. In your view, how were Massachusetts Bay colonists attempting to adapt to these changes? Would you say they were or were not successful?

Many of the people we have been examining chose to adapt by leaving their towns and migrating to the frontier to set up new communities where they could make fresh starts. Many others, however, adapted by migrating to Boston (Source 18). How could you prove this? How did migration to Boston change in character between 1747 and 1771? How did migration affect the towns from which these people migrated (see Source 19)? What were the likely results of that migration?

Our attention now should follow those migrants to Boston. Were these migrants able to improve their collective situation in that large seaport? How could you prove your answer to that question?

At this point we are at source 20, wealth distribution in Boston. Note that Boston is not a farming village like Andover and Concord. Read the set this way: The richest 5% of those living in Boston in 1687 owned 30.2 percent of the town's taxable wealth

(essentially real estate and buildings), but by 1771 the richest 5 percent owned 48.7 percent of the town's taxable wealth; the poorest 30% of those living in Boston in 1687 owned 2.6 percent of the town's taxable wealth, but by 1771 the poorest 30 percent owned 0.1 percent of the town's taxable wealth. Read the chart the same way for the groups in between. As you examine the chart, note which groups were gaining in wealth and which groups were losing in wealth.

Sources 21 and 22 are different ways of looking at the same problem. How are those sources related to one another? How can you link them back to the chain you have made?

At this point, you should be able to answer the central questions:

1. What important trends regarding growth, change, and maturation affected the people of colonial Massachusetts Bay?
2. How were people likely to think and feel about those trends?
3. How might those trends have contributed to the decision of Massachusetts Bay colonists to revolt against Great Britain?

EPILOGUE

Many of the men who fought on the Patriot side in either the Continental Line (the troops under the central government, the United States Army) or the Massachusetts Bay militia came from the towns, farms, and seaports of Massachusetts Bay. If asked why they had endured such hardships to fight against the mother country, most probably they would have said that

CHAPTER 3

RHYTHMS OF
COLONIAL LIFE:
THE STATISTICS
OF COLONIAL
MASSA-
CHUSETTS BAY

they were fighting for liberty and independence—and undoubtedly they were. But we now realize that a number of other factors were present that may very well have provided strong reasons for these men to contest the British. Whether they fully understood these forces can never be known with certainty because very few left any written record that might help us comprehend their thoughts or behavior.

The American Revolution was a momentous event not just for Americans but ultimately for many other people as well. As Ralph Waldo Emerson wrote years later, it was a "shot heard 'round the world." The American Revolution was the first anticolonial rebellion that was successful on the first try, and as such it provided a model for others in Latin America and elsewhere. As a revolt against authority, the American Revolution made many European rulers tremble because if the ideas contained in the Declaration of Independence (especially that of the right of revolution against unjust rulers) ever became widespread, their own tenures might well be doomed. And, beginning with the French Revolution, this is precisely what happened; gradually, crowns began to topple all across the Continent. Indeed, many would have agreed with the Frenchman Turgot, who, writing of America in the 1780s, noted the following:

This people is the hope of the human race. It may become the model. It ought to show the world, by facts, that men can be free and yet peaceful, and may dispense with the chains in which tyrants and knaves ... have presumed to bind them.... The Americans should be an example of political, religious, commercial and industrial liberty. The asylum they offer to the oppressed of every nation, the avenue of escape they open, will compel governments to be just and enlightened.[13]

The revolution obviously brought independence and in the long run became one of the significant events in world history. But did it alter or reverse the economic and social trends that, as we have seen, were affecting the men, women, and children of colonial New England? In 1818, the United States Congress passed an act providing pensions for impoverished veterans of the War of Independence and their widows. Congressmen believed that there were approximately 1,400 poor veterans and widows who were still alive. Yet an astounding 30,000 applied for pensions, 20,000 of whom were ultimately approved to receive these benefits. Clearly the American Revolution, although an event that had worldwide significance, did not necessarily change the lives of all the men and women who participated in it. Or did it?

13. Richard Price, *Observations on the Importance of the American Revolution, and the Means of Making It a Benefit to the World* (London: printed for T. Cadell, 1785), pp. 102, 123.

CHAPTER FOUR

WHAT REALLY HAPPENED IN THE BOSTON MASSACRE? THE TRIAL OF CAPTAIN THOMAS PRESTON

THE PROBLEM

On the chilly evening of March 5, 1770, a small group of boys began taunting a British sentry (called a "Centinel" or "Sentinel") in front of the Boston Custom House. Pushed to the breaking point by this goading, the soldier struck one of his tormenters with his musket. Soon a crowd of fifty or sixty gathered around the frightened soldier, prompting him to call for help. The officer of the day, Captain Thomas Preston, and seven British soldiers hurried to the Custom House to protect the sentry.

Upon arriving at the Custom House, Captain Preston must have sensed how precarious his position was. The crowd had swelled to more than one hundred, some anxious for a fight, others simply curiosity seekers, and still others called from their homes by the town's church bells, a traditional signal that a fire had broken out. Efforts by Preston and others to calm the crowd proved useless. And because the crowd had enveloped Preston and his men as it had the lone sentry, escape was nearly impossible.

What happened next is a subject of considerable controversy. One of the soldiers fired his musket into the crowd, and the others followed suit, one by one. The colonists scattered, leaving five dead[1] and six wounded,

1. Those killed were Crispus Attucks (a black seaman in his forties, who also went by the name of Michael Johnson), James Caldwell (a sailor), Patrick Carr (an immigrant from Ireland who worked as a leather-breeches maker), Samuel Gray (a rope-maker), and Samuel Maverick (a seventeen-year-old apprentice).

CHAPTER 4

WHAT REALLY
HAPPENED IN
THE BOSTON
MASSACRE? THE
TRIAL OF
CAPTAIN
THOMAS
PRESTON

some of whom were probably innocent bystanders. Preston and his men quickly returned to their barracks, where they were placed under house arrest. They were later taken to jail and charged with murder.

Preston's trial began on October 24, 1770, delayed by the authorities in an attempt to cool the emotions of the townspeople. John Adams, Josiah Quincy, and Robert Auchmuty had agreed to defend Preston, even though the former two were staunch Patriots. They believed that the captain was entitled to a fair trial and did their best to defend him. After a difficult jury selection, the trial began. It lasted for four days, an unusually long trial for the times. The case went to the jury at 5:00 P.M. on October 29. Although it took the jury only three hours to reach a verdict, the decision was not announced until the following day.

In this chapter you will be using portions of the evidence given at the murder trial of Captain Thomas Preston to reconstruct what actually happened on that March 5, 1770, evening in Boston, Massachusetts. Was Preston guilty as charged? Or was he innocent? Only by reconstructing the event that we call the Boston Massacre will you be able to answer these questions.

BACKGROUND

The town of Boston[2] had been uneasy throughout the first weeks of 1770. Tension had been building since the early 1760s because the town was increasingly affected by the forces of migration, change, and maturation. The protests against the Stamp Act had been particularly bitter there, and men such as Samuel Adams were encouraging their fellow Bostonians to be even bolder in their remonstrances. In response, in 1768 the British government ordered two regiments of soldiers to Boston to restore order and enforce the laws of Parliament. "They will not *find* a rebellion," quipped Benjamin Franklin of the soldiers, "they may indeed *make* one" (italics added).

Instead of bringing calm to Boston, the presence of soldiers only increased tensions. Incidents between Bostonians and redcoats were common on the streets, in taverns, and at the places of employment of British soldiers who sought part-time jobs to supplement their meager salaries. Known British sympathizers and informers were harassed, and crown officials were openly insulted. Indeed, the town of Boston seemed to be a powder keg just waiting for a spark to set off an explosion.

On February 22, 1770, British sympathizer and informer Ebenezer Richardson tried to tear down an anti-

2. Although Boston was one of the largest urban centers in the colonies, the town was not incorporated as a city. Several attempts were made, but residents opposed them, fearing they would lose the institution of the town meeting.

British sign. He was followed to his house by an angry crowd that proceeded to taunt him and break his windows with stones. One of the stones struck Richardson's wife. Enraged, he grabbed a musket and fired almost blindly into the crowd. Eleven-year-old Christopher Seider[3] fell to the ground with eleven pellets of shot in his chest. The boy died eight hours later. The crowd, by now numbering about one thousand, dragged Richardson from his house and through the streets, finally delivering him to the Boston jail. Four days later the town conducted a huge funeral for Christopher Seider, probably arranged and organized by Samuel Adams. Seider's casket was carried through the streets by children, and approximately two thousand mourners (one-seventh of Boston's total population) took part.

All through the next week Boston was an angry town. Gangs of men and boys roamed the streets at night looking for British soldiers foolish enough to venture out alone. Similarly, off-duty soldiers prowled the same streets looking for someone to challenge them. A fight broke out at a ropewalk between some soldiers who worked there part-time and some unemployed colonists.

With large portions of both the Boston citizenry and the British soldiers inflamed, an incident on March 5 touched off an ugly confrontation that took place in front of the Custom House, a symbol of British authority over the colonies. Both sides sought to use the event to support their respective causes. But Samuel Adams, a struggling attorney with a flair for politics and propaganda, clearly had the upper hand. The burial of the five "martyrs" was attended by almost every resident of Boston, and Adams used the event to push his demands for British troop withdrawal and to heap abuse on the mother country. Therefore, when the murder trial of Captain Thomas Preston finally opened in late October, emotions had hardly diminished.

Crowd disturbances had been an almost regular feature of life, in both England and America. Historian John Bohstedt has estimated that England was the scene of at least one thousand crowd disturbances and riots between 1790 and 1810. Colonial American towns were no more placid; demonstrations and riots were almost regular features of the colonists' lives. Destruction of property and burning of effigies were common in these disturbances; in August 1765 in Boston, for example, crowds protesting against the Stamp Act burned effigies and destroyed the homes of stamp distributor Andrew Oliver and Massachusetts Lieutenant Governor Thomas Hutchinson. Indeed, it was almost as if the entire community was willing to countenance demonstrations and riots as long as they were confined to parades, loud gatherings, and limited destruction of property. In almost no cases were there any deaths, and the authorities seldom fired on the crowds. Yet on March 5, 1770, both the crowd and the soldiers acted uncharacteristically. The result was the tragedy that

3. Christopher Seider is sometimes referred to as Christopher Snider.

CHAPTER 4

WHAT REALLY
HAPPENED IN
THE BOSTON
MASSACRE? THE
TRIAL OF
CAPTAIN
THOMAS
PRESTON

colonists dubbed the "Boston Massacre." Why did the crowd and the soldiers behave as they did? .

To repeat, your task is to reconstruct the so-called Boston Massacre so as to understand what really happened on that fateful evening. Spelling and punctuation in the evidence have been modernized only to clarify the meaning.

THE METHOD

Many students (and some historians) like to think that facts speak for themselves. This is especially tempting when analyzing a single incident like the Boston Massacre, many eyewitnesses of which testified at the trial. However, discovering what really happened, even when there are eyewitnesses, is never quite that easy. Witnesses may be confused at the time, they may see only part of the incident, or they may unconsciously "see" only what they expect to see. Obviously, witnesses may also have some reasons to lie. Thus the testimony of witnesses must be carefully scrutinized, for both what the witnesses *mean* to tell us and other relevant information as well. Therefore, historians approach such testimony with considerable skepticism and are concerned not only with the testimony itself but also with the possible motives of the witnesses.

Neither Preston nor the soldiers testified at the captain's trial because English legal custom prohibited defendants in criminal cases from testifying in their own behalf (the expectation was that they would perjure themselves). One week after the massacre, however, in a sworn deposition Captain Preston gave his side of the story. Although the deposition was not introduced at the trial and therefore the jury was not aware of what Preston himself had said, we have reproduced a portion of Preston's deposition for you to examine. How does Preston's deposition agree or disagree with other eyewitnesses' accounts?

No transcript of Preston's trial survives, if indeed one was ever made. Trial testimony comes from an anonymous person's summary of what each person said, the notes of Robert Treat Paine (one of the lawyers for the prosecution), and one witness's (Richard Palmes's) reconstruction of what his testimony and the cross-examination had been. Although historians would prefer to use the original trial transcript and would do so if one were available, the anonymous summary, Paine's notes, and one witness's recollections are acceptable substitutes because probably all three people were present in the courtroom (Paine and Palmes certainly were) and the accounts tend to corroborate one another.

Almost all the witnesses were at the scene, yet not all their testimony is of equal merit. First try to reconstruct the scene itself—the actual order in which the events occurred and where the various participants were standing. Whenever possible, look for corroborating testimony—two or more reliable witnesses who heard or saw the same things.

Be careful to use all the evidence. You should be able to develop some reasonable explanation for the conflicting testimony and those things that do not fit into your reconstruction very well.

Almost immediately you will discover that some important pieces of evidence are missing. For example, it would be useful to know the individual backgrounds and political views of the witnesses. Unfortunately, we know very little about the witnesses themselves, and we can reconstruct the political ideas of only about one-third of them. Therefore you will have to rely on the testimonies given, deducing which witnesses were telling the truth, which were lying, and which were simply mistaken.

The fact that significant portions of the evidence are missing is not disastrous. Historians seldom have all the evidence they need when they attempt to tackle a historical problem. Instead, they must be able to do as much as they can with the evidence that is available, using it as completely and imaginatively as they can. They do so by asking questions of the available evidence. Where were the witnesses standing? Which one(s) seem more likely to be telling the truth? Which witnesses were probably lying? When dealing with the testimony of the witnesses, be sure to determine what is factual from what is a witness's opinion. A rough sketch of the scene has been provided. How can it help you?

Also included in the evidence is Paul Revere's famous engraving of the incident, probably plagiarized from a drawing by artist Henry Pelham. It is unlikely that either Pelham or Revere was an eyewitness to the Boston Massacre, yet Revere's engraving gained widespread distribution, and most people—in 1770 and today—tend to recall that engraving when they think of the Boston Massacre. Do not examine the engraving until you have read the trial account closely. Can Revere's engraving help you find out what really happened that night? How does the engraving "fit" the eyewitnesses' accounts? How do the engraving and the accounts differ? Why?

Keep the central question in mind: what really happened in the Boston Massacre? Throughout this exercise, you will be trying to determine whether or not an order to fire was actually given. If so, by whom? If not, how can you explain why shots were fired? As commanding officer, Thomas Preston was held responsible and charged with murder. You might want to consider the evidence available to you as either a prosecution or defense attorney. Which side had the stronger case?

CHAPTER 4

WHAT REALLY
HAPPENED IN
THE BOSTON
MASSACRE? THE
TRIAL OF
CAPTAIN
THOMAS
PRESTON

THE EVIDENCE

1. Site of the Boston Massacre, Town House Area, 1770.

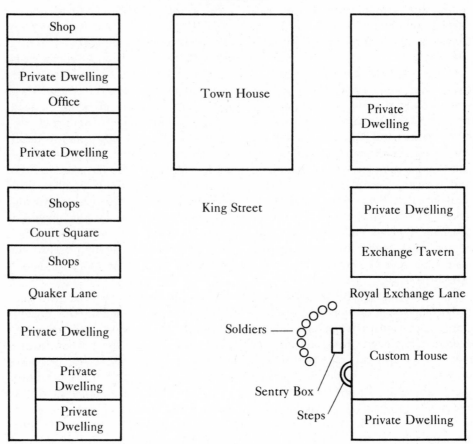

Source 2 from *Publications of The Colonial Society of Massachusetts*, Vol. VII
(Boston: The Colonial Society Of Massachusetts, 1905), pp. 8–9.

2. Deposition of Captain Thomas Preston, March 12, 1770 (Excerpt).

The mob still increased and were outrageous, striking their clubs or blud-
geons one against another, and calling out, come on you rascals, you bloody
backs, you lobster scoundrels, fire if you dare, G-d damn you, fire and be
damned, we know you dare not, and much more such language was used.
At this time I was between the soldiers and the mob, parleying with, and
endeavoring all in my power to persuade them to retire peaceably, but to no
purpose. They advanced to the points of the bayonets, struck some of them
and even the muzzles of the pieces, and seemed to be endeavoring to close
with the soldiers. On which some well behaved persons asked me if the guns
were charged. I replied yes. They then asked me if I intended to order the
men to fire. I answered no, by no means, observing to them that I was advanced before the muzzles of the men's pieces, and must fall a sacrifice if
they fired; that the soldiers were upon the half cock[4] and charged bayonets,
and my giving the word fire under those circumstances would prove me to
be no officer. While I was thus speaking, one of the soldiers having received
a severe blow with a stick, stepped a little to one side and instantly fired. . . .
On this a general attack was made on the men by a great number of heavy
clubs and snowballs being thrown at them, by which all our lives were in
imminent danger, some persons at the same time from behind calling out,
damn your bloods—why don't you fire. Instantly three or four of the soldiers
fired. . . . On my asking the soldiers why they fired without orders, they said
they heard the word fire and supposed it came from me. This might be the
case as many of the mob called out fire, fire, but I assured the men that I
gave no such order; that my words were, don't fire, stop your firing. . . .[5]

4. The cock of a musket had to be fully drawn back (cocked) for the musket to fire. In half
cock, the cock was drawn only halfway back so that priming powder could be placed in the
pan. The musket, however, would not fire at half cock. This is the origin of "Don't go off half
cocked."
5. Depositions were also taken from the soldiers, three of whom claimed, "We did our Captain's orders and if we don't obey his commands should have been confined and shot. . . ."
As with Preston's deposition, the jury was not aware of that statement. In addition, ninety-
six depositions were taken from townspeople.

CHAPTER 4

WHAT REALLY
HAPPENED IN
THE BOSTON
MASSACRE? THE
TRIAL OF
CAPTAIN
THOMAS
PRESTON

Source 3 from Hiller B. Zobel, ed., *The Legal Papers of John Adams*, Vol. III (Cambridge, Mass.: Belknap Press of Harvard University Press, 1965), pp. 46–98.

3. The Trial of Captain Thomas Preston *(Rex v. Preston),* October 24–29, (Excerpt).

Witnesses for the King (Prosecution)

Edward Gerrish

I heard a noise about 8 o'clock and went down to Royal Exchange Lane. Saw some Persons with Sticks coming up Quaker Lane. I said [to the sentry] Capt. Goldsmith owed my fellow Apprentice. He said he was a Gentlemen and would pay every body. I said there was none in the Regiment. He asked for me. I went to him, was not ashamed of my face. . . . The Sentinel left his Post and Struck me. I cried. My fellow Apprentice and a young man came up to the Sentinel and called him Bloody back. He called to the Main Guard. . . . There was not a dozen people when the Sentinel called the Guard.[6]

Thomas Marshall

The People kept gathering. I saw no uneasiness with the Centinel. A Party then came down from the Guard [House] I thought to relieve him. I heard one Gun. Thought it was to alarm the Barracks. A little space after another, and then several. I stood within 30 feet of the Centinel and must have seen any disturbance. . . . Between the firing the first and second Gun there was time enough for an Officer to step forward and to give the word Recover if he was so minded.

Ebenezer Hinkley

Just after 9 o'clock heard the Cry of Fire. I saw the party come out of the Guard House. A Capt. cried out of the Window "fire upon 'em damn 'em." I followed 'em down before the Custom House door. Capt. Preston was out and commanded 'em. They drew up and charged their Bayonets. Montgomery[7] pushed at the people advancing. In 2 or 3 minutes a Boy threw

---

6. Ironically, the person who had as much to do with bringing on the Boston Massacre as anyone, apprentice Edward Gerrish, was at home when the firing broke out.
7. Montgomery, one of the soldiers, almost undoubtedly fired the first gun.

a small stick over hand and hit Montgomery on Breast. Then I heard the word fire in ¼ minute he fired. I saw some pieces of Snow as big as Egg thrown. 3 or 4 thrown at the same time of pushing on the other End of the file, before 1st gun fired. The body of People about a Rod[8] off. People said Damn 'em they durst not fire don't be afraid. No threats. . . . I was a Rod from Capt. Preston. Did not hear him give Order to fire. ½ minute from 1st Gun to 2d. same to 3d. The others quicker. I saw no people striking the Guns or Bayonets nor pelting 'em. I saw Preston between people and Soldiers. I did not see him when 1st firing.

Peter Cunningham

Upon the cry of fire and Bells ringing went into King Street, heard the Capt. say Turn out the Guard. Saw the Centinel standing on the steps of the Custom house, pushing his Bayonet at the People who were about 30 or 40. Captain came and ordered the Men to prime and load.[9] He came before 'em about 4 or 5 minutes after and put up their Guns with his Arm. They then fired and were priming and loading again. I am pretty positive the Capt. bid 'em Prime and load. I stood about 4 feet off him. Heard no Order given to fire. The Person who gave Orders to Prime and load stood with his back to me, I did not see his face only when he put up their Guns. I stood about 10 or 11 feet from the Soldiers, the Captain about the midway between.

Alexander Cruikshanks

As the Clock struck 9 I saw two Boys abusing the Centinel. They said you Centinel, damned rascally Scoundrel Lobster[10] Son of a Bitch and desired him to turn out. He told them it was his ground and he would maintain it and would run any through who molested or attempted to drive him off. There was about a dozen standing at a little distance. They took no part. He called out Guard several times and 7 or 8 Soldiers with Swords Bayonets and one with a large Tongs in his hand came. I saw the two Boys going to

8. A rod equals 16.5 feet.
9. Muskets were loaded with powder, wadding, a ball, and more wadding from the muzzle. Then the hammer (see Source 5) was drawn back halfway, and powder was poured into the small pan under the hammer. A small piece of flint was attached to the cock (see Source 5) so that, when the trigger was pulled, the cock would come down and the flint would make a spark that would ignite the gunpowder in the pan. The fire would then travel into the breech to ignite the powder there and fire the gun. If the powder in the pan exploded but did not ignite the powder in the breech, the result was a "flash in the pan" and a musket that did not fire.
10. The British soldiers' coats from the rear bore a slight resemblance to the back of a lobster.

CHAPTER 4

WHAT REALLY
HAPPENED IN
THE BOSTON
MASSACRE? THE
TRIAL OF
CAPTAIN
THOMAS
PRESTON

the Men who stood near the Centinel. They returned with a new Edition of fresh Oaths, threw Snow Balls at him and he then called Guard several times as before.

William Wyatt

I heard the Bell, coming up Cornhill, saw People running several ways. The largest part went down to the North of the Townhouse. I went the South side, saw an officer leading out 8 or 10 Men. Somebody met the officer and said, Capt. Preston for Gods sake mind what you are about and take care of your Men. He went down to the Centinel, drew up his Men, bid them face about, Prime and load. I saw about 100 People in the Street huzzaing, crying fire, damn you fire. In about 10 minutes I heard the Officer say fire. The Soldiers took no notice. His back was to me. I heard the same voice say fire. The Soldiers did not fire. The Officer then stamped and said Damn your bloods fire be the consequences what it will. Immediately the first Gun was fired. I have no doubt the Officer was the same person the Man spoke to when coming down with the Guard. His back was to me when the last order was given. I was then about 5 or 6 yards off and within 2 yards at the first. He stood in the rear when the Guns were fired. Just before I heard a Stick, which I took to be upon a Gun. I did not see it. The Officer had to the best of my knowledge a cloth coloured Surtout[11] on. After the firing the Captain stepd forward before the Men and struck up their Guns. One was loading again and he damn'd 'em for firing and severely reprimanded 'em. I did not mean the Capt. had the Surtout but the Man who spoke to him when coming with the Guard.

John Cole

I saw the officer after the firing and spoke to the Soldiers and told 'em it was a Cowardly action to kill men at the end of their Bayonets. They were pushing at the People who seemed to be trying to come into the Street. The Captain came up and stamped and said Damn their bloods fire again and let 'em take the consequence. I was within four feet of him. He had no surtout but a red Coat with a Rose on his shoulder. The people were quarrelling at the head of Royal Exchange lane.[12] The Soldiers were pushing and striking with the Guns. I saw the People's Arms moving but no Sticks.

11. *Surtout* is the name of a certain type of overcoat.
12. See Source 1 for location of Royal Exchange Lane.

Theodore Bliss

At home. I heard the Bells for fire.[13] Went out. Came to the Town House. The People told me there was going to be a Rumpus with the Soldiers. Went to the Custom house. Saw Capt. Preston there with the Soldiers. Asked him if they were loaded. He said yes. If with Ball. He said nothing. I saw the People throw Snow Balls at the Soldiers and saw a Stick about 3 feet long strike a Soldier upon the right. He sallied and then fired. A little time a second. Then the other[s] fast after one another. One or two Snow balls hit the Soldier, the stick struck, before firing. I know not whether he sallied on account of the Stick or step'd back to make ready. I did not hear any Order given by the Capt. to fire. I stood so near him I think I must have heard him if he had given an order to fire before the first firing. I never knew Capt. Preston before. I can't say whether he had a Surtout on, he was dressed in red. I know him to be the Man I took to be the Officer. The Man that fired first stood next to the Exchange lane. I saw none of the People press upon the Soldiers before the first Gun fired. I did after. I aimed a blow at him myself but did not strike him. I am sure the Captain stood before the Men when the first Gun was fired. I had no apprehension the Capt. did give order to fire when the first Gun was fired. I thought, after the first Gun, the Capt. did order the Men to fire but do not certainly know. I heard the word fire several times but know not whether it came from the Captain, the Soldiers or People. Two of the People struck at the Soldiers after the first Gun. I don't know if they hit 'em. There were about 100 people in the Street. The muzzles of the Guns were behind him. After the first Gun the Captain went quite to the left and I to the right.

Henry Knox

I saw the Captain coming down with his party. I took Preston by the Coat, told him for Gods sake take care of your Men for if they fire your life must be answerable. In some agitation he replied I am sensible of it. A Corporal was leading them. The Captain stopd with me and the Party proceeded to the Centinel the People crying stand by. The Soldiers with their Bayonets charged[14] pushing through the People in order to make way—make way

13. No town in colonial America had a municipal fire department. Whenever a fire broke out, the church bells would be rung and citizens would gather with buckets to put out the fire. In Boston, citizens were required to keep two buckets in their homes and to turn out when the bells were rung.
14. *Bayonets charged* was a position in the manual of arms (see Source 4) in which the musket, with bayonet fixed, was held outward and slightly upward. It would be exceedingly difficult to fire a musket accurately from this position because of the recoil upon firing.

CHAPTER 4

WHAT REALLY
HAPPENED IN
THE BOSTON
MASSACRE? THE
TRIAL OF
CAPTAIN
THOMAS
PRESTON

damn your Bloods. The Captain then left me and went to the Party. I heard the Centinel say damn their bloods if they touch me I will fire. In about 3 minutes after this the party came up. I did not see any thing thrown at the Centinel. I stood at the foot of the Town house when the Guns were fired. I heard the People cry damn your bloods fire on. To the best of my recollection the Corporal had a Surtout on. I had none.

Benjamin Burdick

When I came into King Street about 9 o'Clock I saw the Soldiers round the Centinel. I asked one if he was loaded and he said yes. I asked him if he would fire, he said yes by the Eternal God and pushd his Bayonet at me. After the firing the Captain came before the Soldiers and put up their Guns with his arm and said stop firing, dont fire no more or dont fire again. I heard the word fire and took it and am certain that it came from behind the Soldiers. I saw a man passing busily behind who I took to be an Officer. The firing was a little time after. I saw some persons fall. Before the firing I saw a stick thrown at the Soldiers. The word fire I took to be a word of Command. I had in my hand a highland broad Sword which I brought from home. Upon my coming out I was told it was a wrangle between the Soldiers and people, upon that I went back and got my Sword. I never used to go out with a weapon. I had not my Sword drawn till after the Soldier pushed his Bayonet at me. I should have cut his head off if he had stepd out of his Rank to attack me again. At the first firing the People were chiefly in Royal Exchange lane, there being about 50 in the Street. After the firing I went up to the Soldiers and told them I wanted to see some faces that I might swear to them another day. The Centinel in a melancholy tone said perhaps Sir you may.

Daniel Calef

I was present at the firing. I heard one of the Guns rattle. I turned about and lookd and heard the officer who stood on the right in a line with the Soldiers give the word fire twice. I lookd the Officer in the face when he gave the word and saw his mouth. He had on a red Coat, yellow Jacket and Silver laced hat, no trimming on his Coat.[15] The Prisoner is the Officer I mean. I saw his face plain, the moon shone on it. I am sure of the man though I have not seen him since before yesterday when he came into Court

15. The 29th Regiment, to which Preston belonged, wore uniforms that exactly matched Calef's description.

with others. I knew him instantly. I ran upon the word fire being given about 30 feet off. The officer had no Surtout on.

Robert Goddard

The Soldiers came up to the Centinel and the Officer told them to place themselves and they formd a half moon. The Captain told the Boys to go home least there should be murder done. They were throwing Snow balls. Did not go off but threw more Snow balls. The Capt. was behind the Soldiers. The Captain told them to fire. One Gun went off. A Sailor or Townsman struck the Captain. He thereupon said damn your bloods fire think I'll be treated in this manner. This Man that struck the Captain came from among the People who were seven feet off and were round on one wing. I saw no person speak to him. I was so near I should have seen it. After the Capt. said Damn your bloods fire they all fired one after another about 7 or 8 in all, and then the officer bid Prime and load again. He stood behind all the time. Mr. Lee went up to the officer and called the officer by name Capt. Preston. I saw him coming down from the Guard behind the Party. I went to Gaol the next day being sworn for the Grand Jury to see the Captain. Then said pointing to him that's the person who gave the word to fire. He said if you swear that you will ruin me everlastingly. I was so near the officer when he gave the word fire that I could touch him. His face was towards me. He stood in the middle behind the Men. I looked him in the face. He then stood within the circle. When he told 'em to fire he turned about to me. I lookd him in the face.

Diman Morton

Between 9 and 10 I heard in my house the cry of fire but soon understood there was no fire but the Soldiers were fighting with the Inhabitants. I went to King Street. Saw the Centinel over the Gutter, his Bayonet breast high. He retired to the steps—loaded. The Boys dared him to fire. Soon after a Party came down, drew up. The Captain ordered them to load. I went across the Street. Heard one Gun and soon after the other Guns. The Captain when he ordered them to load stood in the front before the Soldiers so that the Guns reached beyond him. The Captain had a Surtout on. I knew him well. The Surtout was not red. I think cloth colour. I stood on the opposite corner of Exchange lane when I heard the Captain order the Men to load. I came by my knowledge of the Captain partly by seeing him lead the Fortification Guard.

CHAPTER 4

WHAT REALLY
HAPPENED IN
THE BOSTON
MASSACRE? THE
TRIAL OF
CAPTAIN
THOMAS
PRESTON

Nathaniel Fosdick

Hearing the Bells ring, for fire I supposed I went out and came down by the Main Guard. Saw some Soldiers fixing their Bayonets on. Passed on. Went down to the Centinel. Perceived something pass me behind. Turned round and saw the Soldiers coming down. They bid me stand out of the way and damnd my blood. I told them I should not for any man. The party drew up round the Centinel, faced about and charged their Bayonets. I saw an Officer and said if there was any disturbance between the Soldiers and the People there was the Officer present who could settle it soon. I heard no Orders given to load, but in about two minutes after the Captain step'd across the Gutter. Spoke to two Men—I don't know who—then went back behind his men. Between the 4th and 5th men on the right. I then heard the word fire and the first Gun went off. In about 2 minutes the second and then several others. The Captain had a Sword in his hand. Was dressd in his Regimentals. Had no Surtout on. I saw nothing thrown nor any blows given at all. The first man on the right who fired after attempting to push the People slipped down and drop'd his Gun out of his hand. The Person who stepd in between the 4th and 5th Men I look upon it gave the orders to fire. His back was to me. I shall always think it was him. The Officer had a Wig on. I was in such a situation that I am as well satisfied there were no blows given as that the word fire was spoken.

Isaac Pierce

The Lieut. Governor asked Capt. Preston didn't you know you had no power to fire upon the Inhabitants or any number of People collected together unless you had a Civil Officer to give order. The Captain replied I was obliged to, to save my Sentry.

Joseph Belknap

The Lieut. Governor said to Preston Don't you know you can do nothing without a Magistrate. He answered I did it to save my Men.

Witnesses for the Prisoner (Preston)

Edward Hill

After all the firing Captain Preston put up the Gun of a Soldier who was going to fire and said fire no more you have done mischief enough.

Richard Palmes

Somebody there said there was a Rumpus in King Street. I went down. When I had got there I saw Capt. Preston at the head of 7 or 8 Soldiers at the Custom house drawn up, their Guns breast high and Bayonets fixed. Found Theodore Bliss talking with the Captain. I heard him say why don't you fire or words to that effect. The Captain answered I know not what and Bliss said God damn you why don't you fire. I was close behind Bliss. They were both in the front. Then I step'd immediately between them and put my left hand in a familiar manner on the Captains right shoulder to speak to him. Mr. John Hickling then looking over my shoulder I said to Preston are your Soldiers Guns loaded. He answered with powder and ball. Sir I hope you dont intend the Soldiers shall fire on the Inhabitants. He said by no means. The instant he spoke I saw something resembling Snow or Ice strike the Grenadier on the Captains right hand being the only one then at his right. He instantly stepd one foot back and fired the first Gun. I had then my hand on the Captains shoulder. After the Gun went off I heard the word fire. The Captain and I stood in front about half between the breech and muzzle of the Guns. I dont know who gave the word fire. I was then looking on the Soldier who fired. The word was given loud. The Captain might have given the word and I not distinguish it. After the word fire in about 6 or 7 seconds the Grenadier on the Captains left fired and then the others one after another. The Captain stood still till the second Gun was fired. After that I turned and saw the Grenadier who fired first attempting to prick me by the side of the Captain with his Bayonet. I had a large Stick in my hand. I struck over hand and hit him in his left arm. Knocked his hand from his Gun. The Bayonet struck the Snow and jarr'd the breech out of his hand. I had not before struck at any body. Upon that I turnd, thinking the other would do the same and struck at any body at first and hit Preston. In striking him my foot slip'd and my blow fell short and hit him, as he afterwards told me, on the arm. When I heard the word fire the Captains back was to the Soldiers and face to me. Before I recovered the Soldier who fired the first Gun was attempting again to push me through. I tossed my Stick in

CHAPTER 4

WHAT REALLY
HAPPENED IN
THE BOSTON
MASSACRE? THE
TRIAL OF
CAPTAIN
THOMAS
PRESTON

his face. He fell back and I jump'd towards the land. He push'd at me there and fell down. I turn'd to catch his Gun. Another Soldier push'd at me and I ran off. Returnd soon and saw the dead carrying off and the party was gone. The Gun which went off first had scorched the nap of my Surtout at the elbow. I did not hear the Captain speak after he answered me. Was there but about ¾ of a minute in the whole. There was time enough between the first and second Gun for the Captain to have spoke to his Men. He stood leaning on the dagger in the scabbard. At the time of the firing there was between 50 and 80 People at some distance not crowding upon the Soldiers and thin before them.

"Q. Did you situate yourself before Capt. Preston, in order that you might be out of danger, in case they fired?

"A. I did not apprehend myself in any danger.

"Q. Did you hear Captain Preston give the word *Fire*?

"A. I have told your Honors, that after the first gun was fired, I heard the word, *fire!* but who gave it, I know not.

"Q. Do you think it was possible Capt. Preston should give the word *fire,* and you not be certain he gave it?

"A. I think it was.

Matthew Murray

I heard no order given. I stood within two yards of the Captain. He was in front talking with a Person, I don't know who. I was looking at the Captain when the Gun was fired.

Andrew, a Negro servant to Oliver Wendell[16]

I jump'd back and heard a voise cry fire and immediately the first Gun fired. It seemed to come from the left wing from the second or third man on the left. The Officer was standing before me with his face towards the People. I am certain the voice came from beyond him. The Officer stood before the Soldiers at a sort of a corner. I turned round and saw a Grenadier who stood on the Captain's right swing his Gun and fire. I took it to be Killeroy. I look'd a little to the right and saw a Man drop. The Molatto was killed by the first Gun by the Grenadier on the Captains Right. I was so frightened, after, I did not know where I was. . . .

16. Andrew was Oliver Wendell's slave. Wendell appeared in court to testify as to Andrew's veracity.

Daniel Cornwall

Capt. Preston was within 2 yards of me—before the Men—nearest to the right—facing the Street. I was looking at him. Did not hear any order. He faced me. I think I should have heard him. I directly heard a voice say Damn you why do you fire. Don't fire. I thought it was the Captain's then. I now believe it. . . .

William Sawyer

The people kept huzzaing. Damn 'em. Daring 'em to fire. Threw Snow balls. I think they hit 'em. As soon as the Snow balls were thrown and a club a Soldier fired. I heard the Club strike upon the Gun and the corner man next the lane said fire and immediately fired. This was the first Gun. As soon as he had fired he said Damn you fire. I am so sure that I thought it was he that spoke. That next Gun fired and so they fired through pretty quick.

Jane Whitehouse

A Man came behind the Soldiers walked backwards and forward, encouraging them to fire. The Captain stood on the left about three yards. The man touched one of the Soldiers upon the back and said fire, by God I'll stand by you. He was dressed in dark colored clothes. . . . He did not look like an Officer. The man fired directly on the word and clap on the Shoulder. I am positive the man was not the Captain. . . . I am sure he gave no orders. . . . I saw one man take a chunk of wood from under his Coat throw it at a Soldier and knocked him. He fell on his face. His firelock[17] was out of his hand. . . . This was before any firing.

Newton Prince, a Negro, a member of the South Church

Heard the Bell ring. Ran out. Came to the Chapel. Was told there was no fire but something better, there was going to be a fight. Some had buckets and bags and some Clubs. I went to the west end of the Town House where [there] were a number of people. I saw some Soldiers coming out of the Guard house with their Guns and running down one after another to the Custom house. Some of the people said let's attack the Main Guard, or the Centinel who is gone to King street. Some said for Gods sake don't lets touch

17. *Firelock* is a synonym for a musket.

CHAPTER 4

WHAT REALLY
HAPPENED IN
THE BOSTON
MASSACRE? THE
TRIAL OF
CAPTAIN
THOMAS
PRESTON

the main Guard. I went down. Saw the Soldiers planted by the Custom house two deep. The People were calling them Lobsters, daring 'em to fire saying damn you why don't you fire. I saw Capt. Preston out from behind the Soldiers. In the front at the right. He spoke to some people. The Capt. stood between the Soldiers and the Gutter about two yards from the Gutter. I saw two or three strike with sticks on the Guns. I was going off to the west of the Soldiers and heard the Guns fire and saw the dead carried off. Soon after the Guard Drums beat to arms. The People whilst striking on the Guns cried fire, damn you fire. I have heard no Orders given to fire, only the people in general cried fire.

James Woodall

I saw one Soldier knocked down. His Gun fell from him. I saw a great many sticks and pieces of sticks and Ice thrown at the Soldiers. The Soldier who was knocked down took up his Gun and fired directly. Soon after the first Gun I saw a Gentleman behind the Soldiers in velvet of blue or black plush trimmed with gold. He put his hand toward their backs. Whether he touched them I know not and said by God I'll stand by you whilst I have a drop of blood and then said fire and two went off and the rest to 7 or 8. . . . The Captain, after, seemed shocked and looked upon the Soldiers. I am very certain he did not give the word fire.

Cross-Examination of Captain James Gifford

Q. Did you ever know an officer order men to fire with their bayonets charged [Source 4]?
A. No, Officers never give order to fire from charged bayonet. They would all have fired together, or most of them.

Thomas Handaside Peck

I was at home when the Guns were fired. I heard 'em distinct. I went up to the main guard and addressed myself to the Captain and said to him What have you done? He said, Sir it was none of my doings, the Soldiers fired of their own accord, I was in the Street and might have been shot. His character is good as a Gentleman and Soldier. I think it exceeds any of the Corps.

Lieutenant Governor Thomas Hutchinson

I was pressed by the people almost upon the Bayonets. The People cried the Governor. I called for the Officer. He came from between the Ranks. I did not know him by Moon light. I had heard no circumstances. I inquired with some emotion, How came you to fire without Orders from a Civil Magistrate? I am not certain of every word. I cannot recollect his answer. It now appears to me that it was imperfect. As if he had more to say. I remember by what he said or his actions I thought he was offended at being questioned. Before I could have his full answer the people cried to the Town house, to the Town house. A Gentleman by me (Mr. Belknap) was extremely civil. I thought he press'd my going into the Town house from a concern for my safety. I was carried by the crowd into the Council Chamber. After some hours Capt. Preston was brought there to be examined. I heard him deny giving Orders. I am very sure it did not occur to me that he had said anything in answer to my question in the Street which would not consist with this denial. My intention in going up was to enquire into the affair. I have no particular intimacy with Capt. Preston. His general character is extremely good. Had I wanted an Officer to guard against a precipitate action I should have pitched upon him as soon as any in the Regiment.

The Evidence was ended.

Closing Arguments

For the Defense

[No transcript of John Adams's closing arguments exists. From his notes, however, we can reconstruct his principal arguments. Adams began by citing cases that ruled that "it is always safer to err in acquitting rather than punishing" when there was doubt as to the defendant's guilt. He also argued that there was ample provocation and that Preston was merely defending himself and his men and was, in all, a victim of self-defense. Adams then reviewed the evidence, stating that there was no real proof that Preston had ordered his men to fire into the crowd. Adams also called into question the testimony of the prosecution witnesses, saying that Robert Goddard "is not capable of making observations" and that other witnesses were in error (he made much of the surtout). Of Wyatt, he called him "diabolically malicious."]

Conclusion of Prosecution's Summary to the Jury

Now Gentlemen the fact being once proved, it is the prisoner's part to justify or excuse it, for all killing is, *prima facie,* Murder. They have attempted to

CHAPTER 4

WHAT REALLY
HAPPENED IN
THE BOSTON
MASSACRE? THE
TRIAL OF
CAPTAIN
THOMAS
PRESTON

prove, that the People were not only the aggressors, but attacked the Soldiers with so much Violence, that an immediate Danger of their own Lives, obliged them to fire upon the *Assailants,* as they are pleased to call them. Now this *violent Attack* turns out to be nothing more, than a few Snow-balls, thrown by a parcel of *Boys;* the most of them at a considerable distance, and as likely to hit the Inhabitants as the Soldiers (*all this is but* which is a common Case in the Streets of Boston at that Season of the Year, when a Number of People are collected in a Body), and one Stick, that struck Grenadier, but was not thrown with sufficient force to wound, or even sally him; whence then this Outrage, fury and abuse so much talk'd of? The Inhabitants collected, Many of them from the best of Motives, to make peace; and some out of mere Curiosity, and what was the Situation of Affairs when the Soldiers begun the fire? In addition to the Testimony of many others, you may collect it from the Conduct of Mr. Palmes, a Witness on whom they principally build their Defence. Wou'd he place himself before a party of Soldiers, and risque his Life at the Muzzels of their Guns, when he thought them under a Necessity of firing to defend their Life? 'Tis absurd to suppose it; and it is impossible you should ever seriously believe, that their Situation could either justify or excuse their . . . Conduct. I would contend, as much as any Man, for the tenderness and Benignity of the Law; but, if upon such trifling and imaginary provocation, Men may o'er leap the Barriers of Society, and carry havock and Desolation among their defenceless Fellow Subjects; we had better resign and unmeaning title to protection in Society and range the Mountains uncontrol'd. Upon the whole Gentlemen the facts are with you, and I doubt not, you will find such a Verdict as the Laws of God, of Nature and your own Conscience will ever approve.

Sources 4 and 5 from Anthony D. Darling, *Red Coat and Brown Bess,* Historical Arms Series, No. 12 (Bloomfield, Ontario). Courtesy of Museum Restoration Service, © 1970, 1981.

4. The Position of "Charged Bayonets."

5. Detail of a Musket.

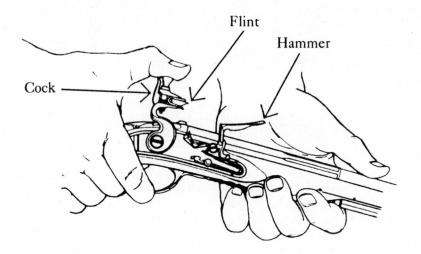

CHAPTER 4

WHAT REALLY
HAPPENED IN
THE BOSTON
MASSACRE? THE
TRIAL OF
CAPTAIN
THOMAS
PRESTON

6. Paul Revere's Engraving of the Boston Massacre.

[Notice how he has dubbed the Custom House "Butcher's Hall."]

QUESTIONS TO CONSIDER

In reconstructing the event, begin by imagining the positions of the various soldiers and witnesses. Where were the soldiers standing? Where was Captain Preston standing? Which witnesses were closest to Preston (that is, in the best positions to see and hear what happened)? Where were the other witnesses? Remember that the event took place around 9:00 P.M. when Boston was totally dark.

Next, read closely Preston's deposition and the trial testimony. What major points did Preston make in his own defense? Do you find those points plausible? More important, do the witnesses who were closest to Preston agree or disagree with his recounting, or with each other's? On what points? Be as specific as possible.

Now consider the other witnesses, those who were not so near. What did they hear? What did they see? To what degree do their testimonies agree or disagree, both with each other and with Preston and those closest to him?

Lawyers for both sides spent considerable time trying to ascertain what Captain Preston was wearing on that evening. Why did they consider this important? Based on the evidence, what do you think Preston was wearing on the evening of March 5, 1770? What conclusions could you draw from that?

The attorneys also were particularly interested in the crowd's behavior *prior to* the firing of the first musket. Why did they consider that important? How would you characterize the crowd's behavior? Are you suspicious of testimony that is at direct odds with your conclusion about this point?

Particularly damning to Preston was the testimony given by Thomas Marshall, Ebenezer Hinkley, William Wyatt, John Cole, Daniel Calef, Robert Goddard, Isaac Pierce, and Joseph Belknap.

In what ways were these accounts damaging? Are there any significant flaws in their testimony?

Several witnesses (especially Jane Whitehouse) tell a quite different story. To what extent is her recounting of the event plausible? Is it corroborated by other witnesses?

We included Paul Revere's engraving, even though he probably was not an eyewitness, because by the time of Preston's trial, surely all the witnesses would have seen it and, more importantly, because later Americans obtained their most lasting visual image of the event from that work. How does the engraving conform to what actually happened? How does it conflict with your determination of what actually took place? If there are major discrepancies, why do you think this is so (Revere certainly knew a number of the eyewitnesses and could have ascertained the true facts from them)?

After you have answered these questions and carefully weighed the eyewitnesses' evidence, answer the central question: what really happened in the Boston Massacre?

EPILOGUE

In the trial of Thomas Preston, the jury took only three hours to reach its verdict: not guilty. The British officer was quickly packed off to England, where he received a pension of £200 per year from the King "to compensate him for his suffering." He did not participate in the American Revolution and died in 1781. Of the eight soldiers (the sentry plus the seven men Preston brought to the Custom House), six were acquitted, and two were convicted of manslaughter and punished by being branded on the thumb. From there they disappeared into the mists of history.

CHAPTER 4

WHAT REALLY
HAPPENED IN
THE BOSTON
MASSACRE? THE
TRIAL OF
CAPTAIN
THOMAS
PRESTON

On the road to the American Revolution, many events stand out as important or significant. The Boston Massacre is one such event. However, we must be careful in assessing its importance. After all, the colonists and the mother country did not finally resort to arms until five years after this dramatic event. By that time, most of those killed on King Street on March 5 had been forgotten.

Yet the Boston Massacre and other events helped shape an attitude Americans held as to what their own revolution had been all about. To most Americans, the British were greedy, heartless tyrants who terrorized a peaceful citizenry. More than one hundred years after the event, the Massachusetts legislature authorized a memorial honoring the "martyrs" to be placed on the site of the "massacre" (over the objections of the Massachusetts Historical Society). The Bostonians' convictions were bolstered by Irish immigrants whose ancestors had known British "tyranny" first hand, and the Bostonians remained convinced that the American Revolution had been caused by Britain's selfishness and oppression. As we can see in the Boston Massacre, the road to evolution was considerably more complicated than that.

Today the site of the Boston Massacre is on a traffic island beside the Old State House (formerly called the Town House and seen in the background of Paul Revere's famous engraving) in the midst of Boston's financial district. With the exception of the State House (now a tasteful museum), the site is ringed by skyscrapers that house, among others, the Bank of Boston and the Bank of New England. Thousands of Bostonians and tourists stand on the Boston Massacre site every day, waiting for the traffic to abate.

Many years ago John Adams said that "the foundation of American independence was laid" on the evening of March 5, 1770. Although he may have overstated the case, clearly many Americans have come to see the event as a crucial one in the coming of their revolution against Great Britain. Now that you have examined the evidence, do you think the Boston Massacre of March 5, 1770, was a justifiable reason for rebellion against the mother country? Could the crowd action on that evening secretly have been directed by the Patriot elite, or was it a spontaneous demonstration of anti-British fury? Why was Paul Revere's engraving at such variance with what actually took place?

Few Americans have stopped to ponder what actually happened on that fateful evening. Like the American Revolution itself, the answer to that question may well be more complex than we think.

CHAPTER FIVE

THE FIRST AMERICAN PARTY SYSTEM: THE PHILADELPHIA CONGRESSIONAL ELECTION OF 1794

For weeks prior to the federal congressional elections of 1794, the city of Philadelphia, the nation's temporary capital, was in a state of extreme political excitement. Not since the battle in Pennsylvania over the ratification of the United States Constitution had the city been the scene of such political tension and argument. The political factions that had appeared like small clouds over the first administration of President George Washington had grown immensely, and by 1794 in Philadelphia they were on the verge of becoming distinct political parties.

Federalist Thomas Fitzsimons, a congressman since the beginning of the new government, was challenged by wealthy merchant and Democratic-Republican John Swanwick. Friends of the two contestants filled the air with vicious charges and countercharges in hopes of attracting voters to their respective candidates. Fitzsimons's supporters called Swanwick an "unstable, avaricious upstart who was unknown as a public figure until he 'herded with [the people's] enemies [the Democratic-Republicans], and became their tool.'" Swanwick's friends nicknamed Fitzsimons "Billy the Fidler" and portrayed him as a mindless sycophant of Secretary of the Treasury Alexander Hamilton. Meetings were held in various parts of the city to endorse one candidate or the other, and Philadelphia's newspapers were filled with charges and countercharges. Although many people were disturbed by these eruptions in what they considered a still fragile nation, unquestionably the growing factions had broken the political calm. Would political parties shatter the new republic or strengthen it? In Philadelphia in 1794, opinion was divided.

Challenger John Swanwick won a stunning victory over incumbent Thomas Fitzsimons, carrying seven of the city's

CHAPTER 5
THE FIRST
AMERICAN
PARTY SYSTEM:
THE
PHILADELPHIA
CONGRESSIONAL
ELECTION OF
1794

twelve wards and collecting 56 percent of the votes cast. Federalism in Philadelphia had been dealt a severe blow.

In this chapter you will be analyzing the evidence to determine *why* the lesser-known Swanwick won the election. What factors do you think were responsible for his victory? You will not be relying on just one or two types of evidence, as in previous chapters, you will be examining myriad evidence to answer that question.

BACKGROUND

The years between 1789 and 1801 were crucial ones for the young nation. To paraphrase a comment of Benjamin Franklin, Americans by 1789 (the first year of the Washington administration) had proved themselves remarkably adept at *destroying* governments: in the American Revolution they had ended British rule of the thirteen colonies, and in the Constitutional Convention of 1787 they had ultimately destroyed the United States' first attempt at self-government, the Articles of Confederation. But they had yet to prove that they could *build* a central government that could protect their rights and preserve order and independence. For that reason the period from 1789 to 1801 was important in terms of the survival of the new republic.

Many important questions confronted the nation's citizens during those difficult years. Could the new government create a financial system that would pay off the public debt, encourage commerce, manufacturing, and investments, and establish a workable federal tax program? Was the central government strong enough to maintain order and protect citizens on the expanding frontier? Could the nation's leaders conceive a foreign policy that would maintain peace, protect international trade, and honor previous treaty commitments? To what extent should national interests overrule the interests and views of the several states?

A much larger question concerned republicanism itself. No republican experiment of this magnitude had ever been tried before, and a number of Americans expressed considerable fears that the experiment might not survive. Some people, such as Rufus King of New York,[1] wondered whether the people possessed sufficient intelligence and virtue to be trusted to make wise decisions and choose proper leaders. Others, such as John Adams of Massachusetts, doubted that a government without titles, pomp, or ceremony would command the respect and allegiance of common men and women. Still others, such

---

1. Rufus King (1755–1827) was a native of Massachusetts who moved to New York in 1786. He was a U.S. senator from 1789 to 1796 and minister to Great Britain from 1796 to 1803. He supported Alexander Hamilton's financial plans. In 1816, he was the Federalist candidate for president, losing in a landslide to James Monroe.

as William L. Smith of South Carolina,[2] feared that the new government was not strong enough to maintain order and enforce its will throughout the huge expanse of its domain. And finally, men such as Patrick Henry of Virginia and Samuel Adams of Massachusetts were afraid that the national government would abandon republican principles in favor of an aristocratic despotism. Hence, although most Americans were republican in sentiment, they strongly disagreed about the best ways to preserve republicanism and the dangers it faced. Some Americans openly distrusted "the people"—Alexander Hamilton of New York once called them a "headless beast." Others were wary of the government itself, even though George Washington had been chosen as its first president.

Much of the driving force of the new government came from Alexander Hamilton, the first Secretary of the Treasury. Hamilton used his closeness to Washington and his boldness and imagination to fashion policies that set the new nation on its initial course. His scheme for paying the national and state debts, creating a semipublic national bank, and instituting a policy of taxation bound the people and the states closer to the central government. His forcefulness concerning the Whiskey Rebellion of 1794 made it clear that the government could protect its citizens and enforce its laws on the vast and faraway frontier. His fa-

voritism toward Great Britain caused him to meddle in the business of Secretary of State Thomas Jefferson and served to redirect American foreign policy to a proBritish orientation. Indeed, using the popular Washington as a shield (as he later admitted), Hamilton became the most powerful figure in the new government and the one most responsible for making that new government workable.

It is not surprising, however, that these issues and policies provoked sharp disagreements that eventually created two rival political factions: the Federalists (led by Hamilton) and the Democratic-Republicans (led by James Madison and Thomas Jefferson). Federalists generally advocated a strong central government, a broad interpretation of the Constitution, full payment of national and state debts, the establishment of the Bank of the United States, encouragement of commerce, and a pro-British foreign policy. Democratic-Republicans generally favored a central government with limited powers, a strict interpretation of the Constitution, a pro-French foreign policy, and opposed the Bank.[3]

First appearing in Congress in the early 1790s, these two relatively stable factions gradually began taking their ideas to the voters, creating the seeds of what would become by the 1830s America's first political party system. Although unanticipated by the men who drafted the Constitution, this party system became a central

2. William L. Smith (1758–1812) was a Federalist congressman from South Carolina and later United States minister to Portugal. He was a staunch supporter of Alexander Hamilton.

3. These are general tendencies. Some Federalists and Democratic-Republicans did not stand with their respective factions on all these issues.

CHAPTER 5

THE FIRST
AMERICAN
PARTY SYSTEM:
THE
PHILADELPHIA
CONGRESSIONAL
ELECTION OF
1794

feature of American political life, so much so that today it would probably be impossible to conduct the affairs of government or hold elections without it.

Yet Americans of the 1790s did not foresee this evolution. Many feared the rise of these political factions, believing that the new government was not strong enough to withstand their increasingly vicious battles. Most people did not consider themselves members of either political faction, and there were no highly organized campaigns or platforms to bind voters to one faction or another. It was considered bad form for candidates to openly seek office (one *stood* for office but never *ran* for office), and appeals to voters were usually made by friends or political allies of the candidates. Different property qualifications for voting in each state limited the size of the electorate, and in the 1790s most states did not let the voters select presidential electors. All these factors impeded the rapid growth of the modern political party system.

Still, political battles during the 1790s grew more intense and ferocious. As Hamilton's economic plans and Federalism's pro-British foreign policy (the climax of which was the Jay Treaty of 1795) became clearer, Democratic-Republican opposition grew more bitter. Initially the Federalists had the

upper hand, perhaps because of that group's identification with President Washington. But gradually the Democratic-Republicans gained strength, so much so that by 1800 their titular leader Thomas Jefferson was able to win the presidential election and put an end to Federalist control of the national government.

How can we explain the success of the Democratic-Republicans over their Federalist opponents? To answer this question, it is necessary to study in depth several key elections of the 1790s. Although many such contests are important for understanding the eventual Democratic-Republican victory in 1800, we have selected for further examination the 1794 race for the federal congressional seat from the city of Philadelphia. Because that seat had been held by a Federalist since the formation of the new government, this election was both an important test of strength of the rival Democratic-Republicans and representative of similar important contests being held in that same year in New York, Massachusetts, Maryland, and elsewhere. Because Philadelphia was the nation's capital in 1794, political party development was more advanced there than in other towns and cities of the young republic, thus offering us a harbinger of things to come nationwide.

THE METHOD

Observers of modern elections use a variety of methods to analyze political contests and determine why particular candidates won or lost. Some of the more important methods are:

1. *Study the candidates*—How a candidate projects him- or herself may be crucial to the election's outcome. Candidates have backgrounds, voting records, personalities, and idiosyncracies voters can assess. Candidates travel extensively, are seen by voters either in person or on television, and have several opportunities to appeal to the electorate. Post-election polls have shown that many voters respond as much to the candidates as people (a strong leader, a warm person, a confident leader, and so forth) as they do to the candidates' ideas. For example, in 1952, voters responded positively to Dwight Eisenhower even though many were not sure of his positions on a number of important issues. Similarly, in 1980 Ronald Reagan proved to be an extremely attractive presidential candidate, as much for his personal style as for his ideas and policies.

2. *Study the issues*—Elections often give citizens a chance to clarify their thinking on leading questions of the day. To make matters more complicated, certain groups (economic, ethnic, and interest groups, for example) respond to issues in different ways. The extent to which candidates can identify the issues that concern voters and can speak to these issues in an acceptable way can well mean the difference between victory and defeat. For example, in 1976, candidate Jimmy Carter was able to tap voters' post–Watergate disgust with corruption in the federal government and defeat incumbent Gerald Ford by speaking to that issue.

3. *Study the campaigns*—Success in devising and implementing a campaign strategy in modern times has been a crucial factor in the outcomes of elections. How does the candidate propose to deal with the issues? How are various interest groups to be lured under the party banner? How will money be raised, and how will it be spent? Will the candidate debate her or his opponent? Will the candidate make many personal appearances, or will she or he conduct a "front-porch" campaign? How will the candidate's family, friends, and political allies be used? Which areas (neighborhoods, regions, states, sections) will be targeted for special attention? To many political analysts, it is obvious that a number of superior candidates have been unsuccessful because of poorly run campaigns. By the same token, many less-than-superior candidates have won elections because of effectively conducted campaigns.

4. *Study the voters*—Recently the study of elections has become more sophisticated. Polling techniques have revealed that people similar in demographic variables such as age, sex, race, income, marital status, ethnic group, and religion tend to vote in similar fashions. For example, urban blacks voted overwhelmingly for Jimmy Carter in 1976.

CHAPTER 5

THE FIRST
AMERICAN
PARTY SYSTEM:
THE
PHILADELPHIA
CONGRESSIONAL
ELECTION OF
1794

These sophisticated polling techniques, also used for Gallup polls, Nielsen television ratings, and predicting responses to new consumer products, rest on important assumptions about human behavior. One assumption is that human responses tend to be strongly influenced (some say *determined*) by demographic variables; similar people tend to respond similarly to certain stimuli (such as candidates and campaigns). Another assumption is that these demographic patterns are constant and do not change rapidly. Finally, it is assumed that if we know how some of the people responded to certain stimuli, we can calculate how others possessing the same demographic variables will respond to those same stimuli.

Although there are many such patterns of voting behavior, they are easily observable. After the demographic variables that influence these patterns have been identified, a demographic sample of the population is created. Thus fifty white, male, middle-aged, married, Protestant, middle-income voters included in a sample might represent perhaps 100,000 people who possess these same variables. The fifty in the sample would then be polled to determine how they voted, and from this information we could infer how the 100,000 voted. Each population group in the sample would be polled in similar fashion. By doing this we can know with a fair amount of precision who voted for whom, thereby understanding which groups within the voting population were attracted to which candidate. Of course, the answer to why they were attracted still must be sought with one of the other methods: studying the candidates, studying the issues, and studying the campaigns.

These four approaches are methods for analyzing modern electoral contests. In fact, most political analysts use a combination of these approaches. But can these methods be used to analyze the 1794 congressional election in Philadelphia? Neither candidate openly sought the office, and neither made appearances in his own behalf. Although there certainly were important issues, neither political faction drew up a platform to explain to voters where its candidate stood on those issues. Neither political faction conducted an organized campaign. No polls were taken to determine voter concerns. At first glance, then, it appears that most if not all of these approaches to analyzing modern elections are useless in any attempt to analyze the 1794 Fitzsimons-Swanwick congressional contest.

These approaches, however, are not as useless as they initially appear. Philadelphia in 1794 was not a large city—it contained only about 45,000 people—and many voters knew the candidates personally because both were prominent figures in the community. Their respective backgrounds were generally well known. Moreover, Fitzsimons, as the incumbent, had a voting record in Congress, and most voters would have known how Swanwick stood on the issues, either through Swanwick's friends or through the positions he took as a member of the Democratic Society. Furthermore, the Federalists and Democratic-Republicans had taken general positions on some of the important issues. In addition, we are able to establish with a fair amount of certainty which voters cast ballots for Fitzsimons and which supported Swanwick. Finally, it is possible to identify important trends and events occurring in Philadelphia. In sum, although we might not have all the evidence we would like to have (historians almost never do), intelligent uses of the evidence at our disposal enables us to analyze the 1794 election with all or most of the approaches used in analyzing modern political contests.

As you examine the various types of evidence, divide it into four groups, one group for each general approach used in analyzing elections (candidates, issues, campaign, voters). For example, there are two excerpts from Philadelphia newspapers (one Federalist and one Democratic-Republican) dealing with the excise tax and the Whiskey Rebellion in western Pennsylvania. In what group would you put this evidence? Follow this procedure for all the evidence, noting that occasionally a piece of evidence could fit into more than one group. Such an arrangement of the evidence will give you four ways to analyze why the 1794 congressional election in Philadelphia turned out the way it did. Then, having examined and analyzed the evidence by groups, you will have to assess what principal factors explained Swanwick's upset victory.

THE EVIDENCE

1. The Candidates.

Thomas Fitzsimons (1741–1811) was born in Ireland and migrated to the colonies sometime before the Revolution, probably in 1765. He entered commerce as a clerk, worked his way up in his firm, and secured his position by marrying into the principal merchant's family. Fitzsimons served as a captain of the Pennsylvania militia during the Revolution, was a member of the Continental Congress in 1782 and 1783, and was elected to the Pennsylvania state house of representatives in 1786 and 1787. He was a delegate to the Constitutional Convention in 1787, was a signer of the Constitution, and was elected to the federal House of Representatives in 1788. He was a member of the Federalist inner circle in Philadelphia and a firm supporter of Alexander Hamilton's policies. He was a strong supporter of the excise tax (see approach 2 in the "Questions to Consider" section), was an instrumental figure in the compromise that brought the national capital to Philadelphia for ten years (1790–1800), and helped draft the legislation chartering the Bank of the United States in 1791. He was one of the original founders and directors of the Bank of North America, the director and president of the

CHAPTER 5

THE FIRST
AMERICAN
PARTY SYSTEM:
THE
PHILADELPHIA
CONGRESSIONAL
ELECTION OF
1794

Insurance Company of North America, and a key figure in dispensing federal patronage in Philadelphia. He was a Roman Catholic.

John Swanwick (1740–1798) was born in England. He and his family arrived in the colonies in the early 1770s. His father was a wagonmaster and minor British government official. During the Revolution, his father became a Tory and was exiled, but John Swanwick embraced the Patriot cause. In 1777, he was hired as a clerk in the merchant firm of Robert Morris. His fluency in both French and German made him invaluable to the firm, and he quickly rose to full partnership in 1783, the firm then being known as Willing, Morris & Swanwick. In 1794, he bought out Morris's share in the company. He was one of Philadelphia's leading export merchants, was a stockholder in the Bank of North America, and held a number of minor offices (under Morris) in the Confederation government. He supported the federal Constitution and Hamilton's early financial policies. Swanwick was elected to the state legislature in 1792. By 1793, he had drifted away from Federalism and had become a Democratic-Republican. In 1794, he joined the Pennsylvania Democratic Society and was soon made an officer. Swanwick also was an officer in a society that aided immigrants. He opposed the excise tax but thought the Whiskey Rebellion (see Approach 2 in the "Questions to Consider" section) in western Pennsylvania was the wrong method of protest. He wrote poetry and was never admitted to Philadelphia's social elite. He owned a two-hundred-acre country estate. He was a member of the Protestant Episcopal Church.

Source 2 from *Gazette of the United States* (a pro-Federalist Philadelphia newspaper), August 10, 1794.

2. A Pro-Federalist View of the Excise Tax and the Whiskey Rebellion.

. . . These Societies [the Democratic Societies],[4] strange as it may seem, have been formed in a free elective government for the sake of *preserving liberty*. And what is the liberty they are striving to introduce? It is the liberty of reviling the rulers who are chosen by the people and the government under which they live. It is the liberty of bringing the laws into contempt and

4. Democratic Societies were organizations composed principally of artisans and laborers and founded by Democratic-Republican leaders as political pressure groups against the Washington administration. Many Federalists believed that some Democratic Society members had been behind the Whiskey Rebellion. President Washington condemned the societies in 1794.

persuading people to resist them [a reference to the Whiskey Rebellion]. It is the liberty of condemning every system of Taxation because they have resolved that they will not be subject to laws—that they will not pay any taxes. To suppose that societies were formed with the purpose of opposing and with the hope of destroying government, might appear illiberal provided they had not already excited resistance to the laws and provided some of them had not publicly avowed their opinions that they *ought not to pay any taxes*. . . .

Source 3 from *General Advertiser* (a pro-Democratic-Republic Philadelphia newspaper), August 20, 1794.

3. A Pro-Democratic-Republican View of the Excise Tax and the Whiskey Rebellion.

As violent means appear the desire of high toned government men, it is to be hoped that those who derive the most benefit from our revenue laws will be the foremost to march against the Western insurgents. Let stock-holders, bank directors, speculators and revenue officers arrange themselves immediately under the banner of the treasury, and try their prowess in arms as they have done in calculation. The prompt recourse to hostilities which two certain great characters [Hamilton and Washington?] are so anxious for, will, no doubt, operate upon the knights of our country to appear in military array, and then the poor but industrious citizen will not be obliged to spill the blood of his fellow citizen before conciliatory means are tried. . . .

Source 4 from Harold C. Syrett, ed., *The Papers of Alexander Hamilton,* Vol. XVII (New York: Columbia University Press, 1972), pp. 15–19.

4. Alexander Hamilton to President Washington, August 2, 1794.

If the Judge shall pronounce that the case described in the second section of that Act [authorizing the calling out of the militia] exists, it will follow that a competent force of Militia should be called forth and employed to suppress the insurrection and support the Civil Authority in effectuating Obedience to the laws and punishment of Offenders.

It appears to me that the very existence of Government demands this course and that a duty of the highest nature urges the Chief Magistrate to pursue it.

CHAPTER 5

THE FIRST
AMERICAN
PARTY SYSTEM:
THE
PHILADELPHIA
CONGRESSIONAL
ELECTION OF
1794

Source 5 from Paul L. Ford, ed., *Writings of Thomas Jefferson,* Vol. VI (New York: G. P. Putnam's Sons, 1895), pp. 516–519.

5. Thomas Jefferson to James Madison, December 28, 1794.

And with respect to the transactions against the excise law [the Whiskey Rebellion], it appears to me that you are all swept away in the torrent of governmental opinion, or that we do not know what these transactions have been. We knew of none which, according to the definitions of the law, have been anything more than riotous. . . . The excise law is an infernal one. . . . The information of our militia, returned from the Westward, is uniform, that the people there let them pass quietly; they were objects of their laughter, not of their fear.

6. Excise Tax Statistics.

There were 27 snuff and tobacco factories in Philadelphia, employing more than 400 workers. The city's sugar refineries produced 350,000 pounds of sugar in 1794. All these items came under the excise tax, which added approximately 25 percent to a product's cost.

7. Swanwick and the Democratic Society.

Swanwick was a member of the Democratic Society of Pennsylvania. The society passed a resolution opposing the excise tax. The president condemned the society in 1794, saying that he believed that it and and other similar societies were responsible for the Whiskey Rebellion. The society endorsed Swanwick in 1794 and worked actively in his behalf.

Sources 8 and 9 from Billy G. Smith, "The Best Poor Man's Country: Living Standards of the 'Lower Sort' in Late Eighteenth Century Philadelphia," *Working Papers from the Regional Economic History Research Center* (Wilmington, Del.: Eleutherian Mills-Hagley Foundation, 1979), pp. 57–70. For household budgets, Smith calculated the costs of food, rent, fuel, and clothing and then established how much of these items were consumed.

8. Cost of Living Index, Philadelphia[5] (Base Year 1762 = 100).

Year	Food Cost	Firewood	Clothing	Household Budget
1788	92	74	139	123
1789	94	76	82	115
1790	109	79	92	131
1791	114	97	92	131
1792	114	106	110	136
1793	131	111	119	144
1794	142	130	137	158

9. Index of Wages, Philadelphia (Base Year 1762 = 100).

Year	Laborers	Tailors	Shoemakers
1788	117	84	77
1789	88	79	72
1790	86	100	58
1791	97	82	63
1792	119	109	75
1793	117	82	206
1794	143	123	122

5. An index number is a statistical measure designed to show changes in a variable (such as wages, prices, etc.) over time. A base year is selected and given the value of 100. The index for subsequent years is then expressed as a percentage of the base year.

10. Philadelphia Wards, 1794.

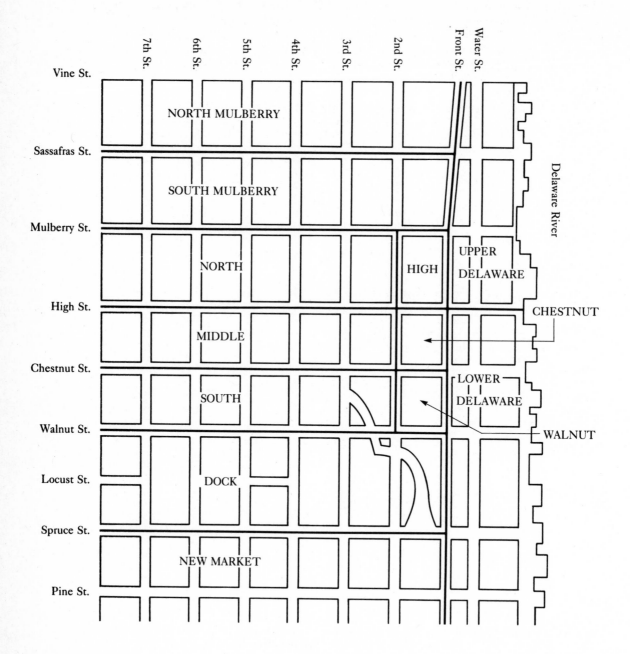

11. A Sample of Occupations by Ward (Males Only), Philadelphia, 1794.[6]

	Upper Delaware	North Mulberry	South Mulberry	High	North	Chestnut	Middle	Walnut	South	Dock	New Market	Lower Delaware	Occupation Totals
Gentleman	3	22	31	7	21	1	15	2	8	17	25	5	157
Merchant	76	47	65	47	90	38	63	20	26	101	83	43	699
Artisan	95	353	338	33	183	46	164	48	73	131	222	71	1,757
Laborer	18	93	103	10	70	7	27	8	12	38	56	1	443
Shopkeeper	13	24	39	24	44	9	23	4	6	7	35	8	236
Inn and Tavern Keeper	8	17	12	3	13	5	22	3	4	12	11	6	116
Captain	6	17	14	0	3	0	1	4	1	7	37	0	90
Government employee	2	12	13	0	16	2	13	1	7	14	18	0	98
Seaman	7	15	5	1	3	1	2	2	2	9	21	2	70
Teacher	1	5	12	0	6	0	2	0	3	5	6	0	40
Doctor	1	3	10	3	5	3	2	3	6	10	9	0	55
Grocer	10	22	20	3	37	2	20	0	5	25	34	6	184
Clergy	0	5	8	0	0	0	3	0	3	4	4	0	27
Lawyer	0	3	11	2	1	0	4	1	13	12	5	1	53
Clerk	5	16	18	3	7	1	12	1	4	10	12	1	90
Broker	0	1	2	0	3	2	4	4	3	2	1	0	22
Other	1	5	0	1	3	1	0	0	1	1	2	0	15
Unknown	1	7	14	1	1	0	2	0	1	2	8	0	37
Ward totals	247	667	715	138	506	118	379	101	178	407	589	144	

6. Sample taken from the Philadelphia city directory for 1794. Poor people were notoriously undercounted in city directories, as were nonpermanent residents, such as seamen.

CHAPTER 5

THE FIRST
AMERICAN
PARTY SYSTEM:
THE
PHILADELPHIA
CONGRESSIONAL
ELECTION OF
1794

Source 12 from James Hardie, *The Philadelphia Directory and Register* (Philadelphia, 1794).

12. First-Person Account of the Yellow Fever.

Having mentioned this disorder to have occasioned great devastation in the year 1793, a short account of it may be acceptable to several of our readers. . . .

This disorder made its first appearance toward the latter end of July, in a lodging house in North Water Street; and for a few weeks seemed entirely confined to that vicinity. Hence it was generally supposed to have been imported and not generated in the city. This was the opinion of Doctors Currie, Cathrall and many others. It was however combated by Dr. Benjamin Rush, who asserts that the contagion was generated from the stench of a cargo of damaged coffee. . . .

But from whatever fountain we trace this poisoned stream, it has destroyed the lives of many thousands—and many of those of the most distinguished worth. . . . During the month of August the funerals amounted to upwards of three hundred. The disease had then reached the central streets of the city and began to spread on all sides with the greatest rapidity. In September its malignance increased amazingly. Fear pervaded the stoutest heart, flight became general, and terror was depicted on every countenance. In this month 1,400 more were added to the list of mortality. The contagion was still progressive and towards the end of the month 90 & 100 died daily. Until the middle of October the mighty destroyer went on with increasing havoc. From the 1st to the 17th upwards of 1,400 fell victims to the tremendous malady. From the 17th to the 30th the mortality gradually decreased. In the whole month, however, the dead amounted to upwards of 2,000—a dreadful number, if we consider that at this time near one half of the inhabitants had fled. Before the disorder became so terrible, the appearance of Philadelphia must to a stranger have seemed very extraordinary. The garlic, which chewed as a preventative[,] could be smelled at several yards distance, whilst other[s] hoped to avoid infection by a recourse to smelling bottles, handkerchiefs dipped in vinegar, camphor bags, &c. . . .

During this melancholy period the city lost ten of her most valuable physicians, and most of the others were sick at different times. The number of deaths in all amounted to 4041.[7]

7. The population of Philadelphia (including suburbs) was 42,444 in 1790.

Sources 13 and 14 from L. H. Butterfield, ed., *Letters of Benjamin Rush*[8], Vol. II (Princeton, N.J.: Published for the American Philosophical Society, 1951) pp. 644–645, 657–658.

13. Benjamin Rush to Mrs. Rush, August 29, 1793, on the Yellow Fever.

Be assured that I will send for you if I should be seized with the disorder, for I conceive that it would be as much your duty not to desert me in that situation as it is now mine not to desert my patients. . . .

Its symptoms are very different in different people. Sometimes it comes on with a chilly fit and a high fever, but more frequently it steals on with headache, languor, and sick stomach. These symptoms are followed by stupor, delirium, vomiting, a dry skin, cool or cold hands and feet, a feeble slow pulse, sometimes below in frequency the pulse of health. The eyes are at first suffused with blood, they afterwards become yellow, and in most cases a yellowness covers the whole skin on the 3rd or 4th day. Few survive the 5th day, but more die on the 2 and 3rd days. In some cases the patients possess their reason to the last and discover much less weakness than in the last stage of common fevers. One of my patients stood up and shaved himself on the morning of the day he died. Livid spots on the body, a bleeding at the nose, from the gums, and from the bowels, and a vomiting of black matter in some instances close the scenes of life. The common remedies for malignant fevers have all failed. Bark, wine, and blisters make no impression upon it. Baths of hot vinegar applied by means of blankets, and the cold bath have relieved and saved some. . . .

This day I have given mercury, and I think with some advantage. . . .

8. Dr. Benjamin Rush (1745–1813) was a Pennsylvanian who was graduated from the College of New Jersey (Princeton, 1760) and studied medicine at the College of Philadelphia and the University of Edinburgh. Practicing medicine in Philadelphia, he was elected to the Continental Congress in 1776 and was a signer of the Declaration of Independence. He supported the ratification of the Constitution. By 1794, he had changed allegiances and was considered a Democratic-Republican. He participated in many reform movements, including the abolition of slavery, the end to capital punishment, temperance, an improved educational system, and prison reform. His protégé, Dr. Michael Leib, was extremely active in Democratic-Republican politics.

Most physicians in Philadelphia in 1794 were Federalists. The majority fled the city when the fever broke out. Of the doctors who stayed, Rush was one of the most prominent.

CHAPTER 5

THE FIRST
AMERICAN
PARTY SYSTEM:
THE
PHILADELPHIA
CONGRESSIONAL
ELECTION OF
1794

14. Benjamin Rush to Mrs. Rush, September 10, 1793, on the Yellow Fever.

My dear Julia,

Hereafter my name should be Shadrach, Meshach, or Abednego, for I am sure the preservation of those men from death by fire was not a greater miracle than my preservation from the infection of the prevailing disorder. I have lived to see the close of another day, more awful than any I have yet seen. Forty persons it is said have been buried this day, and I have visited and prescribed for more than 100 patients. Mr. Willing is better, and Jno. Barclay is out of danger. Amidst my numerous calls to the wealthy and powerful, I do not forget the poor, well remembering my dream in the autumn of 1780. . . .

15. Sampling of Deaths from Yellow Fever, Philadelphia, 1793 Epidemic.[9]

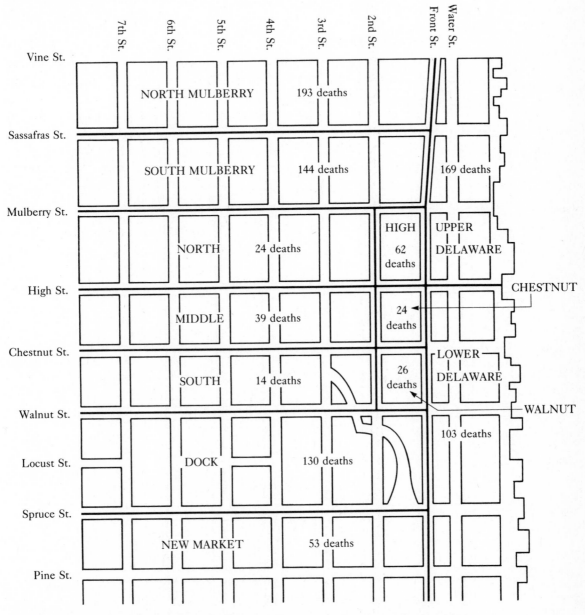

9. Sample taken from Philadelphia newspapers. After a time, officials simply stopped recording the names of those who died, except for prominent citizens. Therefore, although James Hardie reported that 4,041 people had died, one scholar has estimated the death toll as high as 6,000, roughly one out of every seven Philadelphians.

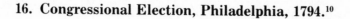

16. Congressional Election, Philadelphia, 1794.[10]

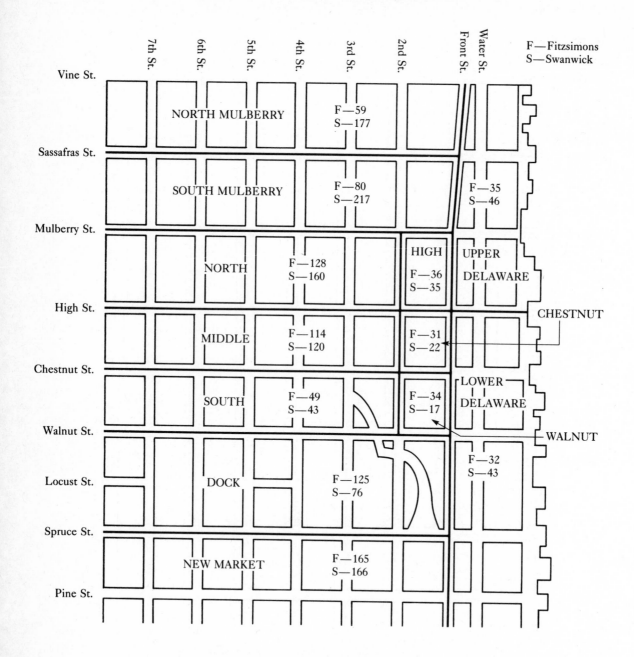

10. Total votes: Swanwick, 1,122; Fitzsimons, 888.

[108]

QUESTIONS TO CONSIDER

No single method of analyzing elections will give you the answer to the central question of why John Swanwick was able to defeat Thomas Fitzsimons. Instead, you must use all four approaches, grouping the evidence by approach and determining what each approach tells you about why the election turned out as it did.

Before examining each group of evidence, however, try to discover who tended to vote for each candidate. Source 11 shows occupations by wards. Although there are exceptions, occupations can often be used to establish a person's wealth and status. Today many people introduce themselves by telling their name, occupation, and address. What are these people really saying? Examine carefully the occupational makeup of each ward. Then look at the map in Source 10. Where do the bulk of laborers live? Artisans (skilled laborers)? Merchants? How could you use this evidence to determine who tended to support Fitzsimons and Swanwick?

Having established who tended to vote for Fitzsimons and who tended to vote for Swanwick, you are ready to answer the question of why one of the candidates was more appealing to the majority of Philadelphia voters. Here is where the four major approaches explained earlier can be brought into play.

1. *Candidates*—Source 1 supplies biographical information about the two candidates. Do not neglect to study the additional material on Swanwick (Source 7); this is material that voters not personally acquainted with the candidates would have known. What are the significant points of comparison and contrast between the candidates?

One significant point of difference is religion. Fitzsimons was a Roman Catholic, and Swanwick belonged to the Protestant Episcopal Church. Most of Philadelphia's voters were Protestant, the two largest denominations being Lutheran and Quaker. Was religion a factor in this election? How can you prove that it was or was not?

One interesting point in Swanwick's biographical sketch is that, although wealthy, he was never admitted to Philadelphia's social elite circles, a fact that probably some of the voters knew. Do you think this was an important consideration in the voters' minds? How would you prove your point?

2. *Issues*—There were a number of issues in this election, and it was fairly clear how each faction stood on those issues. Two of the most important issues were the excise tax (Sources 2, 3, 6, 7) and the Whiskey Rebellion (Sources 4, 5).

In its efforts to raise money, the national government had settled on, among other things, an excise tax on selected products manufactured in the United States. The taxes on tobacco products, sugar products, and distilled spirits raised considerable protest, especially in western Pennsylvania, where whiskey was an important commodity. In that area, farmers tried to prevent the collection of the tax, a protest that

CHAPTER 5

THE FIRST
AMERICAN
PARTY SYSTEM:
THE
PHILADELPHIA
CONGRESSIONAL
ELECTION OF
1794

eventually grew into the Whiskey Rebellion of 1794. In a sense, this was the first real test of the ability of the central government to enforce its laws.

a. Which groups in Philadelphia did the excise tax affect most? How?

b. How did each candidate stand on the excise tax?

c. Which groups of Philadelphians would have been likely to favor their respective positions?

d. How did each faction stand on the Whiskey Rebellion? (See Sources 2 through 5.)

e. How did the candidates stand on this issue?

f. Which groups of Philadelphians would have been likely to favor their respective positions?

3. *Campaign*—Although there were a few mass meetings and some distribution of literature, there was no real campaign in the modern sense. In the absence of an organized campaign, how did voters make up their minds?

4. *Voters*—At the time of the election, other important trends were occurring in Philadelphia that might have influenced voters. For example, review the evidence on the cost of living and wages, compiled by the historian Billy Smith (Sources 8 and 9). What general trends can you observe? Which groups would be most affected by these trends? How would they feel?

Also review the material on the 1793 yellow fever epidemic (Sources 12 through 15), in which more than four thousand recorded deaths (not quite one-tenth of the city's total population) occurred. Why is this material included in the evidence? How does the evidence on the fever relate to other pieces of evidence? Think about where the epidemic broke out. Who lived in that area? James Hardie said that many people fled the city. Who would tend to leave? Who could not leave? What impact might this event have had on the election a year later?[11] By 1794, Dr. Benjamin Rush was a prominent Democratic-Republican. What was his role among the poor Philadelphians? Do you think he might have been influential in the Fitzsimons-Swanwick election? How?

Now you are ready to answer the question of why the 1794 congressional election in Philadelphia turned out the way it did (Source 16). Make sure, however, that your opinion is solidly supported by evidence.

EPILOGUE

As the temporary national capital in 1794, Philadelphia was probably somewhat more advanced than the rest of the nation in the growth of political factions. However, by the presidential election of 1800, most of the country had become involved in the gradual process of party building. By that time the Democratic-Republicans were the dominant political force, aided by more aggressive campaign techniques, their espousal of

11. The fever abated in the autumn of 1793, when frosts killed the fever-bearing mosquitos. At that time, most of those who had fled Philadelphia returned and hence were back in the city by the time of the 1794 election.

a limited national government (which most Americans preferred), their less elitist attitudes, and their ability to brand their Federalist opponents as aristocrats and pro-British monocrats. Although Federalism retained considerable strength in New England and the Middle States, by 1800 it no longer was a serious challenge to the Democratic-Republicans on the national level.

For his part, John Swanwick never saw the ultimate triumph of Democratic-Republicanism because he died in the 1798 yellow fever epidemic in Philadelphia. Fitzsimons never again sought political office, preferring to concentrate his energies on his already successful mercantile and banking career. Hamilton died in a duel with Aaron Burr in 1804. After he left the presidency in 1809, Jefferson retired to his estate Monticello to bask in the glories of being an aging founding father. He died in 1826 at the age of eighty-three.

By 1826, many of the concerns of the Federalist Era had been resolved.

The War of 1812 had further secured American independence, and the death of the Federalist faction had put an end to the notion of government by an entrenched (established) and favored elite. At the same time, however, new issues had arisen to test the durability of the republic and the collective wisdom of its people. After a brief political calm, party battles once again were growing fiercer, as the rise of Andrew Jackson threatened to split the brittle Jeffersonian coalition. Westward expansion was carrying Americans into territories owned by other nations, and few doubted that an almost inevitable conflict lay ahead. American cities, such as Philadelphia, were growing in both population and socioeconomic problems. The twin specters of slavery and sectional conflict were claiming increasing national attention. Whether the political system fashioned in the 1790s could address these crucial issues and trends and at the same time maintain its republican principles was a question that soon would have to be addressed.

THE CLASH
OF POLITICAL PHILOSOPHIES:
THE DEBATE OVER UNIVERSAL SUFFRAGE
IN NEW YORK (1821)

THE PROBLEM

On August 28, 1821, 126 delegates met in the assembly chamber in Albany to revise New York's state constitution. The state's original constitution, drafted and ratified in 1777 in the midst of the War for American Independence, essentially had been left untouched since that date and contained features that many New Yorkers found increasingly intolerable, among them the requirement that only property owners could vote in state elections. The 1777 constitution allowed males who owned real estate (called a *freehold,* which was land that had no mortgage on it) and renters who paid more than 40 shillings in annual rent to cast ballots in assembly elections, but only those who possessed a freehold worth £100 or more could vote for members of the senate and for the governor, thus limiting the voters for senators and governor to less than 40 percent of the adult male population.

Present at the 1821 New York constitutional convention were some of the most talented figures in the state's political history. Daniel D. Tompkins, former governor and in 1821 vice president of the United States, was chosen as president of the convention. Remnants of the nearly dead Federalist party were represented by former U.S. senator Rufus King, New York chief justice Ambrose Spencer, Peter A. Jay (son of Founding Father John Jay), and the brilliant chancellor James Kent. Peter R. Livingston, an aging and wealthy Jeffersonian, spoke for the once mighty Livingston faction. Finally, there were men like the sagacious Martin Van Buren, most of whose political triumphs still lay ahead.

Although the convention dealt with a number of perceived defects of the 1777 constitution, it was the issue of universal male suffrage that elicited the most debate and conflict. Essentially the suffrage debate centered on two questions: (1) Should all property qualifications for voting be elimi-

nated? (2) Should the vote be extended to all adult black males as well as to all adult white males? In this chapter you will be identifying and analyzing the principal arguments on both sides of these two questions. How do those arguments help us understand American political thought in the so-called Age of the Common Man?

BACKGROUND

Many Americans saw the election of General Andrew Jackson to the presidency in 1828 as a victory of the people over the forces of political privilege and vested interests. Although considerably wealthy by 1828, Jackson began life in humbler circumstances and achieved his prosperity through hard work and a measure of good luck; he was truly a "self-made man." Hence, to many Americans, Jackson was the model of what they too could achieve. Moreover, in the War of 1812, the Tennessean had given Americans a genuine war hero and a thrilling victory at New Orleans. Indeed, many Americans turned even Jackson's faults (his legendary stubbornness and hot temper, his tyrannical behavior at New Orleans and later in Florida, his lack of cultural refinements)[1] into political assets, evidence that General Jackson was one of them. The first president to

whom people felt close enough to give a nickname ("Old Hickory"), Andrew Jackson was viewed by his contemporaries as the first "people's president."

In many ways, however, Jackson was the heir of important economic, social, and political forces that he did not create. Collectively, many of these trends can be described as *democratic,*[2] emphasizing social and political equality and the collective wisdom of the common people. After the War of 1812, the rapid increase in geographic mobility to western lands and the nation's mushrooming cities undermined traditional class distinctions and the power of established elite groups. In the West particularly, where expansion had been aided by an 1820 easing of government land sales policies and a revolution in transportation technol-

1. In an expedition against the Seminole Indians in 1818, Jackson apprehended and hanged two British agents, causing a diplomatic dispute between the British and American governments.

2. The term *democratic* refers to the concept of human equality, whereas *Democratic* (with a capital D) refers to the political party of which Jackson was a founder. That party was an outgrowth of the Democratic-Republican party, founded by James Madison and Thomas Jefferson, among others.

CHAPTER 6

THE CLASH OF
POLITICAL
PHILOSOPHIES:
THE DEBATE
OVER
UNIVERSAL
SUFFRAGE IN
NEW YORK (1821)

ogy, new communities and societies were created with new elite groups who viewed eastern aristocrats with suspicion and distrust. Finally, the discrediting of the Federalist party struck an ultimately fatal blow against the major political group advocating rule by the elite and deference to that elite by people "below" them in the economic and social hierarchy.

This democratic spirit could be seen in nearly every aspect of American life. Deference to one's "betters" was all but eradicated, as wealthy travelers discovered in inns, taverns, and hotels when often they were forced to share rooms and dinner tables with "common" people. Nor could one still tell a member of the "better sort" by dress because men and women of other classes (aided by the mass production of inexpensive textiles, apparel, and shoes) began wearing clothing similar in style—if not in quality—to their wealthier and well-born fellow Americans. A generation ago, this democratization of dress would have shocked Americans, but in the new egalitarian atmosphere it was commonplace. Indeed, this democratic impulse permeated American religion, entertainment, plays, and music, and literature that extolled the virtues of the common people was immensely popular. Except inside the well-protected drawing rooms and fashionable parlors of the old elite groups, egalitarianism was a powerful force that reached nearly every crevice of American life.

But Americans did not believe that all should be equal in wealth or power. In the message accompanying his veto of the bill rechartering the Bank of the United States in 1832, Andrew Jack-

son himself wrote, "Distinctions in society will always exist under every just government. Equality of talents, of education, or of wealth can not be produced by human institutions." What Americans expected was that every person have an *equal opportunity* to acquire wealth and power. In this atmosphere, the self-made man was society's hero and was accorded almost as much honor as earlier generations had bestowed on the "well-born," whose wealth and power was inherited or achieved through connections with the established elite. Indeed, the self-made man and the "indolent rich boy" of inherited wealth became powerful images and symbols in American popular culture.

This democratic spirit had a profound effect on American politics. Previously, only the elite sought major offices, and only those who owned property could vote for the candidates. To people imbued with the democratic spirit, such a situation was intolerable. If all men possessed some wisdom, why shouldn't they be allowed to vote for their political officials? Other traditional distinctions had been struck down; this one too must be eliminated.

When Thomas Jefferson won the presidency in 1800,[3] most states still had property qualifications for voting.

3. Because Jefferson and his vice presidential running mate Aaron Burr received the same number of electoral votes in 1800, the contest was thrown into the House of Representatives, where, after 36 ballots, Jefferson finally was chosen president in February 1801. The Twelfth Amendment to the Constitution eliminated the possibility of this problem recurring. It was ratified in June 1804, before the next presidential contest.

New Jersey abolished that restriction in 1807, as did Maryland in 1810. But the big surge toward universal white male suffrage came with the admission of six new states (Indiana, Illinois, Mississippi, Alabama, Missouri, and Maine) between 1816 and 1821, all of whose constitutions granted all adult white males the right to vote.[4] This put additional pressure on states whose Revolutionary War constitutions still withheld the vote from all adult white males. In those states, ambitious men who hoped to break the constitutional stranglehold their elites held over state government saw universal white male suffrage as a means to that end.

Accompanying the rise of this democratic spirit was the breakdown of America's party system, which had been created in the political wars of the 1790s. The death of Federalism left the nation with but one political party, the Democratic-Republicans, yet that party was rent with sectional and ideological factions. Within the Democratic-Republican party, a group of nationalists, led principally by Henry Clay and John Quincy Adams, advocated a strong central government with wide-ranging powers to enhance the nation's economic development. This faction called for the chartering of a new Bank of the United States (the charter of Alexander Hamilton's first Bank of the United States had not been renewed in 1811), federally financed roads and canals, and a protective tariff to aid new American industries. Opposing this intraparty faction was a group of Democratic-Republicans (the most prominent of whom were Martin Van Buren of New York, Thomas Hart Benton of Missouri, John H. Eaton of Tennessee, and Jackson himself) who adhered more closely to traditional Jeffersonian ideas of a limited central government and a strict construction of the Constitution. As states began to institute universal white male suffrage, these factions increasingly appealed to the people, thus giving the voters a greater role than they previously had enjoyed.

In the years since independence, New York had grown more than any other state. Between 1790 and 1820, the state's population had quadrupled, and the sixteen counties in 1790 had expanded to fifty-five by 1820. Two-thirds of the population lived in areas of the state that had been considered the frontier in 1790, and New York City's population had more than doubled since 1800. Most of the city's new people owned no real estate, and many of the settlers who moved into the northern and western regions were not allowed to vote because properties on which leases and mortgages were paid were not considered freeholds. Moreover, many people who settled in the northern and western areas of New York had come from other states, where suffrage requirements were more lenient. These new settlers, many of whom were disfranchised because they did not own their land outright, were outraged

4. Indiana, Illinois, and Missouri had only resident requirements, Maine excluded only paupers, Alabama did not give the vote to some criminals, and Mississippi required that a voter be either a taxpayer or a member of the state militia. However, because militia duty was compulsory, Mississippi essentially kept no adult white males from the polls.

CHAPTER 6

THE CLASH OF
POLITICAL
PHILOSOPHIES:
THE DEBATE
OVER
UNIVERSAL
SUFFRAGE IN
NEW YORK (1821)

that the right to vote had been taken from them. Together with the people of New York City, they called for suffrage reform.

New York also had the largest black population of any state north of the Chesapeake. Slaves from the West Indies had been brought to New Netherland by the Dutch West India Company in 1626, a practice that increased under English rule. The slaves were used primarily as agricultural workers or laborers. By 1749, New York's slave population numbered 10,592 (out of a total population of 73,348), and one-sixth of New York City's population was black. During the colonial period, a number of slave plots and one real uprising (in 1712) had made white settlers extremely distrustful of blacks. Nevertheless, in 1799, New York approved a plan for the gradual emancipation of slaves.[5] Even before then, during the party battles of the 1790s, as evidence shows, some free black renters were voting in New York City. Hence the issue of whether blacks in New York should be included in the move toward universal male suffrage was a real one.

Governor DeWitt Clinton tried to block a constitutional convention in New York, fearing that the new dem-

5. The 1799 plan for gradual emancipation stated that slave children born after July 4, 1799, would achieve freedom at age twenty-five for females and twenty-eight for males. In 1817, the state legislature passed an act that mandated that all those who were still slaves on July 4, 1827, would immediately become free.

ocratic spirit would drive a wedge between him and his Federalist allies and oust him from power. But Clinton could not smother calls for a constitutional convention that would deal with, among other things, the franchise. Reluctantly, Clinton allowed New Yorkers to vote on whether they wanted a constitutional convention. In the vote, New Yorkers asked for a convention, with the western areas and New York City providing the strongest support.

As noted, when the New York constitutional convention opened in August 1821, there was considerable pressure to approve a new constitution granting universal adult male suffrage. Yet it must be remembered that "democracy" was a relatively new concept in 1821. Concerned about the intelligence and virtue of the people, the drafters of the original state constitution (and, indeed, the federal Constitution itself) purposely placed checks in those documents to prevent unbridled rule by the common people. Even in 1821, reformers and conservatives alike looked into a future that no one could predict. Was former U.S. Supreme Court chief justice and New York governor John Jay's belief that "those who own the country ought to govern it" the best approach, or should those who called for all men to vote be heeded? Most governments in the past had been run by propertied and educated elites. In 1821, democracy was an untested and, many believed, dangerous philosophy. Would it undo all the gains that Americans had won?

THE METHOD

First, you must be able to identify and summarize the principal arguments on both sides of the two issues concerning the suffrage (whether to eliminate all property qualifications for voting and whether to extend the vote to all adult black males as well as to all adult white males). Then, by analyzing the evidence, you must determine what the 1821 debate tells us about American political thought in the Age of the Common Man.

The full transcription of the convention debates is well over six hundred pages, so the evidence here is but a small fraction of the total debate. Nevertheless, the major arguments on each side of the question have been reproduced here. Delegates discussed other important constitutional reforms—sometimes at length—but the question of suffrage extension was the most debated issue.

Excerpts from several speeches have been reproduced in the exact order in which they were delivered at the convention. As you read each selection, ask yourself the following questions:

1. With which of the two questions is the speaker concerned (universal suffrage for all adult white males or universal suffrage for white and black males)?
2. What arguments does the speaker offer in support of his position?
3. Is the speaker replying to an earlier speech? If so, does he support or oppose the position of the earlier speaker? What arguments does he offer to support or counter the earlier speaker?

4. How do the arguments made by the speaker help us understand American political thought at the time?

Take notes as you read the selections. Then, having read all the selections, divide the evidence into two categories: one dealing with universal suffrage for adult white males and one with universal suffrage for white and black males. Next, summarize the main points on both sides of both issues. Finally, using your historical imagination, tell what the debates as a whole reveal about American political thought in Age of the Common Man.

One curious thing you will discover is that a number of those delegates who favored universal adult white male suffrage also *opposed* black male suffrage, whereas many of those who opposed lowering voting restrictions for whites actually *favored* black male suffrage. Why do you think this was so? Do the debates offer any clues?

You will also note that the English language in America had changed. It is much easier to understand the rhetoric of nineteenth-century figures than that of people from earlier eras (see the trial of Anne Hutchinson, for example). The democratic impulse affected the language. In the democratic tumult of the early nineteenth century, people were expected to "speak their mind," to do away with "aristocratic frills" in their speech. If one was "running" for office, then one would have to speak more like the voters one courted.

CHAPTER 6

THE CLASH OF
POLITICAL
PHILOSOPHIES:
THE DEBATE
OVER
UNIVERSAL
SUFFRAGE IN
NEW YORK (1821)

THE EVIDENCE

Sources 1 and 2 from *Reports of the Proceedings and Debates of the Convention of 1821, Assembled for the Purpose of Amending the Constitution of the State of New York* (Albany, N.Y.: F. and E. Hosford, 1821), pp. 156, 178–291, 362–377, 661.

1. Convention Speeches.

Ogden Edwards, New York County

Sir, I came not here to flatter the people. I came here to serve the people, by a faithful devotion of my faculties, such as they are, to a subject which most deeply concerns them and their posterity. To accomplish the end for which we are sent, we must form a correct estimate of the character of this people. We have heard much flattery delt out to them; and who would imagine from what we have heard, but that they were all wise, all honest, all, all honourable men. Sir, this is all folly. It is not true, and the people know that it is not true. The truth of the matter is, that the people of this state are like the people of other states. Some of them are wise and some are foolish; some honest and some are knaves. If the people are as they have been represented, how does it happen that your courts of justice are crowded with lawsuits, and your state-prison so filled to overflowing, that it is necessary from time to time to disgorge their foul contents upon the community? Sir, the very existence of civil government is a libel upon the human race. It is enough for us to know, that there is in the people of this, as well as of other states, a fund of good sense, of integrity, and of patriotism, which qualifies them in an eminent degree for the enjoyment of a free government. And it is our business so to organize the government, as that it will most effectually answer the end for which it is established, and that is to protect the virtuous and to punish the vicious; to cast a rampart around the deserving, and to restrain those who will not respect the laws of God or man. We must take things as we find them here. . . .

Nathan Sanford, New York County[6]

The question before us is the right of suffrage—who shall, or who shall not, have the right to vote. The committee have presented the scheme they

---

6. Sanford chaired the committee that drafted the universal white male suffrage proposal.

thought best; to abolish all existing distinctions, and make the right of voting uniform. Is this not right? Where did these distinctions arise? They arose from British precedents. In England, they have their three estates, which must always have their separate interests represented. Here there is but one estate—the people. To me, the only qualification seems to be, the virtue and morality of the people; and if they may be safely entrusted to vote for one class of our rulers, why not for all? In my opinion, these distinctions are fallacious. We have the experience of almost all the other states against them. The principle of the scheme now proposed, is, that those who bear the burthens of the state, should choose those that rule it. There is no privilege given to property, as such; but those who contribute to the public support, we consider as entitled to a share in the election of rulers. The burthens are annual, and the elections are annual, and this appears proper. To me, and the majority of the committee, it appeared the only reasonable scheme that those who are to be affected by the acts of the government, should be annually entitled to vote for those who administer it. Our taxes are of two sorts, on real and personal property. The payment of a tax on either, we thought, equally entitled a man to a vote, and thus we intended to destroy the odious distinctions of property which now exist. But we have considered personal service, in some cases, equivalent to a tax on personal property, as in work on the high roads. This is a burthen, and should entitle those subject to it to equivalent privileges. The road duty is equal to a poll tax on every male citizen of 21 years, of 62½ cents per annum, which is about the value of each individual's work on the road. This work is a burthen imposed by the legislature—a duty required by rulers, and which should entitle those subject to it, to a choice of those rulers. Then, sir, the militia next presents itself; the idea of personal service, as applicable to the road duty, is, in like manner, applicable here; and this criterion has been adopted in other states. In Mississippi, mere enrolment gives a vote. In Connecticut, as is proposed here, actual service, and that without the right of commutation, is required. The duty in the militia is obligatory and onerous. The militia man must find his arms and accoutrements, and lose his time. But, after admitting all these persons, what restrictions, it will be said, are left on the right of suffrage? 1st. The voter must be a citizen. 2d. The service required must be performed within the year, on the principle that taxation is annual, and election annual; so that when the person ceases to contribute or serve, he ceases to vote. . . .

Now, sir, this scheme will embrace almost the whole male population of the state. There is perhaps no subject so purely matter of opinion, as the question how far the right of suffrage may be safely carried. We propose to carry it almost as far as the male population of the state. The Convention

CHAPTER 6

THE CLASH OF
POLITICAL
PHILOSOPHIES:
THE DEBATE
OVER
UNIVERSAL
SUFFRAGE IN
NEW YORK (1821)

may perhaps think this too broad. On this subject we have much experience; yet there are respectable citizens who think this extension of suffrage unfavourable to the rights of property. Certainly this would be a fatal objection, if well founded; for any government, however constituted, which does not secure property to its rightful owners, is a bad government. But how is the extension of the right of suffrage unfavourable to property? Will not our laws continue the same? Will not the administration of justice continue the same? And if so, how is private property to suffer? Unless these are changed, and upon them rest the rights and security of property, I am unable to perceive how property is to suffer by the extension of the right of suffrage. But we have abundant experience on this point in other states. Now, sir, in many of the states the right of suffrage has no restriction; every male inhabitant votes. Yet what harm has been done in those states? What evil has resulted to them from this cause? The course of things in this country is for the extension, and not the restriction of popular rights. I do not know that in Ohio or Pennsylvania, where the right of suffrage is universal, there is not the same security for private rights and private happiness as elsewhere. . . .

John Ross, Genesee County

That all men are free and equal, according to the usual declarations, applies to them only in a state of nature, and not after the institution of civil government; for then many rights, flowing from a natural equality, are necessarily abridged, with a view to produce the greatest amount of security and happiness to the whole community. On this principle the right of suffrage is extended to white men only. But why, it will probably be asked, are blacks to be excluded? I answer, because they are seldom, if ever, required to share in the common burthens or defence of the state. There are also additional reasons; they are a peculiar people, incapable, in my judgment, of exercising that privilege with any sort of discretion, prudence, or independence. They have no just conceptions of civil liberty. They know not how to appreciate it, and are consequently indifferent to its preservation.

Under such circumstances, it would hardly be compatible with the safety of the state, to entrust such a people with this right. It is not thought advisable to permit aliens to vote, neither would it be safe to extend it to the blacks. We deny to minors this right, and why? Because they are deemed incapable of exercising it discreetly, and therefore not safely, for the good of the whole community.—Even the better part of creation[7] as my honourable

7. Ross was referring here to women.

friend from Oneida, (Mr. N. Williams) stiles them, are not permitted to participate in this right. No sympathies seemed to be awakened in their behalf, nor in behalf of the aborigines, the original and only rightful proprietors of our soil—a people altogether more acute and discerning, and in whose judicious exercise of the right I should repose far more confidence, than in the African race. In nearly all the western and southern states, indeed many others, even in Connecticut, where steady habits and correct principles prevail, the blacks are excluded. And gentlemen have been frequently in the habit of citing the precedents of our sister states for our guide; and would it not be well to listen to the decisive weight of precedents furnished in this case also? . . .

Peter A. Jay, Westchester County

The chairman of the select committee has given a fair and candid exposition of the reasons that induced them to make the report now under consideration, and on the motives by which they were governed. He has clearly stated why they were desirous of extending the right of suffrage to some who did not at present enjoy it, but he has wholly omitted to explain why they deny it to others who actually possess it. The omission, however, has been supplied by one of his colleagues, who informed us that all who were not white ought to be excluded from political rights, because such persons were incapable of exercising them discreetly, and because they were peculiarly liable to be influenced and corrupted. . . .

Why, sir, are these men to be excluded from rights which they possess in common with their countrymen? What crime have they committed for which they are to be punished? Why are they, who were born as free as ourselves, natives of the same country, and deriving from nature and our political institutions, the same rights and privileges which we have, now to be deprived of all those rights, and doomed to remain forever as aliens among us? We are told, in reply, that other states have set us the example. It is true that other states treat this race of men with cruelty and injustice, and that we have hitherto manifested towards them a disposition to be just and liberal. Yet even in Virginia and North Carolina, free people of colour are permitted to vote, and if I am correctly informed, exercise that privilege. In Pennsylvania, they are much more numerous than they are here, and there they are not disfranchised, nor has any inconvenience been felt from extending to all men the rights which ought to be common to all. In Connecticut, it is true, they have, for the last three years adopted a new constitution which prevents people of colour from acquiring the right of suffrage in future, yet even

CHAPTER 6

THE CLASH OF
POLITICAL
PHILOSOPHIES:
THE DEBATE
OVER
UNIVERSAL
SUFFRAGE IN
NEW YORK (1821)

there they have preserved the right to all those who previously possessed it. . . .

But we are told by one of the select committee, that people of colour are incapable of exercising the right of suffrage. I may have misunderstood that gentleman; but I thought he meant to say, that they laboured under a physical disability. It is true that some philosophers have held that the intellect of a black man is naturally inferior to that of a white one; but this idea has been so completely refuted, and is now so universally exploded, that I did not expect to have heard of it in an assembly so enlightened as this, nor do I now think it necessary to disprove it. That in general the people of colour are inferior to the whites in knowledge and in industry, I shall not deny. You made them slaves, and nothing is more true than the ancient saying, "The day you make man a slave takes half his worth away." Unaccustomed to provide for themselves, and habituated to regard labour as an evil, it is no wonder that when set free, they should be improvident and idle, and that their children should be brought up without education, and without prudence or forethought. But will you punish the children for your own crimes; for the injuries which you have inflicted upon their parents? Besides, sir, this state of things is fast passing away. Schools have been opened for them, and it will, I am sure, give pleasure to this committee to know, that in these schools there is discovered a thirst for instruction, and a progress in learning, seldom to be seen in the other schools of the state. They have also churches of their own, and clergymen of their own colour, who conduct their public worship with perfect decency and order, and not without ability. . . .

Robert Clarke, Delaware County

My honourable colleague has told us, "that these people are not liable to do military duty, and that as they are not required to contribute to the protection or defence of the state, they are not entitled to an equal participation in the privileges of its citizens." But, sir, whose fault is this? Have they ever refused to do military duty when called upon? It is haughtily asked, who will stand in the ranks, shoulder to shoulder, with a negro? I answer, no one in time of peace; no one when your musters and trainings are looked upon as mere pastimes; no one when your militia will shoulder their muskets and march to their trainings with as much unconcern as they would go to a sumptuous entertainment, or a splendid ball. But, sir, when the hour of danger approaches, your "white" militia are just as willing that the man of colour should be set up as a mark to be shot at by the enemy, as to be set up themselves. In the war of the revolution, these people helped to fight

[122]

your battles by land and by sea. Some of your states were glad to turn out corps of coloured men, and to stand "shoulder to shoulder" with them. In your late war they contributed largely towards some of your most splendid victories. On Lakes Erie and Champlain, where your fleets triumphed over a foe superior in numbers, and engines of death, they were manned in a large proportion with men of colour. And in this very house, in the fall of 1814, a bill passed receiving the approbation of all the branches of your government, authorizing the governor to accept the services of a corps of 2000 free people of colour. Sir, these were times which tried men's souls. In these times it was no sporting matter to bear arms. These were times when a man who shouldered his musket, did not know but he bared his bosom to receive a death wound from the enemy ere he laid it aside; and in these times these people were found as ready and as willing to volunteer in your service as any other. They were not compelled to go, they were not drafted. No, your pride had placed them beyond your compulsory power. But there was no necessity for its exercise; they were volunteers; yes, sir, volunteers to defend that very country from the inroads and ravages of a ruthless and vindictive foe, which had treated them with insult, degradation, and slavery. Volunteers are the best of soldiers; give me the men, whatever be their complexion, that willingly volunteer, and not those who are compelled to turn out; such men do not fight from necessity, nor from mercenary motives, but from principle. Such men formed the most efficient corps for your country's defence in the late war; and of such consisted the crews of your squadrons on Erie and Champlain, who largely contributed to the safety and peace of your country, and the renown of her arms. Yet, strange to tell, such are the men whom you seek to degrade and oppress.

There is another consideration which I think important. Our government is a government of the people, supported and upheld by public sentiment; and to support and perpetuate our free institutions, it is our duty and our interest to attach to it all the different classes of the community. Indeed there should be but one class. Then, sir, is it wise, is it prudent, is it consistent with sound policy, to compel a large portion of your people and their posterity, forever to become your enemies, and to view you and your political institutions with distrust, jealousy, and hatred, to the latest posterity; to alienate one portion of the community from the rest, and from their own political institutions? I grant you, sir, that in times of profound peace, their numbers are so small that their resentment could make no serious impression. But, sir, are we sure; can we calculate that we are always to remain in a state of peace? That our tranquility is never again to be disturbed by invasion or insurrection? And, sir, when that unhappy period arrives, if they, justly incensed by the accumulated wrongs which you heap upon them,

CHAPTER 6

THE CLASH OF
POLITICAL
PHILOSOPHIES:
THE DEBATE
OVER
UNIVERSAL
SUFFRAGE IN
NEW YORK (1821)

should throw their weight in the scale of your enemies, it might, and most assuredly would, be severely felt. Then your gayest and proudest militiamen that now stand in your ranks, would rather be seen "shoulder to shoulder" with a negro, than have him added to the number of his enemies, and meet him in the field of battle. . . .

But it is said these people are incapable of exercising the right of suffrage judiciously; that they will become the tools and engines of aristocracy, and set themselves up in market, and give their votes to the highest bidder; that they have no will or judgment of their own, but will follow implicitly the dictates of the purse-proud aristocrats of the day, on whom they depend for bread. This may be true to a certain extent; but, sir, they are not the only ones who abuse this privilege: and if this be a sufficient reason for depriving any of your citizens of their just rights, go on and exclude also the many thousands of white fawning, cringing sycophants, who look up to their more wealthy and more ambitious neighbours for direction at the polls, as they look to them for bread. But although most of this unfortunate class of men may at present be in this dependent state, both in body and mind, yet we ought to remember, that we are making our constitution, not for a day, nor a year, but I hope for many generations; and there is a redeeming spirit in liberty, which I have no doubt will eventually raise these poor, abused, unfortunate people, from their present degraded state, to equal intelligence with their more fortunate and enlightened neighbours. . . .

Col. Samuel Young, Saratoga County

The gentleman who had just sat down had adverted to the declaration of independence to prove that the blacks are possessed of "certain unalienable rights." But is the right of voting a natural right? If so, our laws are oppressive and unjust. A natural right is one that is born with us. No man is born twenty-one years old, and of course all restraint upon the natural right of voting, during the period of nonage, is usurpation and tyranny. This confusion arises from mixing natural with acquired rights. The right of voting is adventitious. It is resorted to only as a means of securing our natural rights.

In forming a constitution, we should have reference to the feelings, habits, and modes of thinking of the people. The gentleman last up has alluded to the importance of regarding public sentiment. And what is the public sentiment in relation to this subject? Are the negroes permitted to a participation in social intercourse with the whites? Are they elevated to public office? No, sir—public sentiment forbids it. This they know; and hence they are prepared to sell their votes to the highest bidder. In this manner you introduce corruption into the very vitals of the government.

A few years ago a law was made requiring the clerks of the respective counties to make out a list of jurymen. Was a negro ever returned upon that list? If he were, no jury would sit with him. Was a constable ever known to summon a negro as a juror, even before a justice of the peace in a matter of five dollars amount? Never,—but gentlemen who would shrink from such an association, would now propose to associate with him in the important act of electing a governor of the state.

This distinction of colour is well understood. It is unnecessary to disguise it, and we ought to shape our constitution so as to meet the public sentiment. If that sentiment should alter—if the time should ever arrive when the African shall be raised to the level of the white man—when the distinctions that now prevail shall be done away—when the colours shall intermarry—when negroes shall be invited to your tables—to sit in your pew, or ride in your coach, it may then be proper to institute a new Convention, and remodel the constitution so as to conform to that state of society. . . .

The minds of the blacks are not competent to vote. They are too much degraded to estimate the value, or exercise with fidelity and discretion that important right. It would be unsafe in their hands. Their vote would be at the call of the richest purchaser. If this class of people should hereafter arrive at such a degree of intelligence and virtue, as to inspire confidence, then it will be proper to confer this privilege upon them. At present emancipate and protect them; but withhold that privilege which they will inevitably abuse. Look to your jails and penitentiaries. By whom are they filled? By the very race, whom it is now proposed to cloth with the power of deciding upon your political rights. . . .

Chief Justice Ambrose Spencer, Albany County[8]

He said he would explain what he believed to be the origin of this sentiment in favour of extending the elective franchise. The western part of this state has increased with an almost unexampled rapidity, with a virtuous and intelligent people—I speak of those who hold lands by virtue of contracts. They have gone on improving their estates, and paying as far as they could; but in very few cases have they completed their payments, and merely for

---

8. Spencer introduced an amendment restoring property requirements to voters for state senators.

CHAPTER 6
THE CLASH OF
POLITICAL
PHILOSOPHIES:
THE DEBATE
OVER
UNIVERSAL
SUFFRAGE IN
NEW YORK (1821)

the want of a form of a deed, they have been excluded from the right of voting. A short time since, attempts had been made in the legislature to invest them with the privilege of voting, as being equitable freeholders, but the attempt did not succeed; and their condition certainly does appear to call for some relief.

I have believed, and do still believe, said Mr. S. that we are called on to extend the right of suffrage, as far as the interests of the community will permit; but I do think we cannot contemplate carrying it to the full extent recommended in the report, without knowing that we are not giving it to those people who will nominally enjoy the right, but to those who feed and clothe them. I shall vote against striking out the word white, on the ground that it is necessary for securing our own happiness. I cannot say I would deprive those people, who have acquired property, of the privilege of voting; but I cannot consent to extend it to others, in whose hands it will be as much abused as by these coloured people. I am willing to extend the right of suffrage as far as my conscience will admit; but I never can agree to extend it so far, as to deprive the agricultural interests of this state of the rights which they ought to enjoy. I never can consent to extend this right, and make an aristocracy by giving the man who has the longest purse, the power to control the most votes. . . .

Chancellor James Kent, Albany County

Let us recall our attention, for a moment, to our past history. This state has existed for forty-four years under our present constitution, which was formed by those illustrious sages and patriots who adorned the revolution. It has wonderfully fulfilled all the great ends of civil government. During that long period, we have enjoyed in an eminent degree, the blessings of civil and religious liberty. We have had our lives, our privileges, and our property, protected. We have had a succession of wise and temperate legislatures. The code of our statute law has been again and again revised and corrected, and it may proudly bear a comparison with that of any other people. We have had, during that period, (though I am, perhaps, not the fittest person to say it) a regular, stable, honest, and enlightened administration of justice. All the peaceable pursuits of industry, and all the important interests of education and science, have been fostered and encouraged. We have trebled our numbers within the last twenty-five years, have displayed mighty resources, and have made unexampled progress in the career of prosperity and greatness.

Our financial credit stands at an enviable height; and we are now successfully engaged in connecting the great lakes with the ocean by stupendous canals, which excite the admiration of our neighbours, and will make a conspicuous figure even upon the map of the United States.

These are some of the fruits of our present government; and yet we seem to be dissatisfied with our condition, and we are engaged in the bold and hazardous experiment of remodelling the constitution. Is it not fit and discreet: I speak as to wise men; is it not fit and proper that we should pause in our career, and reflect well on the immensity of the innovation in contemplation? Discontent in the midst of so much prosperity, and with such abundant means of happiness, looks like ingratitude, and as if we were disposed to arraign the goodness of Providence. Do we not expose ourselves to the danger of being deprived of the blessings we have enjoyed? . . .

The senate has hitherto been elected by the farmers of the state—by the free and independent lords of the soil, worth at least $250 in freehold estate, over and above all debts charged thereon. The governor has been chosen by the same electors, and we have hitherto elected citizens of elevated rank and character. Our assembly has been chosen by freeholders, possessing a freehold of the value of $50, or by persons renting a tenement of the yearly value of $5, and who have been rated and actually paid taxes to the state. By the report before us, we propose to annihilate, at one stroke, all those property distinctions and to bow before the idol of universal suffrage. That extreme democratic principle, when applied to the legislative and executive departments of government, has been regarded with terror, by the wise men of every age, because in every European republic, ancient and modern, in which it has been tried, it has terminated disastrously, and been productive of corruption, injustice, violence, and tyranny. And dare we flatter ourselves that we are a peculiar people, who can run the career of history, exempted from the passions which have disturbed and corrupted the rest of mankind? If we are like other races of men, with similar follies and vices, then I greatly fear that our posterity will have reason to deplore in sackcloth and ashes, the delusion of the day.

It is not my purpose at present to interfere with the report of the committee, so far as respects the qualifications of electors for governor and members of assembly. I shall feel grateful if we may be permitted to retain the stability and security of a senate, bottomed upon the freehold property of the state. Such a body, so constituted, may prove a sheet anchor amidst the future factions and storms of the republic. The great leading and governing interest of this state, is, at present, the agricultural; and what madness would it be to commit that interest to the winds. The great body of the peo-

CHAPTER 6

THE CLASH OF
POLITICAL
PHILOSOPHIES:
THE DEBATE
OVER
UNIVERSAL
SUFFRAGE IN
NEW YORK (1821)

ple, are now the owners and actual cultivators of the soil. With that whole-some population we always expect to find moderation, frugality, order, hon-esty, and a due sense of independence, liberty, and justice. It is impossible that any people can lose their liberties by internal fraud or violence, so long as the country is parcelled out among freeholders of moderate possessions, and those freeholders have a sure and efficient control in the affairs of the government. Their habits, sympathies, and employments, necessarily in-spire them with a correct spirit of freedom and justice; they are the safest guardians of property and the laws: We certainly cannot too highly appre-ciate the value of the agricultural interest: It is the foundation of national wealth and power. According to the opinion of her ablest political econo-mists, it is the surplus produce of the agriculture of England, that enables her to support her vast body of manufacturers, her formidable fleets and armies, and the crowds of persons engaged in the liberal professions, and the cultivation of the various arts.

Now, sir, I wish to preserve our senate as the representative of the landed interest. I wish those who have an interest in the soil, to retain the exclusive possession of a branch in the legislature, as a strong hold in which they may find safety through all the vicissitudes which the state may be destined, in the course of Providence, to experience. I wish them to be always enabled to say that their freeholds cannot be taxed without their consent. The men of no property, together with the crowds of dependants connected with great manufacturing and commercial establishments, and the motley and unde-finable population of crowded ports, may, perhaps, at some future day, under skilful management, predominate in the assembly, and yet we should be perfectly safe if no laws could pass without the free consent of the owners of the soil. That security we at present enjoy; and it is that security which I wish to retain.

The apprehended danger from the experiment of universal suffrage ap-plied to the whole legislative department, is no dream of the imagination. It is too mighty an excitement for the moral constitution of men to endure. The tendency of universal suffrage, is to jeopardize the rights of property, and the principles of liberty. There is a constant tendency in human society, and the history of every age proves it; there is a tendency in the poor to covet and to share the plunder of the rich; in the debtor to relax or avoid the obligation of contracts; in the majority to tyranize over the minority, and trample down their rights; in the indolent and the profligate, to cast the whole burthens of society upon the industrious and the virtuous; and *there is a tendency in ambitious and wicked men, to inflame these combustible materials*. It requires a vigilant government, and a firm administration of justice, to counteract that tendency. Thou shalt not covet; thou shalt not steal; are divine injunctions induced by this miserable depravity of our nature. Who can undertake to calculate with any precision, how many millions of people, this great state will contain in the course of this and the next century, and who can estimate the future extent and magnitude of our commercial ports? The disproportion between the men of property, and the men of no property, will be in every society in a ratio to its commerce, wealth, and population. We are no longer to remain plain and simple republics of farmers, like the New-England colonists, or the Dutch settlements on the Hudson. We are fast becoming a great nation, with great commerce, manufactures, population, wealth, luxuries, and with the vices and miseries that they engender. One seventh of the population of the city of Paris at this day subsists on charity, and one third of the inhabitants of that city die in the hospitals; what would become of such a city with universal suffrage? France has upwards of four, and England upwards of five millions of manufacturing and commercial labourers without property. Could these kingdoms sustain the weight of universal suffrage? The radicals in England, with the force of that mighty engine, would at once sweep away the property, the laws, and the liberties of that island like a deluge.

The growth of the city of New-York is enough to startle and awaken those who are pursuing the *ignis fatuus*[9] of universal suffrage.

In 1773	it had	21,000 souls.
1801	"	60,000 do.
1806	"	76,000 do.
1820	"	123,000 do.

It is rapidly swelling into the unwieldly population, and with the burdensome pauperism, of an European metropolis. New-York is destined to become the future London of America; and in less than a century, that city, with the operation of universal suffrage, and under skilful direction, will govern this state.

The notion that every man that works a day on the road, or serves an idle hour in the militia, is entitled as of right to an equal participation in the whole power of the government, is most unreasonable, and has no foundation in justice. We had better at once discard from the report such a nominal test of merit. If such persons have an equal share in one branch of the legislature, it is surely as much as they can in justice or policy demand. Society is an association for the protection of property as well as of life, and the individual who contributes only one cent to the common stock, ought not to have the same power and influence in directing the property concerns of the partnership, as he who contributes his thousands. He will not have the same

9. *Ignis fatuus*—literally, a "foolish fire," although a loose translation might be "mad rage."

[129]

CHAPTER 6

THE CLASH OF
POLITICAL
PHILOSOPHIES:
THE DEBATE
OVER
UNIVERSAL
SUFFRAGE IN
NEW YORK (1821)

inducements to care, and diligence, and fidelity. His inducements and his temptation would be to divide the whole capital upon the principles of an agrarian law.

Liberty, rightly understood, is an inestimable blessing, but liberty without wisdom, and without justice, is no better than wild and savage licentiousness. The danger which we have hereafter to apprehend, is not the want, but the abuse, of liberty. We have to apprehend the oppression of minorities, and a disposition to encroach on private right—to disturb chartered privileges—and to weaken, degrade, and overawe the administration of justice; we have to apprehend the establishment of unequal, and consequently, unjust systems of taxation, and all the mischiefs of a crude and mutable legislation. A stable senate, exempted from the influence of universal suffrage, will powerfully check these dangerous propensities, and such a check becomes the more necessary, since this Convention has already determined to withdraw the watchful eye of the judicial department from the passage of laws. . . .

I hope, sir, we shall not carry desolation through all the departments of the fabric erected by our fathers. I hope we shall not put forward to the world a new constitution, as will meet with the scorn of the wise, and the tears of the patriot.

Peter R. Livingston, Dutchess County

Allusions had been made to the formation of the constitution under which we live; and what was the first feature in our remonstance against the usurpations of Britain? Was it not that taxation and representation were reciprocal; and that no imposition could be laid upon us without our consent? Was it the paltry tax on tea that led to the revolution? No, sir; it was the *principle,* for which we contended; and the same principle, in my judgment, requires a rejection of the proposition now on your table. But we are asked, what evidence we have that the people want this extension of suffrage? Sir, 74,000 witnesses testified, last spring, that they wanted it. Meetings and resolutions, public prints, and conversation have united to require it.

It is concluded, however, that the measure proposed by the original amendment jeopardizes the landed interest. Sir, it is the landed interest, in common with others, that have demanded this measure at our hands; and will they resort to projects which are calculated to injure ourselves? France has been alluded to. The French revolution, sir, has produced incalculable blessings to that country. Before that revolution one third of the property of the kingdom was in the hands of the clergy; the rest in the hands of the nobility. Where the interest of one individual has been sacrificed, the interests of thousands have been promoted. After dining with that friend of universal liberty, the patriotic La Fayette, he once invited me to a walk upon the top of his house, that commanded a view of all the surrounding country. Before the revolution, said he, all the farms and hamlets you can see were mine. I am now reduced to a thousand acres, and I exult in the diminution, since the happiness of others is promoted by participation.

This, sir, is the language of true patriotism; the language of one whose heart, larger than his possessions, embraced the whole family of man in the circuit of its beneficence. And shall we, with less ample domains, refuse to our poorer neighbours the common privileges of freemen?

But, sir, we are told and warned of the rotten boroughs of England. By whom are they owned? By men of wealth. They confer the right of representation on the few, to the exclusion of the many. They are always found in the views of the monarch; and while aristocracy is supported by the house of lords, the house of commons is borne down by the boroughs.

It is said that wealth builds our churches, establishes our schools, endows our colleges, and erects our hospitals. But have these institutions been raised without the hand of labour? No, sir; and it is the same hand that has levelled the sturdy oak, the lofty pine, and the towering hemlock, and subdued your forests to a garden. It is not the fact, in this country, that money controls labour; but labour controls money. When the farmer cradles his wheat and harvests his hay, he does not find the labourer on his knees before him at the close of the day, solicitous for further employment; but it is the farmer who takes off his hat, pays him his wages, and requests his return on the morrow. . . .

Abraham Van Vechten, Albany County

Some of the opposers of the amendment before us, object to it, because, as they allege, it is founded in aristocratic principles. I must confess, sir, that this objection has at least the merit of novelty. A landed aristocracy composed of the great body of yeomen of this state, is, I apprehend, an anomaly. I have sometimes heard the holders of overgrown estates in lands, called aristocrats, but until now, I never heard that the prescribed freehold qualification of $250 for electors of the senate, was considered an aristocratic feature in our constitution. What! the common farmers—the stable pillars of the state, a body of aristocrats? If the ownership of fifty, or an hundred, or two hundred acres of our soil, converts the owner into an aristocrat, then,

CHAPTER 6

THE CLASH OF
POLITICAL
PHILOSOPHIES:
THE DEBATE
OVER
UNIVERSAL
SUFFRAGE IN
NEW YORK (1821)

according to the estimate of the gentleman from Dutchess (Mr. Livingston) two-thirds of the present electors of this state are aristocrats—and hence proceeds, I presume, the solicitude of the remaining one-third, that the right of suffrage may be extended, so as to countervail the aristocratic influence of the farmers, by a class of voters, who, *for the want of real property, are more democratic, and of course more independent.*

The time has been, when a large portion of the real property of the state was vested in a few men of wealth, but that time is past. Our large landed estates are rapidly dividing, and the facilities given to promote their division, by the operation of the statute for regulating descents and abolishing entails, will in a few years break them up. There is, therefore, no ground for apprehension from that quarter.

Daniel D. Tompkins, Richmond County

Property, sir, when compared with our other essential rights, is insignificant and trifling. "Life, liberty, and *the pursuit of happiness*"—not of property— are set forth in the declaration of independence as cardinal objects. Property is not even named. . . .

David Buel, Jr., Rensselaer County

A man who is possessed of a piece of land worth $250 for his own life, or the life of another person, is a freeholder, and has the right to vote for governor and senators. But one who has an estate in ever so valuable a farm, for 999 years, or any other definite term, however long, is not a freeholder and cannot vote. The absurdity of the distinction, at this day, is so glaring as to require no comment. Yet there are numerous farmers, in different parts of the state, who are excluded from the right of suffrage on this absurd distinction between freehold and leasehold estates. No person will now pretend that a farmer who holds his land by a thousand years lease is less attached to the soil, or less likely to exercise the privilege of freeman discreetly, than a freeholder. We shall not, I trust, be accused of want of respect to settled institutions, if we expunge such glaring absurdities from our constitution. It is supposed, however, by the honourable member before me (Chancellor Kent) that landed property will become insecure under the proposed extension of the right of suffrage, by the influx of a more dangerous population. That gentleman has drawn a picture from the existing state of society in European kingdoms, which would be indeed appalling, if we could suppose such a state of society could exist here. But are arguments, drawn from the state of society in Europe, applicable to our situation? I think the concessions of my honourable friend from Albany, who last addressed the committee, (Mr. Van Vechten) greatly weaken the force of the arguments of his honour the Chancellor.

There are in my judgment, many circumstances which will forever preserve the people of this state from the vices and the degradation of European population, beside those which I have already taken notice of. The provision already made for the establishment of common schools, will, in a very few years, extend the benefit of education to all our citizens. The universal diffusion of information will forever distinguish our population from that of Europe. Virtue and intelligence are the true basis on which every republican government must rest. When these are lost, freedom will no longer exist. The diffusion of education is the only sure means of establishing these pillars of freedom. I rejoice in this view of the subject, that our common school fund will (if the report on the legislative department be adopted,) be consecrated by a constitutional provision; and I feel no apprehension, for myself, or my posterity, in confiding the right of suffrage to the great mass of such a population as I believe ours will always be. The farmers in this country will always out number all other portions of our population. Admitting that the increase of our cities, and especially of our commercial metropolis, will be as great as it has been hitherto; it is not to be doubted that the agricultural population will increase in the same proportion. The city population will never be able to depress that of the country. New-York has always contained about a tenth part of the population of the state, and will probably always bear a similar proportion. Can she, with such a population, under any circumstances, render the property of the vast population of the country insecure? It may be that mobs will occasionally be collected, and commit depredations in a great city; but, can the mobs traverse our immense territory, and invade the farms, and despoil the property of the landholders? And if such a state of things were possible, would a senate, elected by freeholders, afford any security? It is the regular administration of the laws by an independent judiciary, that renders property secure against private acts of violence. And there will always be a vast majority of our citizens interested in preventing legislative injustice. . . .

Our community is an association of persons—of human beings—not a partnership founded on property. The declared object of the people of this state in associating, was, to "establish such a government as they deemed best calculated to secure the rights and liberties of the good people of the state, and most conducive to their happiness and safety." Property, it is admitted, is one of the rights to be protected and secured; and although the

CHAPTER 6

THE CLASH OF
POLITICAL
PHILOSOPHIES:
THE DEBATE
OVER
UNIVERSAL
SUFFRAGE IN
NEW YORK (1821)

protection of life and liberty is the highest object of attention, it is certainly true, that the security of property is a most interesting and important object in every free government. Property is essential to our temporal happiness; and is necessarily one of the most interesting subjects of legislation. The desire of acquiring property is a universal passion. I readily give to property the important place which has been assigned to it by the honourable member from Albany (Chancellor Kent.) To property we are indebted for most of our comforts, and for much of our temporal happiness. The numerous religious, moral, and benevolent institutions which are every where established, owe their existence to wealth; and it is wealth which enables us to make those great internal improvements which we have undertaken. Property is only one of the incidental rights of the person who possesses it; and, as such, it must be made secure; but it does not follow, that it must therefore be represented specifically in any branch of the government. . . .

Elisha Williams, Columbia County

The gentleman from New-York, (Mr. Radcliff,) has contended that, by nature, all were endowed with the right of suffrage; and he calls upon us to show that universal suffrage would be dangerous to the best interests of the state. Sir, the burden of proof rests upon the gentleman himself, not on us; the constitution on this occasion, holds the negative; and I call upon him to point out the danger to be apprehended from the exercise of this elective power by the yeomanry of the country. Have the freeholders exercised it tyrannically? Let their wide liberality—their expanded charities—give the answer. . . .

Who are they who will protect the landed interest of this state, better than its owners; or better determine when a direct tax is necessary and proper to be imposed on their farms; and better judges what laws are calculated to advance the agricultural interests of the state? Sir, they are the ring streaked and speckled population of our large towns and cities, comprising people of every kindred and tongue. They bring with them the habits, vices, political creeds, and nationalities of every section of the globe; they have fled from oppression, if you please, and have habitually regarded sovereignty and tyranny as identified; they are men, whose wants, if not whose vices, have sent them from other states and countries, to seek bread by service, if not by plunder; whose means and habits, whose best kind of ambition and only sort of industry, all forbid their purchasing in the country and tilling the soil. Would the state be better governed—would the landed interest be better protected, by the suffrages of such men, than by the ballots of freeholders? Mr. Jefferson has said, sir, that great cities were upon the body politic great sores. In mentioning the name of this illustrious statesman with commendation, I am aware that I may fall under the lash of the honourable gentleman from Richmond, for most certainly I have never been an admirer of the gun-boat system.[10] But, however that may be, his old adherents and universal admirers, cannot object to his authority, because he may be cited by one, who has not assented to all his views; and adopting his sentiment as already expressed, I would not, certainly I would not, if I could prevent it, carry, by absorption, the contents of those sores through the whole political body. These cities are filled with men too rich, or too poor to fraternize with the yeomen of the country; and I warn my fellow freeholders of the dangers which must attend the surrender of this most inestimable of privileges—this attribute of sovereignty. On whom do the burthens of government fall, in peace and in war? On you. Your freeholds cannot escape taxation—they cannot elude the vigilance of the assessor, and though encumbered to their whole value, they must pay on their entire amount. When danger threatens, to whom must you look for support? Is your militia called for, he who has no interest in your soil, swings his pack, and is away, leaving the farmer and the farmer's son, to abide the draft, and defend the life, liberty, and property of themselves and the community. They are identified with the interest of the state. I would to heaven, the entire mass of the freeholders of this state were here present, to decide upon this all-important question—to determine whether they would wantonly cast away this saving power—this long-enjoyed attribute of sovereignty, granted to them, at first, by the whole population, and which would constitute the richest inheritance they could transmit to posterity. Among the blessings which a moderate portion of property confers, the right of suffrage is conspicuous; and the attainment of this right, holds out a strong inducement to that industry and economy, which are the life of society. If you *bestow* on the idle and profligate, the privileges which should be purchased only by industry, frugality, and character, will they ever be at the trouble and pains to earn those privileges? No, sir; and the prodigal waste of this invaluable privilege—this attribute of sovereignty—like indiscriminate and misguided charity, will multiply the evils which it professes to remedy. Give the people, to the extent contended for, one department of the government, as a means of security from possible oppression; but preserve, I conjure you, to the faithful citizen, as his best

10. When he was president, Jefferson advocated abolishing large and expensive naval vessels and replacing them with small gunboats. The gunboats proved ineffective.

CHAPTER 6

THE CLASH OF
POLITICAL
PHILOSOPHIES:
THE DEBATE
OVER
UNIVERSAL
SUFFRAGE IN
NEW YORK (1821)

recompense—as the richest gem he can hoard—and as the sheet-anchor of the republic, the freehold right of suffrage for the senate. If the time shall ever come, when the poverty shall be arrayed in hostility against the wealth of the state; when the needy shall be excited to ask for a *division* of your property, as they now ask for the right of governing it, I would then have a senate composed of men, each selected from a district where he should be known, by the yeomanry of the country—by the men who, if I may venture upon the exquisite figure of the eloquent gentleman from Dutchess, "wake their own ploughs with the dawn, and rouse their harrows with the lark."

But we are told this distinction is odious, aristocratic, and perpetuating a privileged order. Has it come to this? Does the possession of a small farm, or a modest house and lot in town, render the owner odious in the eyes of the people? Who ever before heard of a privileged order of all the freeholders of the state—of an aristocracy of two-thirds of the whole body of the people— of 250 dollar aristocrats? The idea admits not of a serious refutation.

One argument which has been pressed upon this committee, I confess I never expected to hear in this hall; it is, that "the people *demand* this right;" that is to say, in point of fact, those who will not exercise their faculties and industry so as to make themselves owners of a real estate of $250 dollars, *demand* that you surrender to them rights which are now, and have been for more than forty years, attached to freeholds. Sir, if it be just and safe to confer this right, it should be bestowed gratuitously; nothing should be yielded to this menacing demand. If this demand were presented in a different shape—if you were called upon to bestow so much of your freeholds upon these unqualified demandants as would enable them to vote against you, would you advocate that claim—would you yield to it? I know, sir, that one honourable gentleman has pointed out the blessings which would flow from yielding this boon to our brethren in distress. He has witnessed the exultation of the patriot La Fayette, in the victory of republicanism over his own property. The honourable gentleman was taken, by the noble marquis, to the terrace of the splendid chateau of Le Grange. Before him, as far as the eye could stretch, lay the rich domain. "But yesterday," exclaimed the imperial republican, "but yesterday this vast territory was my property: it was dotted with cottages filled with my vassals: Mark the blessings of *la grande revolution;* those who were then hewers of wood and drawers of water, the vassals of my estate, are now the legitimate sovereigns of republican France—the lords of their own soil." How long, Mr. Chairman, if we yield to this demand, will it be, in all human probability, before those, who now modestly ask no more than a right to govern our property—they having none themselves to engross their attention, or require their care—will appear armed with the elective power of the state, to *consummate* to us, the rich blessings conferred on the vassals of Le Grange by the French revolution? If this surrender be now made, how long before a demand of the property itself may be expected? Never, Mr. Chairman, never, til now, have I understood that our dearest rights were at the disposal of those who might think proper to demand them. . . .

Martin Van Buren, Otsego County

Mr. Van Buren, said he was opposed to the amendment under consideration, offered by the gentleman from Albany, (Chief Justice Spencer) and he would beg the indulgence of the committee, for a short time, while he should attempt to explain the reasons, which, in his opinion, required its rejection. The extreme importance which the honourable mover had attached to the subject, and the sombre and frightful picture which had been drawn by his colleague, (the Chancellor) of the alarming consequences, which would result from the adoption of a course, different from the one recommended, rendered it a duty, which those, who entertained a contrary opinion, owed to themselves and their constituents, to explain the motives which governed them. If a stranger had heard the discussions on this subject, and had been unacquainted with the character of our people, and the character and standing of those, who find it their duty to oppose this measure, he might well have supposed, that we were on the point of prostrating with lawless violence, one of the fairest and firmest pillars of the government, and of introducing into the sanctuary of the constitution, a mob or a rabble, violent and disorganizing, as were the Jacobins of France; and furious and visionary as the radicals of England, are, by some gentlemen, supposed to be. The honourable gentleman from Albany (the Chancellor) tells us, that if we send the constitution to the people, without the provision contemplated by the proposition now under consideration, it will meet with scorn of the wise, and be hailed with exultation by the vicious and the profligate. He entertained, he said, a high personal respect for the mover of this amendment, and also for his learned colleague, who had so eloquently and pathetically described to them the many evils and miseries which its rejection would occasion; he declared his entire conviction of his sincerity in what he had uttered, his simplicity of character, he had himself so feelingly described, his known candour and purity of character would forbid any one to doubt, that he spoke the sentiments of his heart. But believing as he did, that those fears and apprehensions were wholly without foundation, it could not be expected, that he would suffer them to govern his conduct. . . .

He had no doubt but the honourable gentlemen who had spoken in favour

CHAPTER 6

THE CLASH OF
POLITICAL
PHILOSOPHIES:
THE DEBATE
OVER
UNIVERSAL
SUFFRAGE IN
NEW YORK (1821)

of the amendment, had suffered from the fearful forebodings which they had expressed. That ever to be revered band of patriots who made our constitution, entertained them also, and therefore they engrafted in it the clause which is now contended for. But a full and perfect experience had proved the fallacy of their speculations, and they were now called upon again to adopt the exploded notion; and on that ground, to disfranchise, if not a majority, nearly a moiety, of our citizens. He said he was an unbeliever in the speculations and mere theories on the subject of government, of the best and wisest men, when unsupported by, and especially when opposed to, experience. He believed with a sensible and elegant modern writer, "That constitutions are the work of time, not the invention of ingenuity; and that to frame a complete system of government, depending on habits of reverence and experience, was an attempt as absurd as to build a tree, or manufacture an opinion."

All our observation, he said, united to justify this assertion—when they looked at the proceedings of the Convention which adopted the constitution of the United States, they could not fail to be struck by the extravagance, and, as experience had proved, the futility of the fears and hopes that were entertained and expressed, from the different provisions of that constitution, by the members. The venerable and enlightened Franklin, had no hope if the president had the qualified negative, that it would be possible to keep him honest; that the extensive power of objecting to laws, would inevitably lead to the bestowment of doucers to prevent the exercise of the power; and many, very many of the members, believed that the general government, framed as it was, would, in a few years, prostrate the state governments. While, on the other hand, the lamented Hamilton, Mr. Madison, and others, distressed themselves with the apprehension, that unless they could infuse more vigour into the constitution they were about to adopt, the work of their hands could not be expected to survive its framers. Experience, the only unerring touchstone, had proved the fallacy of all those speculations, as it had also those of the framers of our state constitution, in the particular now under consideration; and having her records before them, he was for being governed by them. . . .

The next consideration which had been pressed upon the committee by the honourable mover of the amendment, was, the apprehension that the persons employed in the manufactories which now were, or which, in the progress of time, might be established amongst us, would be influenced by their employers. So far as it respected the question before the committee, said Mr. V. B. it was a sufficient answer to the argument, that if they were so influenced, they would be enlisted on the same side, which it was the object of the amendment to promote, on the side of property. If not—if they were independent of the influence of their employers, they would be safe depositories of the right. For no man, surely, would contend that they should be deprived of the right of voting on account of their poverty, except so far as it might be supposed to impair their independence, and the consequent purity of the exercise of that invaluable right. . . .

If he could possibly believe, added Mr. V. B. that any portion of the calamitous consequences could result from the rejection of the amendment, which had been so feelingly pourtrayed by the honourable gentleman from Albany, (Mr. Kent,) and for whom he would repeat the acknowledgment of his respect and regard, he would be the last man in society who would vote for it. But, believing, as he conscientiously did, that those fears were altogether unfounded; hoping and expecting that the happiest results would follow from the abolition of the freehold qualification, and hoping too, that caution and circumspection would preside over the settlement of the general right of suffrage, which was hereafter to be made, and knowing, besides, that this state, in abolishing the freehold qualifications, would but be uniting herself in the march of principle, which had already prevailed in every state of the union, except two or three, including the royal charter of Rhode-Island, he would cheerfully record his vote against the amendment.

Jonas Platt, Oneida County

Mr. Platt moved to expunge the proviso in the first section, which declares that no person, *other than a white man,* shall vote, unless he have a freehold estate of the value of $250. He said, I am not disposed, sir, to turn knight-errant in favour of the men of colour. But the obligations of justice are eternal and indispensable: and this proviso involves a principle which, upon reflection, I cannot concede, or compromise as a matter of expediency. I am aware of the intrinsic difficulty of this subject. The evils of negro slavery are deep rooted, and admit of no sudden and effectual remedy. In the act of doing justice, we are bound to consider consequences. With such a population as that of Virginia, or the Carolinas, a sudden emancipation, and permission to the negroes to vote, would be incompatible with the public safety: and necessity creates a law for itself. But, sir in this state there is no grounds for such a plea. I admit, that most of the free negroes in our state, are unfit to be entrusted with the right of suffrage; they have neither sufficient intelligence, nor a sufficient degree of independence, to exercise that right in a safe and proper manner. I would exclude the great mass of them,

CHAPTER 6

THE CLASH OF
POLITICAL
PHILOSOPHIES:
THE DEBATE
OVER
UNIVERSAL
SUFFRAGE IN
NEW YORK (1821)

but not by this unjust and odious discrimination of colour. We are under no necessity of adopting such a principle, in laying the foundation of our government. Let us attain this object of exclusion, by fixing such a uniform standard of qualification, as would not only exclude the great body of free men of colour, but also a large portion of ignorant and depraved white men, who are as unfit to exercise the power of voting as the men of colour. By adopting the principle of universal suffrage, in regard to white men, we create the necessity, which is now pleaded as an excuse for this unjust discrimination. Our republican text is, that all men are born equal, in civil and political rights; and if this proviso be ingrafted into our constitution, the practical commentary will be, that a portion of our free citizens shall not enjoy equal rights with their fellow citizens. All freemen, of African parentage, are to be constitutionally degraded: no matter how virtuous or intelligent. Test the principle, sir, by another example. Suppose the proposition were, to make a discrimination, so as to exclude the descendants of German, or Low Dutch, or Irish ancestors; would not every man be shocked at the horrid injustice of the principle? It is in vain to disguise the fact; we shall violate a sacred principle, without any necessity, if we retain this discrimination. We say to this unfortunate race of men, purchase a freehold estate of $250 value, and you shall then be equal to the white man, who parades one day in the militia, or performs a day's work on the highway. Sir, it is adding mockery to injustice. We know that, with rare exceptions, they have not the means of purchasing a freehold: and it would be unworthy of this grave Convention to do, *indirectly,* an act of injustice, which we are unwilling openly to avow. The real object is, to exclude the oppressed and degraded sons of Africa; and, in my humble judgment, it would better comport with the dignity of this Convention to speak out, and to pronounce the sentence of perpetual degradation, on negroes and their posterity for ever, than to establish a test, which we know they cannot comply with, and which we do not require of others. . . .

In our own state, public sentiment has been totally changed on the subject of negro slavery. About sixty years ago, an act of our colonial assembly was passed, with this disgraceful preamble: "whereas justice and good policy require, that the African slave-trade should be liberally encouraged." And within the last forty years, I remember, in the sale of negroes, it was no uncommon occurrence to witness the separation of husband and wife, and parents and children, without their consent, and under circumstances which forbid all hope of their ever seeing each other again in this world. And this was done without apparent remorse or compunction, and with as little reluctance on the part of buyer and seller, as we now feel in separating a span of horses, or a yoke of oxen. But I thank God, that a sense of justice and mercy has in a good measure regenerated the hearts of men. A rapid emancipation has taken place; and we approach the era, when, according to the existing law, slavery will be abolished in this state.

But, sir, we owe to that innocent and unfortunate race of men, much more than mere emancipation. We owe to them our patient and persevering exertions, to elevate their condition and character, by means of moral and religious instruction. And I rejoice that by the instrumentality of Sunday schools and other benevolent institutions, many of them promise fair to become intelligent, virtuous, and useful citizens. Judging from our experience of the last fifty years; what may we not reasonably expect, in the next half century? Sir, if we adopt the principle of this proviso, I hope and believe, that our posterity will blush, when they see the names recorded in favour of such a discrimination.

I beseech gentlemen to consider the enlightened age in which we live! Consider how much has already been accomplished by the efforts of Christian philanthropy! During the last forty years, we have brought up this African race from the house of bondage: We have led them nearly through the wilderness, and shown them the promised land. Shall we now drive them back again into Egypt? I hope not, sir. The light of science, and the heavenly beams of Christianity, are dawning upon them. Shall we extinguish these rays of hope? This is not a mere question of expediency. Man has no right to deal thus with his fellow man; except on the ground of necessity and public safety. It is not pretended that such a reason exists in this case. We shall violate a sacred principle, to avoid, at most a slight inconvenience:—and, if I do not deceive myself, those who shall live fifty years hence, will view this proviso in the same light as we now view the law of our New-England fathers, which punished with death all who were guilty of being Quakers, or the law of our fathers in the colonial assembly of New-York, which offered bounties to encourage the slave trade.

As a republican statesman, I protest against the principle of inequality contained in this proviso. As a man and a father, who expects justice for himself and his children, in this world; and as a Christian, who hopes for mercy in the world to come; I can not, I dare not, consent to this unjust proscription.

CHAPTER 6

THE CLASH OF
POLITICAL
PHILOSOPHIES:
THE DEBATE
OVER
UNIVERSAL
SUFFRAGE IN
NEW YORK (1821)

2. Article Dealing with the Suffrage, Approved by the 1821 Constitutional Convention.

Article Second

SEC. I. Every male citizen, of the age of twenty-one years, who shall have been an inhabitant of this state one year preceding any election, and for the last six months a resident of the town or county where he may offer his vote; and shall have within the year next preceding the election, paid a tax to the state or county, assessed upon his real or personal property; or shall by law be exempted from taxation; or being armed or equipped according to law shall have performed within that year, military duty in the militia of this state; or who shall be exempted from performing military duty in consequence of being a fireman in any city, town, or village in this state; and also, every male citizen of the age of twenty-one years, who shall have been, for three years next preceding such election, an inhabitant of this state; and for the last year, a resident in the town or county, where he may offer his vote; and shall have been within the last year, assessed to labour upon the highways, and shall have performed the labour, or paid an equivalent therefor, according to law; shall be entitled to vote in the town or ward where he actually resides, and not elsewhere, for all officers that now are, or hereafter may be, elective by the people: But no man of colour, unless he shall have been for three years a citizen of this state, and for one year next preceding any election, shall be seized and possessed of a freehold estate of the value of two hundred and fifty dollars, over and above all debts and incumbrances charged thereon; and shall have been actually rated, and paid a tax thereon, shall be entitled to vote at such election. And no person of colour shall be subject to direct taxation, unless he shall be seized and possessed of such real estate as aforesaid.

SEC. II. Laws may be passed, excluding from the right of suffrage, persons who may have been, or may be convicted of infamous crimes.

SEC. III. Laws shall be made for ascertaining by proper proofs, the citizens who shall be entitled to the right of suffrage, hereby established.

SEC. IV. All elections by the citizens, shall be by ballot, except for such town officers, as may by law be directed to be otherwise chosen.

QUESTIONS TO CONSIDER

As noted earlier, the selections from the delegates' speeches are reproduced in the exact order in which they were given. After Edwards offered his opinion about the collective wisdom of the people, and Sanford explained the committee's reasoning in introducing the proposal advocating universal white male suffrage, the next four speakers (Ross, Jay, Clarke, and Young) begin an extended debate over limiting the vote to white men. As you read these selections, you will quickly see that Ross and Young were opposed to black suffrage, whereas Jay and Clarke favored black voting. What were Ross's main objections to black voting? How did Jay and Clarke attempt to counter those objections? Did Young add any points to the debate?

By introducing an amendment that restored a property qualification to voters in state senatorial elections, Ambrose Spencer refocused the debate on the general issue of universal suffrage. What were his arguments against suffrage extension? Was Spencer willing to extend the suffrage somewhat? To whom would he extend the vote, and what was his reasoning?

Chancellor James Kent's remarks, reproduced almost in full, formed a brilliant and well-crafted argument against the democratic impulse and in favor of the old order. Kent's fellow delegates regarded him not as an unthinking reactionary but as the thoughtful defender of tradition. They appear to have treated him with great respect and deference. What principal fears did conservatives such as Kent have about extending the suffrage?

Continue through the remainder of the evidence, asking questions of each speaker. How did Livingston attempt to counter Kent? Did other conservatives share Kent's fears?

Martin Van Buren's speech, reproduced only in part, is regarded as a masterful undercutting of the conservative position. How did Van Buren do this? How effective do you think these arguments were?

After you finish reading the selections from the debates, examine closely the final proposal that the delegates adopted (by a vote of 23 to 15) and the voters of New York ultimately approved. How did that section of the revised constitution deal with the two principal suffrage issues?

One curious aspect of the delegates' voting must be examined with some care. Spencer's amendment to restore property qualifications to senatorial elections failed by a vote of 25 to 16, with all 25 reform-minded delegates voting in a solid bloc. Yet when Jonas Platt's motion to strike the restriction on blacks from the suffrage article was put to a vote, 19 of the reformers voted no, and 15 conservatives voted yes. Why would the reform delegates want to extend the suffrage to only white men? And, equally curiously, why would conservative delegates who favored a limited suffrage support extending the vote to black males? Does any of the evidence help you answer those questions? Does Platt's speech provide a clue?

CHAPTER 6

THE CLASH OF
POLITICAL
PHILOSOPHIES:
THE DEBATE
OVER
UNIVERSAL
SUFFRAGE IN
NEW YORK (1821)

On a broader scale, a good deal of the debate over black male suffrage had to do with the perceived "place" of nonwhites in a society that almost all delegates assumed would be dominated by whites. Note the references to blacks as "aborigines" in several speeches. Was there any consensus among the delegates as to the "place" of blacks in New York? If there were differing opinions, what were they?

Finally, you must determine what the debates in the New York constitutional convention of 1821 tell us about American political thought in the Age of the Common Man. Begin by asking yourself what the delegates thought of human beings (since all political systems rest on a conception of the nature of human beings). Were they virtuous? Could they be trusted with power? What did the delegates believe motivated human behavior? Next, think about how the delegates dealt with the concept of property. Was protection of property a right? Was its protection a primary purpose of government? Were those who owned property different in nature from those who did not? Finally, did the delegates believe that all men were created equal? If so, what did they mean by that phrase? If not, on what were inequalities based (race, sex, class, etc.)? Obviously, the delegates were not of one mind on any of these questions. What, however, do you believe was the *principal* political philosophy in the convention?

EPILOGUE

As with most other states following the War of 1812, New York was profoundly affected by the democratic impulse that swept through many aspects of American life. The state's voters enthusiastically approved the revised constitution, and new voters began using their franchises to elect men more sympathetic to their views. Andrew Jackson was but one product of this trend; another trend was the rise of the second-party system, with Democrats Andrew Jackson, Martin Van Buren, and James K. Polk battling Whigs Henry Clay, Daniel Webster, and William Henry Harrison. Increasingly, candidates for public office began wooing the voters, first with rallies and pamphlets and then with parades, campaign buttons, political cartoons, personal appeals, favors, and, sometimes, outright bribery. By 1840, the modern American political system, with all its strengths and defects, had been born. As candidates became more active in their own behalf, voters correspondingly became more passive, content to be observers of the spectacle of American politics and elections. Candidates tried so much to portray themselves as part of the common people that longtime presidential aspirant Daniel Webster lamented that his political career had been hurt because he had *not* been born in a log cabin.

On the other hand, efforts to extend the suffrage further, to blacks and women, met with stiff resistance in this age of democratic upsurge. In 1846, New Yorkers again revised their constitution, but delegates voted down a proposal granting black males the right to vote (the vote in the constitutional convention was 37 to 63). In 1867, in the aftermath of the Civil War and the emancipation of southern slaves, at still another constitutional convention delegates ignored pleas for women's suffrage but did remove restrictions on black voting. The voters of New York, however, rejected that amendment. Indeed, it took the Fifteenth Amendment to the United States Constitution, which went into effect in 1870, to extend the right to vote to black New Yorkers. As a result, recently freed slaves were voting in the Reconstruction South before blacks were permitted to vote in New York. As for women, they finally achieved the right to vote in New York in 1917. Clearly the democratic spirit of the early nineteenth century was not intended to include all people.

Yet for white males the democratic upsurge appeared real and significant. No matter that the power of business interests and professional politicians actually increased in this period or that securing the vote did not always lead to other gains. Americans had turned their backs on the old order and had cast themselves onto the tempestuous seas whipped up by the winds of democratic rhetoric and spirit. Fearful men such as Chancellor Kent warned of difficulties that might lie ahead, but they were drowned out by the democratic chorus.

AWAY FROM HOME:
THE WORKING GIRLS OF LOWELL

Just before the War of 1812, the successful New England merchant Francis Cabot Lowell toured Great Britain. Among other things, Lowell was very interested in the English textile industry. The invention of the power loom enabled spinning and weaving operations to be combined within one factory, but the factory system had spawned mill towns with overcrowded slums, horrible living conditions, and high death rates. The potential profits the new technology offered were great, yet Lowell knew that Americans already feared the Old World evils that seemed to accompany the factory system.

Back in Boston once again, Lowell and his brother-in-law built a power loom, patented it, raised money, formed a company, and built a textile factory. Realizing that their best source of available labor would be young women from the surrounding New England rural areas and that farm families would have to be persuaded to let their daughters work far from home in the new factories, the company managers developed what came to be known as the Lowell system.

In this chapter, you will be looking at what happened when people's ideas about women's "proper place" conflicted with the labor needs of the new factory system. What did the general public fear? How did the working girls react?

BACKGROUND

By the end of the eighteenth century, the American economy began undergoing a process that historians call modernization. This process involves a number of changes, including the rapid expansion of markets, commercial specialization, improved transportation networks, the growth of credit transactions, the proliferation of towns and cities, and the rise of manufacturing and the factory system. Quite obviously, all these factors are interrelated. Furthermore, such changes always have profound effects on people's lifestyles as well as on the pace of life itself.

While the frontier moved steadily westward, the South was primarily agrarian—tied to cash crops such as cotton and tobacco. New England's economy, however quickly became modernized. Although agriculture was never completely abandoned in New England, by the early 1800s it was increasingly difficult to obtain land, and many small New England farms suffered from soil exhaustion. Young men, of course, could go West—in fact, so many of them left New England that soon there was a "surplus" of young women in the area. In addition, the transformation of New England agriculture and the demise of much of the "putting out" system of the first local textile manufacturing left many single female workers underemployed or unemployed. What were these farmers' daughters supposed to do? What were their options?

At the same time that these economic developments were occurring, ideas about white middle-class women and their place in society were also changing. Historian Barbara Welter described this phenomenon as "the cult of true womanhood,"[1] the emergence of the belief that every (true) woman was "a lady" who behaved in certain ways because of her female nature. True women possessed four virtues: piety, purity, submissiveness, and domesticity. These characteristics, it was thought, were not so much learned as they were biologically natural, simply an inherent part of being born female. Women's magazines, etiquette books for young ladies, sermons and religious tracts, popular short stories and novels—all these sources told women what they were like and how they should feel about themselves. Such sources are called "prescriptive literature" because they literally prescribe how people should—and should not—behave.

What, then, was expected of New England farmers' daughters and other respectable (white) women? They were supposed to be pious, more naturally religious than men (real men might occasionally swear, but real women never did!). Because they were naturally logical and rational, men might pursue education, but true women should not because they might be led into error if they strayed from the Bible. As daughters, wives, or even sisters, women had the

1. Barbara Welter, "The Cult of True Womanhood, 1820–1860," *American Quarterly*, 18 (Summer 1966), 151–174.

important responsibility of being the spiritual uplifters to whom men could turn when necessary.

Just as important as piety was the true woman's purity. This purity was absolute because whereas a man might "sow his wild oats" and then be saved by the love of a good woman, a "fallen woman" could never be saved. In the popular fiction of the period, a woman who had been seduced usually became insane, died, or both. If she had a baby, it also came to a bad end. Only on her wedding night did a true woman surrender her virginity, and then out of duty rather than passion because it was widely believed that pure women were not sexually responsive. In fact, many young women of this era knew nothing at all about their own bodies or the nature of sexual intercourse until they married.

Submission and domesticity were perhaps not as vital as piety and purity. Although women who did not submit to men's leadership were destined to be unhappy (according to the thought of the day), they could correct their mistaken behavior. Men were, after all, stronger and more intelligent, the natural protectors of women. A true woman, wrote then-popular author Grace Greenwood, should be like a "perpetual child," who is always "timid, doubtful, and clingingly dependent." Such pious, pure, submissive women were particularly well suited to the important task of creating a pleasant, cheerful home—a place where men could escape from their worldly struggles and be fed, clothed, comforted, and nursed if they were ill. Even a woman who did not have very much money could create such a haven, people believed, simply by using her natural talents of sewing, cooking, cleaning, and flower arranging.

Simultaneously, then, two important trends were occurring in the early 1800s: the northern economy was modernizing, and sexual stereotypes were developing that assigned very different roles to men and women. Whereas a man should be out in the world of education, work, and politics, a woman's place was in the home, a sphere where she could be sheltered. But what would happen if the economic need for an increased supply of labor clashed with the new ideas about women's place in society? If a young unmarried woman went to work in a factory far away from her parents' farm, would she still be respectable? Where would she live? Who would protect her? Perhaps the experience of factory work itself would destroy those special feminine characteristics all true women possessed. All these fears and more would have to be confronted in the course of the development of the New England textile industry during the 1830s and 1840s.

Although the first American textile mill using water-powered spinning machines was built in 1790, it and the countless other mills that sprung up throughout New England during the next thirty years depended heavily on the putting out system. The mills made only the yarn, which was then distributed ("put out") to women who wove the cloth in their own homes and returned the finished products to the mills. In 1820, two-thirds of all American cloth was still being produced by women working at home. But the pace of modernization accelerated sharply with the formation of the Boston Manufacturing Company, a heavily capitalized firm that purchased a large tract of rural land in the Merrimack River Valley. The Boston Associates adopted the latest technology and, more importantly, concentrated all aspects of cloth production inside their factories. Because they no longer put out work, they had to attract large numbers of workers, especially young women from New England farms, to their mills. Lowell, Massachusetts (the "City of Spindles") and the Lowell mills became a kind of model, an experiment that received a good deal of attention in both Europe and America. As historian Thomas Dublin has shown, most of the young women at the Lowell mills were fifteen to thirty years old, unmarried, and from farm families that were neither the richest nor the poorest in their area. Although some of the Lowell girls occasionally sent small amounts of money back to their families, most used their wages for new clothes, education, and dowries.[2] These wages were significantly higher than those for teaching, farm labor, or domestic services, the three other major occupations open to women.

The factory girls were required to live and eat in boardinghouses run according to company rules and supervised by respectable landladies. The company partially subsidized the cost

of room-and-board and also encouraged the numerous lecture series, evening schools, and church-related activities in Lowell. Girls worked together in the mills, filling the unskilled and semiskilled positions, and men (about one-fourth of the work force) performed the skilled jobs and served as overseers (foremen). Work in the mills was also characterized by strict regulations and an elaborate system of bells that signaled meal times and work times.

During the 1840s, factory girls occasionally published their own magazines, the most famous of which was the *Lowell Offering*. This journal grew out of a working woman's self-improvement society and was sponsored by a local Lowell minister. When the minister was transferred, the mill owners partially subsidized the magazine. The female editors, who were former mill workers, insisted that the magazine was for "literary" work rather than for labor reform. The "Evidence" section presents a description and the rules of Lowell mills and boardinghouses and several selections from the *Lowell Offering* and other sources. The conflict between economic modernization and the cult of true womanhood was indirectly recognized by many New Englanders and directly experienced by the Lowell mill girls. What forms did this conflict take? What kind of fears and anxieties did it reveal? How did the mill girls attempt to cope with this tension?

2. A dowry was the money, goods, or property that a woman brought into her marriage.

THE METHOD

When historians use prescriptive literature as evidence, they ask (1) what message is being conveyed, (2) who is sending the message, (3) why is it being sent, and (4) for whom is it intended? All the evidence you are using in this chapter is in some ways prescriptive—that is, it tells people how women *should* behave.

An early major criticism of the effects of factory work on young women was written by Orestes Brownson, a well-known New England editor and reformer. A sharply contrasting view appears in the excerpts from a brief, popular book about Lowell written by the Reverend Henry Mills in 1845. The Reverend Mills was a local Protestant minister who was asked by the textile company owners to conduct surveys into the workers' habits, health, and moral character. Depending heavily on information provided by company officials, overseers, and landladies, the Reverend Mills published *Lowell, As It Was, and As It Is*.

Yet the controversy continued because only one year later the journal owned by the Lowell Female Labor Reform Association, *Voice of Industry,* painted a much darker picture of the factory girls' "slavery." Although purchased by a militant group of women factory workers, the *Voice* originated as a labor reform paper. Its editorial policy always addressed the larger worker-oriented issues such as the shorter workday and dedicated a special column to women workers' concerns.

The young women who worked in the textile mills also actively participated in the debate. The evidence in the selections from the *Lowell Offering* was written by factory girls during the years 1840 to 1843. Also presented is an excerpt from a book written by Lucy Larcom, one of the few children (under age fifteen) employed in the Lowell mills in the late 1830s. She was a factory girl for more than ten years, after which she went west and obtained a college education. She became a well-known teacher and author when she returned to New England. Larcom published the book about her New England girlhood when she was sixty-five years old. The final set of evidence includes two pictures of "typical" mill girls in 1860 and letters written by mill girls and their families.

First read through the evidence, looking for elements of the cult of true womanhood in the factory girls' writings and in the Lowell system itself. Be sure to consider all four questions: what message is being conveyed? who is sending the message? why is it being sent? for whom is it intended? This will tell you a great deal, not only about the social standards for respectable young white women but also about the fears and anxieties aroused by a factory system that employed women away from their homes.

Reading about how people *should* behave, however, does not tell us how people actually behaved. Remember that the central question of this problem involves a clash—a conflict between ideas (the cult) and reality (the factory system). Go through the evidence again, this time trying to reconstruct what it was really like for the young women who lived and worked in Lowell. Ask yourself to what degree and in what ways they might have deviated from the ideal of "true" women.

Also ask whether they could have achieved this ideal goal—and whether they really wanted to—while working and living in Lowell. In other words, try to clarify in your own mind the forms of the conflict and the reactions (of both society and the young women) to that conflict.

THE EVIDENCE

Source 1 from Orestes A. Brownson, *Boston Quarterly Review,* 3 (July 1840), 368–370.

1. Slave Labor Versus Free Labor.

In regard to labor, two systems obtain: one that of slave labor, the other that of free labor. Of the two, the first is, in our judgment, except so far as the feelings are concerned, decidedly the least oppressive. If the slave has never been a free man, we think, as a general rule, his sufferings are less than those of the free laborer at wages. As to actual freedom, one has just about as much as the other. The laborer at wages has all the disadvantages of freedom and none of its blessings, while the slave, if denied the blessings, is freed from the disadvantages.

We are no advocates of slavery. We are as heartily opposed to it as any modern abolitionist can be. But we say frankly that, if there must always be a laboring population distinct from proprietors and employers, we regard the slave system as decidedly preferable to the system at wages.

It is no pleasant thing to go days without food; to lie idle for weeks, seeking work and finding none; to rise in the morning with a wife and children you love, and know not where to procure them a breakfast; and to see constantly before you no brighter prospect than the almshouse. . . .

It is said there is no want in this country. There may be less in some other countries. But death by actual starvation in this country is, we apprehend, no uncommon occurrence. The sufferings of a quiet, unassuming but useful class of females in our cities, in general seamstresses, too proud to beg or to apply to the almshouse, are not easily told. They are industrious; they do all that they can find to do. But yet the little there is for them to do, and the miserable pittance they receive for it, is hardly sufficient to keep soul and body together. . . .

The average life—working life, we mean—of the girls that come to Lowell, for instance, from Maine, New Hampshire, and Vermont, we have been assured, is only about three years. What becomes of them then? Few of them ever marry;[3] fewer still ever return to their native places with reputations unimpaired. "She has worked in a factory" is almost enough to damn to infamy the most worthy and virtuous girl. . . .

One thing is certain: that, of the amount actually produced by the operative, [the worker] retains a less proportion than it costs the master to feed, clothe, and lodge his slave. Wages is a cunning device of the devil, for the benefit of tender consciences who would retain all the advantages of the slave system without the expense, trouble, and odium of being slaveholders.

Source 2 from the Reverend Henry A. Mills, *Lowell, As It Was, and As It Is* (Lowell, Mass.: Powers, Bagley, and Dayton, 1845).

2. A Lowell Boardinghouse.

[Reverend Mills began by describing the long blocks of boardinghouses, each three stories high, which were built in a style reminiscent of country farmhouses. Clean, well-painted, and neat, these houses contained common eating rooms, parlors, and sleeping rooms for two to six boarders. The boarders, Reverend Mills observed, were sometimes a bit crowded but actually lived under better conditions than seamstresses and milliners in other towns.]

As one important feature in the management of these houses, it deserves to be named that male operatives and female operatives do not board in the same tenement; and the following Regulations, printed by one of the companies, and given to each keeper of their houses, are here subjoined, as a simple statement of the rules generally observed by all the Corporations.

Regulations to be observed by persons occupying the Boarding-houses belonging to the Merrimack Manufacturing company.

They must not board any persons not employed by the company, unless by special permission.

No disorderly or improper conduct must be allowed in the houses.

3. According to historian Thomas Dublin (*Women At Work*, New York: Columbia University Press, 1979), the working women of Lowell tended to marry in about the same proportion as nonworking New England women, although the Lowell women married three to five years later in life and had a distinct tendency to marry men who were tradesmen or skilled workers rather than farmers.

The doors must be closed at 10 o'clock in the evening; and no person admitted after that time, unless a sufficient excuse can be given.

Those who keep the houses, when required, must give an account of the number, names, and employment of their boarders; also with regard to their general conduct and whether they are in the habit of attending public worship.

The buildings, both inside and out, and the yards about them, must be kept clean and in good order. If the buildings or fences are injured, they will be repaired and charged to the occupant.

No one will be allowed to keep swine.

The hours of taking meals in these houses are uniform throughout all the Corporations in the city, and are as follows: Dinner—always at half-past twelve o'clock. Breakfast—from November 1 to February 28, before going to work, and so early as to begin work as soon as it is light; through March at half-past seven o'clock; from April 1 to September 19, at seven o'clock; and from September 20 to October 31, at half-past seven o'clock. Supper—always after work at night, that is, after seven o'clock, from March 20 to September 19; after half-past seven o'clock, from September 20 to March 19. The time allowed for each meal is thirty minutes for breakfast, when that meal is taken after beginning work; for dinner, thirty minutes, from September 1 to April 30; and forty-five minutes from May 1 to August 31.

[The meals might seem rushed, Mills noted, but that was common among all Americans, particularly businesspeople. Working girls could choose whichever boarding-houses they preferred, rents were very low, and their living arrangements were very respectable.]

No tenant is admitted who has not hitherto borne a good character, and who does not continue to sustain it. In many cases the tenant has long been keeper of the house, for six, eight, or twelve years, and is well known to hundreds of her girls as their adviser and friend and second mother. . . .

The influence which this system of boarding-houses has exerted upon the good order and good morals of the place, has been vast and beneficent. It is this system to which we especially referred in our previous chapter on Waltham. By it the care and influence of the superintendent are extended over his operatives, while they are out of the mill, as well as while they are in it. Employing chiefly those who have no permanent residence in Lowell, but are only temporary boarders, upon any embarrassment of affairs they return to their country homes, and do not sink down here a helpless caste, clamouring for work, starving unless employed, and hence ready for a riot, for the destruction of property, and repeating here the scenes enacted in the

manufacturing villages of England. To a very great degree the future condition of Lowell is dependent upon a faithful adhesion to this system; and
it will deserve the serious consideration of those old towns which are now
introducing steam mills, whether, if they do not provide boarding-houses,
and employ chiefly other operatives than resident ones, they be not bringing
in the seeds of future and alarming evil. . . .

To obtain this constant importation of female hands from the country, it
is necessary to secure *the moral protection of their characters while they are
resident in Lowell.* This, therefore, is the chief object of that moral police
referred to, some details of which will now be given.

It should be stated, in the outset, that no persons are employed on the
Corporations who are addicted to intemperance, or who are known to be
guilty of any immoralities of conduct. As the parent of all other vices, intemperance is most carefully excluded. Absolute freedom from intoxicating li-
quors is understood, throughout the city, to be a prerequisite to obtaining
employment in the mills, and any person known to be addicted to their use
is at once dismissed. This point has not received the attention, from writers
upon the moral conditions of Lowell, which it deserves; and we are surprised
that the English traveller and divine, Dr. Scoresby, in his recent book upon
Lowell, has given no more notice to this subject. A more strictly and universally temperate class of persons cannot be found, than the nine thousand
operatives of this city; and the fact is as well known to all others living here,
as it is of some honest pride among themselves. In relation to other immoralities, it may be stated, that the suspicion of criminal conduct, association
with suspected persons, and general and habitual light behavior and conversation, are regarded as sufficient reasons for dismissions, and for which
delinquent operatives are discharged.

*[Reverend Mills also described the discharge system at the factories. For those girls
whose conduct was satisfactory and who had worked at least a year, honorable discharges were issued. Discharge letters could be used as recommendations for another
job. Those who received dishonorable discharges for such infractions as stealing,
lying, leaving the job without permission, or other "improper conduct," however,
would have difficulty finding other employment.]*

So much for honorable discharges. Those dishonorable have another
treatment. The names of all persons dismissed for bad conduct, or who leave
the mill irregularly, are also entered in a book kept for that purpose, and
these names are sent to all the counting-rooms of the city, and are there
entered on *their* books. *Such persons obtain no more employment throughout
the city.* The question is put to each applicant, "Have you worked before in
the city, and if so, where is your discharge?" If no discharge be presented,

an inquiry of the applicant's name will enable the superintendent to know whether that name stands on his book of dishonorable discharges, and he is thus saved from taking in a corrupt or unworthy hand. This system, which has been in operation in Lowell from the beginning, is of great and important effect in driving unworthy persons from our city, and in preserving the high character of our operatives.

[Male overseers, or foremen, were also closely screened and had to possess good moral character. In response to the Reverend's questions about the male overseers, one factory owner responded as follows.]

Lowell, May 10, 1841

Dear Sir:—

I employ in our mills, and in the various departments connected with them, thirty overseers, and as many second overseers. My overseers are married men, with families, with a single exception, and even he has engaged a tenement, and is to be married soon. Our second overseers are younger men, but upwards of twenty of them are married, and several others are soon to be married. Sixteen of our overseers are members of some regular church, and four of them are deacons. Ten of our second overseers are also members of the church, and one of them is the Superintendent of a Sunday School. I have no hesitation in saying that in all the sterling requisites of character, in native intelligence, and practical good sense, in sound morality, and as active, useful, and exemplary citizens, they may, as a class, safely challenge comparison with any class in our community. I know not, among them all, an intemperate man, nor, at this time, even what is called a moderate drinker.

[Furthermore, the girls were expected to obey numerous rules.]

Still another source of trust which a Corporation has, for the good character of its operatives, is the moral control which they have over one another. Of course this control would be nothing among a generally corrupt and degraded class. But among virtuous and high-minded young women, who feel that they have the keeping of their characters, and that any stain upon their associates brings reproach upon themselves, the power of opinion becomes an ever-present, and ever-active restraint. A girl, *suspected* of immoralities, or serious improprieties of conduct, at once loses caste. Her fellow-boarders will at once leave the house, if the keeper does not dismiss the offender. In self-protection, therefore, the matron is obliged to put the offender away. Nor will her former companions walk with, or work with her; till at length, finding herself everywhere talked about, and pointed at, and shunned, she is obliged to relieve her fellow-operatives of a presence which they feel brings disgrace. From this power of opinion, there is no appeal; and as long as it is exerted in favor of propriety of behavior and purity of life, it is one of the most active and effectual safeguards of character.

It may not be out of place to present here the regulations, which are observed alike on all the Corporations, which are given to the operatives when they are first employed, and are posted up conspicuously in all the mills. They are as follows:—

Regulations to be observed by all persons employed by the _____ *Manufacturing Company, in the Factories.*

Every overseer is required to be punctual himself, and to see that those employed under him are so.

The overseers may, at their discretion, grant leave of absence to those employed under them, when there are sufficient spare hands to supply their place; but when there are not sufficient spare hands, they are not allowed to grant leave of absence unless in cases of absolute necessity.

All persons are required to observe the regulations of the room in which they are employed. They are not allowed to be absent from their work without the consent of their overseer, except in case of sickness, and then they are required to send him word of the cause of their absence.

All persons are required to board in one of the boarding-houses belonging to the company, and conform to the regulations of the house in which they board.

All persons are required to be constant in attendance on public worship, at one of the regular places of worship in this place.

Persons who do not comply with the above regulations will not be employed by the company.

Persons entering the employment of the company are considered as engaging to work one year.

All persons intending to leave the employment of the company, are required to give notice of the same to their overseer, at least two weeks previous to the time of leaving.

Any one who shall take from the mills, or the yard, any yarn, cloth, or other article belonging to the company, will be considered guilty of STEAL-ING—and prosecuted accordingly.

The above regulations are considered part of the contract with all persons entering the employment of the _____ MANUFACTURING COMPANY.

All persons who shall have complied with them, on leaving the employment of the company, shall be entitled to an honorable discharge, which will serve as a recommendation to any of the factories in Lowell. No one who shall not have complied with them will be entitled to such a discharge.

———————— ————————, Agent

Source 3 courtesy of Museum of American Textile History.

3. Timetable of the Lowell Mills.

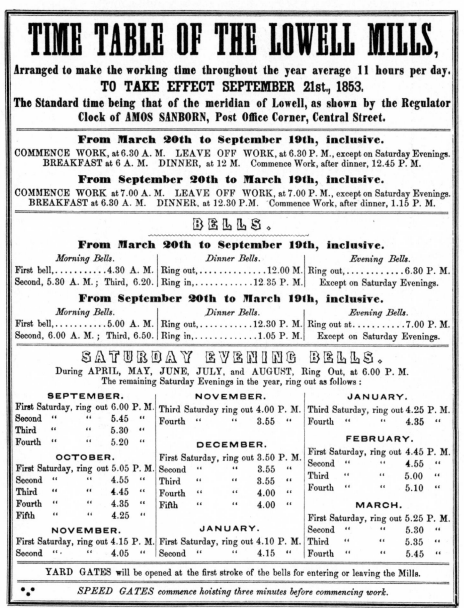

TIME TABLE OF THE LOWELL MILLS,

Arranged to make the working time throughout the year average 11 hours per day.

TO TAKE EFFECT SEPTEMBER 21st., 1853.

The Standard time being that of the meridian of Lowell, as shown by the Regulator Clock of AMOS SANBORN, Post Office Corner, Central Street.

From March 20th to September 19th, inclusive.

COMMENCE WORK, at 6.30 A. M. LEAVE OFF WORK, at 6.30 P. M., except on Saturday Evenings.
BREAKFAST at 6 A. M. DINNER, at 12 M. Commence Work, after dinner, 12.45 P. M.

From September 20th to March 19th, inclusive.

COMMENCE WORK at 7.00 A. M. LEAVE OFF WORK, at 7.00 P. M., except on Saturday Evenings.
BREAKFAST at 6.30 A. M. DINNER, at 12.30 P.M. Commence Work, after dinner, 1.15 P. M.

BELLS.

From March 20th to September 19th, inclusive.

Morning Bells.	Dinner Bells.	Evening Bells.
First bell,..........4.30 A. M.	Ring out,.............12.00 M.	Ring out,.............6.30 P. M.
Second, 5.30 A. M.; Third, 6.20.	Ring in,..........12.35 P. M.	Except on Saturday Evenings.

From September 20th to March 19th, inclusive.

Morning Bells.	Dinner Bells.	Evening Bells.
First bell,..........5.00 A. M.	Ring out,..........12.30 P. M.	Ring out at..........7.00 P. M.
Second, 6.00 A. M.; Third, 6.50.	Ring in,.............1.05 P. M.	Except on Saturday Evenings.

SATURDAY EVENING BELLS.

During APRIL, MAY, JUNE, JULY, and AUGUST, Ring Out, at 6.00 P. M.
The remaining Saturday Evenings in the year, ring out as follows :

SEPTEMBER.	NOVEMBER.	JANUARY.
First Saturday, ring out 6.00 P. M.	Third Saturday ring out 4.00 P. M.	Third Saturday, ring out 4.25 P. M.
Second " " 5.45 "	Fourth " " 3.55 "	Fourth " " 4.35 "
Third " " 5.30 "		
Fourth " " 5.20 "	**DECEMBER.**	**FEBRUARY.**
OCTOBER.	First Saturday, ring out 3.50 P. M.	First Saturday, ring out 4.45 P. M.
First Saturday, ring out 5.05 P. M.	Second " " 3.55 "	Second " " 4.55 "
Second " " 4.55 "	Third " " 3.55 "	Third " " 5.00 "
Third " " 4.45 "	Fourth " " 4.00 "	Fourth " " 5.10 "
Fourth " " 4.35 "	Fifth " " 4.00 "	
Fifth " " 4.25 "		**MARCH.**
NOVEMBER.	**JANUARY.**	First Saturday, ring out 5.25 P. M.
First Saturday, ring out 4.15 P. M.	First Saturday, ring out 4.10 P. M.	Second " " 5.30 "
Second " . " 4.05 "	Second " " 4.15 "	Third " " 5.35 "
		Fourth " " 5.45 "

YARD GATES will be opened at the first stroke of the bells for entering or leaving the Mills.

•.•   *SPEED GATES commence hoisting three minutes before commencing work.*

Penhallow, Printer, Wyman's Exchange, 28 Merrimack St.

Source 4 from *Voice of Industry,* January 2, 1846, in H. R. Warfel et al., eds., *The American Mind* (1937), p. 392.

4. "Slaver" Wagons.

We were not aware, until within a few days, of the *modus operandi* of the factory powers in this village of forcing poor girls from their quiet homes to become their tools and, like the Southern slaves, to give up their life and liberty to the heartless tyrants and taskmasters.

Observing a singular-looking "long, low, black" wagon passing along the street, we made inquiries respecting it, and were informed that it was what we term a "slaver." She makes regular trips to the north of the state [Massachusetts], cruising around in Vermont and New Hampshire, with a "commander" whose heart must be as black as his craft, who is paid a dollar a head for all he brings to the market, and more in proportion to the distance—if they bring them from such a distance that they cannot easily get back.

This is done by "hoisting false colors," and representing to the girls that they can tend more machinery than is possible, and that the work is so very neat, and the wages such that they can dress in silks and spend half their time in reading. Now, is this true? Let those girls who have been thus deceived, answer.

Let us say a word in regard to the manner in which they are stowed in the wagon, which may find a similarity only in the manner in which slaves are fastened in the hold of a vessel. It is long, and the seats so close that it must be very inconvenient.

Is there any humanity in this? Philanthropists may talk of Negro slavery, but it would be well first to endeavor to emancipate the slaves at home. Let us not stretch our ears to catch the sound of the lash on the flesh of the oppressed black while the oppressed in our very midst are crying out in thunder tones, and calling upon us for assistance.

Source 5 from *Lowell Offering*, Series I (1840). Courtesy of Merrimack Valley Textile Museum.

5. Title Page of *Lowell Offering*.

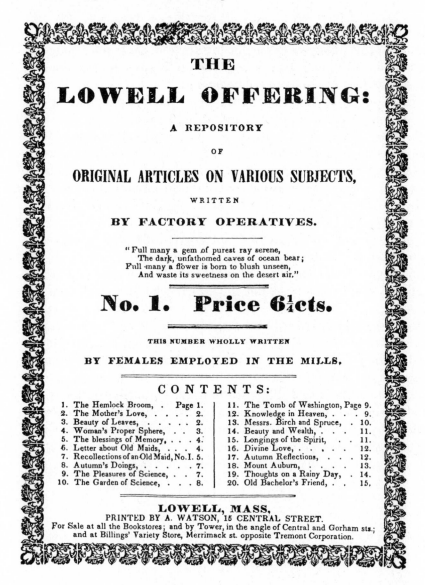

THE

LOWELL OFFERING:

A REPOSITORY

OF

ORIGINAL ARTICLES ON VARIOUS SUBJECTS,

WRITTEN

BY FACTORY OPERATIVES.

"Full many a gem of purest ray serene,
The dark, unfathomed caves of ocean bear;
Full many a flower is born to blush unseen,
And waste its sweetness on the desert air."

No. 1.   Price 6¼cts.

THIS NUMBER WHOLLY WRITTEN

BY FEMALES EMPLOYED IN THE MILLS.

CONTENTS:

LOWELL, MASS,
PRINTED BY A. WATSON, 15 CENTRAL STREET.
For Sale at all the Bookstores; and by Tower, in the angle of Central and Gorham sts.;
and at Billings' Variety Store, Merrimack st. opposite Tremont Corporation.

Source 6 from *Lowell Offering,* Series I (1840), p. 16.

6. Editorial Corner.

The Lowell Offering is strictly what it purports to be, a "Repository of original articles on various subjects, written by Factory Operatives."—The objects of the publication are, to encourage the cultivation of talent; to preserve such articles as are deemed most worthy of preservation; and to correct an erroneous idea which generally prevails in relation to the intelligence of persons employed in the Mills. This number is wholly the offering of Females. . . .

We are persuaded that the citizens generally, and those engaged in the Mills particularly, will feel and manifest a lively interest in the prosperity of the Lowell Offering. That it is faultless—that the severe and captious critic will find no room for his vocation, is not to be expected. Nevertheless, while the work makes no noisy pretensions to superior excellency, it would claim no unusual indulgences. It asks only that, all the circumstances incident to its peculiar character being duly weighed, it shall be fairly and candidly judged. The Editors do not hesitate to say, that they anticipate for a favorable reception at the hands of those who have at heart the interests of that important and interesting portion of our population, whose intellectual elevation and moral welfare it aims to promote. . . .

The critical reader will doubtless discover, in many of the articles making this number of the Offering, words and phrases for which better might be substituted; and also sentences that want the freedom and smoothness of perfect composition. In explanation, the Editors have to say, that, in preparing the articles for the press, while they claimed to exercise the rights usually granted to the editorial fraternity, they resolved carefully to avoid any alteration which might affect the sentiment or style of the several writers. In consequence of this resolution a few expressions and sentences have been allowed to pass, which a less scrupulous regard for strict originality would have rejected. Nevertheless they are quite sure the rule adopted will be approved by all who shall look to the articles of the Offering as evidence of the intellectual and literary power of the writers.

An opinion extensively prevails, not merely beyond the limits of Massachusetts, that the Manufacturing city of Lowell is a nucleus of depravity and ignorance.

Confessedly, wherever there exists *any* depravity or ignorance, there is *too much* of it. We have this to testify however, that they who know least of the people of Lowell, including the Factory Operatives, entertain the most

unworthy and unjust opinions of them. Close personal observations has satisfied us, that in respect of morality and intelligence, they will not suffer in
comparison with the inhabitants of any part of moral and enlightened New
England. We shall have occasion to speak of this subject at considerable
length hereafter. We shall note the unsurpassed (if not unequaled) advantages of education enjoyed by our population; and the extensive means of
information and piety furnished by popular lectures and religious institutions. We shall note the absence of theatres and kindred abominations; the
care taken to exclude unworthy persons from the Corporations, &c.

And as to the intelligence of our people, we may safely present the pages
of the Offering as a testimony against all revilers "who know not whereof
they affirm." Editors who think proper to copy any thing therefrom, are requested to give due credit, and thus assist in the correction of an unwar-
ranted and injurious error.

Sources 7 and 8 from *Lowell Offering,* Series II, Vol. II (1842), p. 192; Series II, Vol.
III (1842), pp. 69–70.

7. Dignity of Labor.

From whence originated the idea, that it was derogatory to a lady's dignity,
or a blot upon the female character, to labor? and who was the first to say,
sneeringly, 'Oh, she *works* for a living'? Surely, such ideas and expressions
ought not to grow on republican soil. The time has been, when ladies of the
first rank were accustomed to busy themselves in domestic employment.

Homer tells us of princesses who used to draw water from the springs,
and wash with their own hands the finest of the linen of their respective
families. The famous Lucretia used to spin in the midst of her attendants;
and the wife of Ulysses, after the siege of Troy, employed herself in weaving,
until her husband returned to Ithaca. And in later times, the wife of George
the Third of England, has been represented as spending a whole evening in
hemming pocket-handkerchiefs, while her daughter Mary sat in the corner,
darning stockings.

Few American fortunes will support a woman who is above the calls of
her family; and a man of sense, in choosing a companion to jog with him
through all the up-hills and down-hills of life, would sooner choose one who
had to work for a living, than one who thought it beneath her to soil her
pretty hands with manual labor, although she possessed her thousands. To
be able to earn one's own living by laboring with the hands, should be reck-

oned among female accomplishments; and I hope the time is not far distant when none of my countrywomen will be ashamed to have it known that they are better versed in useful, than they are in ornamental accomplishments.

C.B.

8. Editorial—Home in a Boarding-House.

[Factory boardinghouses were not really like homes, the editor pointed out. A place to eat and lodge, the boardinghouses often seemed crowded and impersonal.]

But these are all trifles, compared with the perplexities to which we are subjected in other ways; and some of these things might be remedied by the girls themselves. We now allude to the importunities of evening visitors, such as peddlers, candy and newspaper boys, shoe-dealers, book-sellers, &c., &c., breaking in upon the only hours of leisure we can call our own, and proffering their articles with a pertinacity which will admit of no denial. That these evening salesmen are always unwelcome we will not assert, but they are too often inclined to remain where they know they are considered a nuisance. And then they often forget, if they ever knew, the rules of politeness which should regulate all transient visitors. They deal about their hints, inuendoes [*sic*], and low cunning, as though a factory boarding-house was what no boarding-house should ever be.

The remedy is entirely with the girls. Treat all of these comers with a politeness truly lady-like, when they appear as gentlemen, but let your manners change to stern formality when they forget that they are in the company of respectable females. . . .

C.B.

Sources 9 through 11 from *Lowell Offering,* Series I (1840), pp. 17–19, 61, 44–46.

9. Factory Girls.

"She has worked in a factory, *is sufficient to damn to infamy the most worthy and virtuous girl.*"

So says Mr. Orestes A. Brownson; and either this horrible assertion is true, or Mr. Brownson is a slanderer. I assert that it is *not* true, and Mr. B. may consider himself called upon to prove his words, if he can.

This gentleman has read of an Israelitish boy who, with nothing but a stone and sling, once entered into a contest with a Philistine giant, arrayed in brass, whose spear was like a weaver's beam; and he may now see what will probably appear to him quite as marvellous; and that is, that a *factory*

[163]

girl is not afraid to oppose herself to the *Editor of the Boston Quarterly Review.* True, he has upon his side fame, learning, and great talent; but I have what is better than either of these, or all combined, and that is *truth.* Mr. Brownson has not said that this thing should be so; or that he is glad it is so; or that he deeply regrets such a state of affairs; but he has said it *is* so; and *I* affirm that it is *not.*

And whom has Mr. Brownson slandered? A class of girls who in this city alone are numbered by thousands, and who collect in many of our smaller towns by hundreds; girls who generally come from quiet country homes, where their minds and manners have been formed under the eyes of the worthy sons of the Pilgrims, and their virtuous partners, and who return again to become the wives of the free intelligent yeomanry of New England and the mothers of quite a portion of our future republicans. Think, for a moment, how many of the next generation are to spring from mothers doomed to infamy! "Ah," it may be replied, "Mr. Brownson acknowledges that you may still be worthy and virtuous." Then we must be a set of worthy and virtuous idiots, for no virtuous girl of common sense would choose for an occupation one that would consign her to infamy. . . .

That there has been prejudice against us, we know; but it is wearing away, and has never been so deep nor universal as Mr. B's statement will lead many to believe. Even now it may be that "the mushroom aristocracy" and "would-be fashionables" of Boston, turn up their eyes in horror at the sound of those vulgar words, *factory girls; but they* form but a small part of the community, and theirs are not the opinions which Mr. Brownson intended to represent. . . .

[The prejudice against factory girls was connected to the degraded and exploited conditions of European workers, the angry letter writer asserted. "Yankee girls," she said, are independent, and although the work is hard, the wages are better than those in other kinds of employment. It is no wonder, she concluded, that so many intelligent, worthy, and virtuous young women have been drawn to Lowell.]

The erroneous idea, wherever it exists, must be done away, that there is in factories but one sort of girls, and *that* the baser and degraded sort. There are among us *all* sorts of girls. I believe that there are few occupations which can exhibit so many gradations of piety and intelligence; but the majority may at least lay claim to as much of the former as females in other stations of life. . . . The Improvement Circles, the Lyceum and Institute, the social religious meetings, the Circulating and other libraries, can bear testimony that the little time they have is spent in a better manner. Our well filled churches and lecture halls and the high character of our clergymen and lecturers, will testify that the state of morals and intelligence is not low.

Mr. Brownson, I suppose, would not judge of our moral characters by our church-going tendencies; but as many do, a word on this subject may not be amiss. That there are many in Lowell who do not regularly attend any meeting, is as true as the correspondent of the Boston Times once represented it; but for this there are various reasons. . . .

There have also been nice calculations made, as to the small proportion which the amount of money deposited in the Savings Bank bears to that earned in the city; but this is not all that is saved. Some is deposited in Banks at other places, and some is put into the hands of personal friends. Still, much that is earned is immediately, though not foolishly, spent. Much that none but the parties concerned will ever know of, goes to procure comforts and necessaries for some lowly home, and a great deal is spent for public benevolent purposes. . . .

And now, if Mr. Brownson is a *man,* he will endeavor to retrieve the injury he has done; he will resolve that "the dark shall be light, and the wrong made right," and the assertion he has publicly made will be as publicly retracted. If he still doubts upon the subject let him come among us: let him make himself as well acquainted with us as our pastors and superintendents are; and though he will find error, ignorance, and folly among us, (and where would he find them not?) yet he would not see worthy and virtuous girls consigned to infamy, because they work in a factory.

A FACTORY GIRL

10. A Familiar Letter.

Friends and Associates:—

With indescribable emotions of pleasure, mingled with feelings of deepest gratitude to Him who is the Author of every good and perfect gift, I have perused the second and third numbers of the Lowell Offering.

As a laborer among you, (tho' least of all) I rejoice that the time has arrived when a class of laboring females (who have long been made a reproach and byword, by those whom fortune or pride has placed above the avocation by which we have subjected ourselves to the sneers and scoffs of the idle, ignorant and envious part of community,) are bursting asunder the captive chains of prejudice. . . .

I know it has been affirmed, to the sorrow of many a would-be lady, that factory girls and ladies could not be distinguished by their apparel. What a lamentable evil! and no doubt it would be a source of much gratitude to such, if the awful name of "factory girl!" were branded on the forehead of every female who is, or ever was, employed in the Mills. Appalling as the name may sound in the delicate ears of a sensitive lady, as she contrasts the music of her piano with the rumblings of the factory machinery, we would not shrink from such a token of our calling, could the treasures of the mind be there displayed, and merit, in her own unbiased form be stamped there also. . . .

Yours, in the bonds of affection,

DOROTHEA

11. Gold Watches.

It is now nearly a year since an article appeared in the Ladies' Book, in the form of a tale, though it partakes more of the character of an essay. It was written by Mrs. Hale, and exhibits her usual judgment and talent. Her object evidently was to correct the many erroneous impressions which exist in society, with regard to the folly of extravagance in dress, and all outward show. I was much pleased with all of it, with the exception of a single sentence. Speaking of the impossibility of considering dress a mark of distinction, she observed,—(addressing herself, I presume, to the *ladies* of New England,)—"How stands the difference now? Many of the factory girls wear gold watches, and an imitation, at least, of all the ornaments which grace the daughters of our most opulent citizens."

O the times! O the manners! Alas! how very sadly the world has changed! The time was when the *lady* could be distinguished from the *no-lady* by her dress, as far as the eye could reach; but now, you might stand in the same room, and judging by their outward appearance, you could not tell "which was which." Even gold watches are now no *sure* indication—for they have been worn by the lowest, even by "many of the factory girls." No *lady* need carry one now, for any other than the simple purpose of easily ascertaining the time of day, or night, if she so please! . . .

Those who do not labor for their living, have more time for the improvement of their minds, for the cultivation of conversational powers, and graceful manners; but if, with these advantages, they still need richer dress to distinguish them from *us,* the fault must be their own, and they should at least learn to honor merit, and acknowledge talent wherever they see it. . . .

And now I will address myself to my sister operatives in the Lowell factories. Good advice should be taken, from whatever quarter it may come, whether from friend or foe; and part of the advice which Mrs. Hale has given to the readers of the Ladies' Book, may be of advantage to us. Is there not among us, as a class, too much of this striving for distinction in dress? Is it not the only aim and object of too many of us, to wear something a little better than others can obtain? Do we not sometimes see the girl who has half a dozen silk gowns, toss her head, as if she felt herself six times better than her neighbor who has none? . . .

We all have many opportunities for the exercise of the kindly affections, and more than most females. We should look upon one another something as a band of orphans should do. We are fatherless and motherless: we are alone, and surrounded by temptation. Let us caution each other; let us watch over and endeavor to improve each other; and both at our boarding-houses and in the Mill, let us strive to promote each other's comfort and happiness. Above all, let us endeavor to improve ourselves by making good use of the many advantages we here possess. I say let us at least strive to do this; and if we succeed, it will finally be acknowledged that Factory Girls shine forth in ornaments far more valuable than *Gold Watches*.

A FACTORY GIRL

Source 12 from *Lowell Offering*, Series II, Vol. I (1841), p. 32. Courtesy Merrimack Valley Textile Museum.

12. Song of the Spinners.

SONG OF THE SPINNERS.

1. The day is o'er, nor lon-ger we toil and spin; For ev'ning's hush withdraws from the dai-ly din. And now we sing, with gladsome hearts, The theme of the spinner's song, That la-bor to lei-sure a zest imparts, Unknown to the i--dle throng.

2. We spin all day, and then, in the time for rest, Sweet peace is found, A joyous and welcome guest. Des-pite of toil we all agree, or out of the Mills, or in, De-pen-dent on others we ne'er will be, So long as we're a-ble to spin.

Source 13 from Lucy Larcom, *A New England Girlhood* (Boston: Houghton Mifflin, 1889).

13. Selection from *A New England Girlhood*.

During my father's life, a few years before my birth, his thoughts had been turned towards the new manufacturing town growing up on the banks of the Merrimack. He had once taken a journey there, with the possibility in his mind of making the place his home, his limited income furnishing no adequate promise of maintenance for his large family of daughters. From the beginning, Lowell had a high reputation for good order, morality, piety, and all that was dear to the old-fashioned New Englander's heart.

After his death, my mother's thoughts naturally followed the direction his had taken; and seeing no other opening for herself, she sold her small estate, and moved to Lowell, with the intention of taking a corporation-house for mill-girl boarders. Some of the family objected, for the Old World traditions about factory life were anything but attractive; and they were current in New England until the experiment at Lowell had shown that independent and intelligent workers invariably give their own character to their occupation. My mother had visited Lowell, and she was willing and glad, knowing all about the place, to make it our home. . . .

[Because her mother could not earn enough to support the family, Lucy (age eleven) and her sister went to work in the mills.]

So I went to my first day's work in the mill with a light heart. The novelty of it made it seem easy, and it really was not hard, just to change the bobbins on the spinning-frames every three quarters of an hour or so, with half a dozen other little girls who were doing the same thing. When I came back at night, the family began to pity me for my long, tiresome day's work, but I laughed, and said,—

"Why, it is nothing but fun. It is just like play."

And for a little while it was only a new amusement; I liked it better than going to school and "making believe" I was learning when I was not. And there was a great deal of play mixed with it. We were not occupied more than half the time. The intervals were spent frolicking around among the spinning-frames, teasing and talking to the older girls, or entertaining ourselves with games and stories in a corner, or exploring, with the overseer's permission, the mysteries of the carding-room, the dressing-room, and the weaving-room. . . .

There were compensations for being shut in to daily toil so early. The mill itself had its lessons for us. But it was not, and could not be, the right sort of life for a child, and we were happy in the knowledge that, at the longest, our employment was only to be temporary.

When I took my next three months at the grammar school, everything there was changed, and I too was changed. The teachers were kind, and thorough in their instruction; and my mind seemed to have been ploughed up during that year of work, so that knowledge took root in it easily. It was a great delight to me to study, and at the end of the three months the master told me that I was prepared for the high school.

But alas! I could not go. The little money I could earn—one dollar a week, besides the price of my board—was needed in the family, and I must return to the mill. It was a severe disappointment to me, though I did not say so at home. . . .

In the older times it was seldom said to little girls, as it always has been said to boys, that they ought to have some definite plan, while they were children, what to be and do when they were grown up. There was usually but one path open before them, to become good wives and housekeepers. And the ambition of most girls was to follow their mothers' footsteps in this direction; a natural and laudable ambition. But girls, as well as boys, must often have been conscious of their own peculiar capabilities,—must have desired to cultivate and make use of their individual powers. When I was growing up, they had already begun to be encouraged to do so. We were often told that it was our duty to develop any talent we might possess, or at least learn how to do some one thing which the world needed, or which would make it a pleasanter world. . . .

At this time I had learned to do a spinner's work, and I obtained permission to tend some frames that stood directly in front of the river-windows, with only them and the wall behind me, extending half the length of the mill,—and one young woman beside me, at the farther end of the row. She was a sober, mature person, who scarcely thought it worth her while to speak often to a child like me; and I was, when with strangers, rather a reserved girl; so I kept myself occupied with the river, my work, and my thoughts. . . .

The printed regulations forbade us to bring books into the mill, so I made my window-seat into a small library of poetry, pasting its side all over with newspaper clippings. In those days we had only weekly papers, and they had always a "poet's corner," where standard writers were well represented, with anonymous ones, also. I was not, of course, much of a critic. I chose my verses for their sentiment, and because I wanted to commit them to memory; sometimes it was a long poem, sometimes a hymn, sometimes only a stray verse. . . .

Some of the girls could not believe that the Bible was meant to be counted among forbidden books. We all thought that the Scriptures had a right to go wherever we went, and that if we needed them anywhere, it was at our work. I evaded the law by carrying some leaves from a torn Testament in my pocket.

The overseer, caring more for law than gospel, confiscated all he found. He had his desk full of Bibles. It sounded oddly to hear him say to the most religious girl in the room, when he took hers away, "I did think you had more conscience than to bring that book here." But we had some close ethical questions to settle in those days. It was a rigid code of morality under which we lived. Nobody complained of it, however, and we were doubtless better off for its strictness, in the end.

The last window in the row behind me was filled with flourishing house plants—fragrant-leaved geraniums, the overseer's pets. They gave that corner a bowery look; the perfume and freshness tempted me there often. Standing before that window, I could look across the room and see girls moving backwards and forwards among the spinning-frames, sometimes stooping, sometimes reaching up their arms, as their work required, with easy and not ungraceful movements. On the whole, it was far from being a disagreeable place to stay in. The girls were bright-looking and neat, and everything was kept clean and shining. The effect of the whole was rather attractive to strangers. . . .

One great advantage which came to these many stranger girls though being brought together, away from their own homes, was that it taught them to go out of themselves, and enter into the lives of others. Home-life, when one always stays at home, is necessarily narrowing. That is one reason why so many women are petty and unthoughtful of any except their own family's interests. We have hardly begun to live until we can take in the idea of the whole human family as the one to which we truly belong. To me, it was an incalculable help to find myself among so many working-girls, all of us thrown upon our own resources, but thrown much more upon each others' sympathies. . . .

My grandfather came to see my mother once at about this time and visited the mills. When he had entered the room, and looked around for a moment, he took off his hat and made a low bow to the girls, first toward the right, and then toward the left. We were familiar with his courteous habits, partly due to his French descent; but we had never seen anybody bow to a roomful of mill girls in that polite way, and some one of the family afterwards asked him why he did so. He looked a little surprised at the question, but answered promptly and with dignity, "I always take off my hat to ladies."

His courtesy was genuine. Still, we did not call ourselves ladies. We did not forget that we were working-girls, wearing coarse aprons suitable to our work, and that there was some danger of our becoming drudges. I know that sometimes the confinement of the mill became very wearisome to me. In the sweet June weather I would lean far out of the window, and try not to hear the unceasing clash of sound inside. Looking away to the hills, my whole stifled being would cry out

"Oh, that I had wings!"

Still I was there from choice, and

"The prison unto which we doom ourselves,
No prison is."

Source 14 courtesy of Mildred Tunis Tracey Memorial Library, New London, N.H.

14. A "Typical" Factory Girl, Delia Page, c. 1860.

Source 15 courtesy of Merrimack Valley Textile Museum.

15. Two Women Weavers, c. 1860.

Sources 16–21 from Thomas Dublin, ed., *Farm to Factory: Women's Letters, 1830–1860* (New York: Columbia University Press, 1981), pp. 42, 100–104, 170–172.

16. Letter from Sarah Hodgdon.

[In 1830, Sarah Hodgdon (age sixteen) and two friends went to Lowell to work in the textile mills. After approximately ten years of working in various factories, Hodgdon married a shoemaker from her hometown. This is one of her early letters to her mother.]

[June 1830]

Dear mother

I take this opertunity to write to you to informe you that I have gone into the mill and like very well. I was here one week and three days before I went into the mill to work for my board. We boord t[o]gether. I like my boording place very well. I enjoy my health very well. I do not enjoy my mind so well as it is my desire to. I cant go to any meetings except I hire a seat therefore I have to stay home on that account.[4] I desire you pay that it may not be said of me when I come home that I have sold my soul for the gay vanitys of this world. Give my love to my father tell him not to forget me and to my dear sister and to my brothers and to my grammother tell her I do not forget her and to my Aunts and to all my enquiring friends. I want that you should write to me as soon as you can and when you write to me I want that you should write to me the particulars about sister and Aunt Betsy. Dont fail writing. I bege you not to let this scrabling be seen.

Sarah Hodgdon

Mary Hodgdon

17. Letter from Mary Paul.

[Mary Paul left home in 1845 at age fifteen. She worked briefly and unsuccessfully as a domestic servant and then went to Lowell as a factory girl for four years. After leaving the mills, she returned home for a short while and then worked as a seamstress. Next she joined a utopian community, and finally she took a job as a housekeeper. In 1857, Paul married the son of the woman who ran the boardinghouse where Mary had lived in Lowell.]

---

4. Urban churches in this period often charged people who attended services a fee called pew rent.

Saturday Sept. 13th 1845

Dear Father

I received your letter this afternoon by Wm Griffith. . . . I am very glad you sent my shoes. They fit very well indeed they [are] large enough.

I want you to consent to let me go to Lowell if you can. I think it would be much better for me than to stay about here. I could earn more to begin with than I can any where about here. I am in need of clothes which I cannot get if I stay about here and for that reason I want to go to Lowell or some other place. We all think if I could go with some steady girl that I might do well. I want you to think of it and make up your mind. Mercy Jane Griffith[5] is going to start in four or five weeks. Aunt Miller and Aunt Sarah think it would be a good chance for me to go if you would consent—which I want you to do if possible. I want to see you and talk with you about it.

Aunt Sarah gains slowly.

Mary

Bela Paul

18. Letter from Mary Paul.

Lowell Nov 20th 1845

Dear Father

An opportunity now presents itself which I improve in writing to you. I started for this place at the time I talked of which was Thursday. I left Whitneys at nine o'clock stopped at Windsor at 12 and staid till 3 and started again. Did not stop again for any length of time till we arrived at Lowell. Went to a boarding house and staid until Monday night. On Saturday after I got here Luthera Griffith went round with me to find a place but we were unsuccessful. On Monday we started again and were more successful. We found a place in a spinning room and the next morning I went to work. I like very well have 50 cts first payment increasing every payment as I get along in work have a first rate overseer and a very good boarding place. I work on the Lawrence Corporation. Mill is No 2 spinning room. I was very sorry that you did not come to see me start. I wanted to see you and Henry[6] but I suppose that you were otherways engaged. I hoped to see Julius[7] but did not much expect to for I s[up]posed he was engaged in other matters. He got six dollars for me which I was very glad of. It cost me $3.25

5. A friend of Mary's.
6. Mary's thirteen-year-old brother.
7. Mary's twenty-seven-year-old brother.

to come. Stage fare was $3.00 and lodging at Windsor, 25 cts. Had to pay only 25 cts for board for 9 days after I got here before I went into the mill. Had 2.50 left with which I got a bonnet and some other small articles. Tell Harriet Burbank to send me paper. Tell her I shall send her one as soon as possible. You must write as soon as you receive this. Tell Henry I should like to hear from him. If you hear anything from William[8] write for I want to know what he is doing. I shall write to Uncle Millers folks the first opportunity. Aunt Nancy presented me with a new alpacca dress before I came away from there which I was very glad of. I think of staying here a year certain, if not more. I wish that you and Henry would come down here. I think that you might do well. I guess that Henry could get into the mill and I think that Julius might get in too. Tell all friends that I should like to hear from them.

excuse bad writing and mistakes
This from your own daughter

Mary

P.S. Be sure and direct to No. 15 Lawrence Corporation.
Bela Paul

Mary S Paul

19. Letter from Mary Paul.

Lowell Dec 21st 1845

Dear Father

I received your letter on Thursday the 14th with much pleasure. I am well which is one comfort. My life and health are spared while others are cut off. Last Thursday one girl fell down and broke her neck which caused instant death. She was going in or coming out of the mill and slipped down it being very icy. The same day a man was killed by the cars. Another had nearly all of his ribs broken. Another was nearly killed by falling down and having a bale of cotton fall on him. Last Tuesday we were paid. In all I had six dollars and sixty cents paid four dollars and sixty-eight cents for board. With the rest I got me a pair of rubbers and a pair of 50.cts shoes. Next payment I am to have a dollar a week beside my board. We have not had much snow the deepest being not more than 4 inches. It has been very warm for winter. Perhaps you would like something about our regulations about going in and coming out of the mill. At 5 o'clock in the morning the bell rings for the folks to get up and get breakfast. At half past six it rings for the girls to get up and at seven they are called into the mill. At half past 12 we have dinner

---

8. Mary's brother, who was married and living in Tennessee.

are called back again at one and stay till half past seven. I get along very well with my work. I can doff[9] as fast as any girl in our room. I think I shall have frames before long. The usual time allowed for learning is six months but I think I shall have frames before I have been in three as I get along so fast. I think that the factory is the best place for me and if any girl wants employment I advise them to come to Lowell. Tell Harriet that though she does not hear from me she is not forgotten. I have little time to devote to writing that I cannot write all I want to. There are half a dozen letters which I ought to write to day but I have not time. Tell Harriet I send my love to her and all of the girls. Give my love to Mrs. Clement. Tell Henry this will answer for him and you too for this time.

This from
Mary S Paul

Bela Paul
Henry S Paul

20. Letter to Delia Page.[10]

[Delia Page lived with a foster family, the Trussells, because she did not get along well with her stepmother. In 1859, at age eighteen, she went to work at a textile mill in Manchester, New Hampshire, where she fell in love with a mill worker who had evidently deserted his wife and child in Lowell. When reports of Delia's "affair" reached home, her foster family wrote her urgent letters, trying to persuade Delia to reconsider. Eventually, in 1866, she married an eligible, respectable, single man.]

New London Sept. 7, 1860

Dear Delia,

I should thank you for your very good letter. I am glad to know your health is good. I trust I shall ever feel a deep interest in your welfare.

You say you are not so much in love as we imagine; if so I am very glad of it. Not that I should not be willing you should love a worthy object but the one refered to is no doubt an *unworthy* one; and should you fix you affections on him, it will cause you sorrow such as you never knew; indeed we believe it would be *your ruin*. We have no reason to think, his pretensions notwithstanding, that he has any *real love for you*. Your father Trussell has told or rather written you what he has learned about him. I fear it will be hard for you to believe it, but if you will take the trouble to inquire, I think you will

---

9. A doffer replaces empty bobbins on the spinning frames with full ones.
10. Delia Page's photograph is shown in Source 14.

find it all true. He probably is incapable of even friendship, and in his apparent regard for you, is actuated by *low, base, selfish* motives.

I think you will sooner or later come to this conclusion respecting him. The sooner the better. Your reputation your happines all you hold dear are I fear at stake. You have done well, let not your high hopes be blasted. Do the best you can, keep no company but good and you stand fair to get a good husband, one who has a real regard for you. But if you keep this man's company, the virtuous must shun you. You will not like to read this. My only excuse for writing is that I am very anxious about you. If my anxiety is unfounded so much the better. Unfounded it cannot be if you are keeping the company of an unprincipled libertine.

Your affectionate Mother Trussell

21. Letter to Delia Page.

[Sept. 7 1860]

My Dear Delia,

I am going to trouble you a little longer (I speak for the whole family now). In your situation you must necessarily form many new acquaintance[s] and amongst them there will be not a few who will assure you of their friendship and seek your confidence. The less worthy they are the more earnestly they will seek to convince you of their sincerity. You spoke of one girl whom you highly prised. I hope she is all that you think her to be. If so you are certainly fortunate in making her acquaintance.

But the best have failings & I should hardly expect one of her age a safe counciler in all cases. You must in fact rely upon a principal of morality within your own bosom and if you [are] at a loss you may depend upon the council of Mrs. Piper.[11] A safe way is not to allow yourself to say or do anything that you would not be willing anyone should know if necessary. You will say Humpf think I cant take care of myself. I have seen many who thought so and found their mistake when ruined. My dear girl. We fear much for those we love much, or the fear is in porportion [*sic*] to the Love. And though I have no reason to think that you go out nights or engage in anything that will injure your health or morrals yet the love I have for you leads me to fear lest among so much that is pleasant but evil you may be injured before you are aware of danger.

11. The Pipers were Trussell family friends who lived in Manchester.

And now my Dear Girl I will finish by telling you what you must do for me.

You must take care of my little factory girl. Dont let her expose her health if you do she will be sick and loose [*sic*] all she has earned. Don't let her do any thing any time that she would be ashamed to have her father know. If you do she may loose her charracter. Try to have her improve some every day that she may be the wealthiest most respected & best beloved of all her sisters, brothers & kindred & so be fitted to make the best of husbands the best of wives.

[Luther M Trussell]

QUESTIONS TO CONSIDER

Why did Brownson (Source 1) believe that slaves were better off than free laborers? What did he imply about women who work? What major advantages did Reverend Mills observe in the Lowell system (Source 2)? In what important ways did the system (the factories and the boardinghouses) regulate the girls' lives? How did it protect the morals of its female employees? Of course, not all girls lived up to these standards. What did they do? How were they punished? Do you think Reverend Mills presented a relatively unbiased view? Why or why not? In what ways did the author of the article in *Voice of Industry* (Source 4) believe factory girls were being exploited?

Look carefully at the title page (Source 5) and the first editorial of the *Lowell Offering* (Source 6). What do they tell you about the factory girls, their interests, and their concerns? Was C. B. (Source 7) upholding the cult of true womanhood in her article about the dignity of labor? How did "home" in the boardinghouse (Source 8) differ from the girls' real homes? Based on what you read in Reverend Mills's account, in what ways might a boardinghouse have been similar to the girls' real homes?

The next three letters were written by girls who were rather angry. How did "a factory girl" (Source 9) try to disprove Brownson's view? What fears and anxieties did this letter and the one from Dorothea (Source 10) reveal? What were these two girls trying to prove? The third letter writer (Source 11) retained her sense of humor, but she too was upset. In this case, the offensive remark to which she referred appeared in *Godey's Lady's Book,* the most popular American women's magazine of the period, and was written by the highly respected Sarah Josepha Hale (the magazine's editor and author of "Mary Had a Little Lamb"). What had Mrs. Hale written? What was the factory girl's response? What advice did she give her coworkers about fashion? About being a true woman? Even the "Song of the Spinners" (Source 12) contains a message. What do the lyrics tell you about the spinners' values and attitudes toward work?

What were the other realities of factory girls' lives? What does the bell schedule (Source 3) tell you? How would you describe the image the pictures of the mill girls present (Sources 14 and 15)? What hopes (and fears) did the correspondence between the mill girls and their families (Sources 16 through 21) express? Why did Lucy Larcom (Source 13) have to go to work in the mills when she was so young? How did she feel about the work when she was a child? What contrast did she draw between young boys' and young girls' upbringings in the early nineteenth century? Did she and the other girls always obey the factory rules? What advantages did she discover in her factory experience? What were the disadvantages?

Now that you are thoroughly familiar with the ideas about how the working girls of Lowell were supposed to behave and the realities of the system under which they lived, you are ready to frame an answer to the central question: how did people react when the needs of a modernizing economy came into conflict with the ideas about the women's place in society?

EPILOGUE

The Lowell system was a very real attempt to prevent the spread of the evils associated with the factory system and to make work in the textile mills "respectable" for young New England women. And working conditions in Lowell indeed were considerably better than in most New England mill towns. However, several major strikes (or "turnouts," as they were called) occurred in the Lowell mills in the mid-1830s, and by the mid-1840s Lowell began to experience serious labor problems. To remain competitive yet at the same time maximize profits, companies introduced the "speed up" (a much faster work pace) and the "stretch out" (one worker was put in charge of more machinery—sometimes as many as four looms). The mills also cut wages, even though boardinghouse rents were rising. In Lowell, workers first tried to have the length of the working day reduced and, as did many other American workers, united in support of the Ten-Hour Movement. When women workers joined such protests, they further challenged the ideas embodied in the cult of true womanhood—especially that of submissiveness.

Even before the strikes, the Lowell system was breaking down as more and more mills, far larger than their predecessors, were built. Construction of private housing (especially tenements) expanded, and a much smaller proportion of mill hands lived in boarding-houses. Both housing and neighborhoods became badly overcrowded. By 1850, mill owners were looking for still other ways besides the speed up and stretch out to reduce the cost of labor. They found their answer in the waves of Irish immigrating to America to escape the economic hardships so widespread in their own country. Fewer and fewer "Yankee girls" were recruited for work in the textile mills. At one Lowell company, for example, the number of native-born girls declined from 737 in 1836 to 324 in 1860, although the total number of female workers remained constant. Irish men, women, and increasing numbers of children filled the gap because as wages declined, a family income became a necessity.

By 1860, what Reverend Mills had characterized as "the moral and intellectual advantages" of the Lowell system had come to an end. Indeed, many Americans could see little or no difference between our own factory towns and those of Europe.

CHAPTER EIGHT

THE "PECULIAR INSTITUTION":
SLAVES TELL
THEIR OWN STORY

THE PROBLEM

With the establishment of its new government in 1789, the United States became a virtual magnet for foreign travelers, perhaps never more so than during the three decades immediately preceding our Civil War. Middle to upper class, interested in everything from politics to prison reform to botanical specimens to the position of women in American society, these curious travelers fanned out across the United States, and almost all wrote about their observations in letters, pamphlets, and books widely read on both sides of the ocean. Regardless of their special interests, however, few travelers failed to notice—and comment on—the "peculiar institution" of African American slavery.

As were many nineteenth-century women writers, English author Harriet Martineau was especially interested in those aspects of American society that affected women and children. She was appalled by the slave system, believing it degraded marriage by allowing southern white men to exploit female slaves sexually, a practice that often produced mulatto children born into slavery.

The young Frenchman Alexis de Tocqueville came to study the American penitentiary system and stayed to investigate politics and society. In his book *Democracy in America* (1842), Tocqueville expressed his belief that American slaves had completely lost their African culture—their customs, languages, religions, and even the memories of their countries. An English novelist who was enormously popular in the United States, the crusty Charles Dickens, also visited in 1842. He spent very little time in the South but collected (and published) advertisements for runaway slaves that contained gruesome descriptions

CHAPTER 8

THE "PECULIAR
INSTITUTION":
SLAVES TELL
THEIR OWN
STORY

of their burns, brandings, scars, and iron cuffs and collars. As Dickens departed for a steamboat trip to the West, he wrote that he left "with a grateful heart that I was not doomed to live where slavery was, and had never had my senses blunted to its wrongs and horrors in a slave-rocked cradle."[1]

In the turbulent 1850s, Fredrika Bremer, a Swedish novelist, traveled throughout the United States for two years and spent considerable time in South Carolina, Georgia, and Louisiana. After her first encounters with African Americans in Charleston, Bremer wrote to her sister that "they are ugly, but appear for the most part cheerful and well-fed."[2] Her subsequent trips to the plantations of the backcountry, however, increased her sympathy for slaves and her distrust of white southerners' assertions that "slaves are the happiest people in the world."[3] In fact, by the end of her stay, Bremer was praising the slaves' morality, patience, talents, and religious practices.

These travelers—and many more—added their opinions to the growing literature about the nature of American slavery and its effects. But the overwhelming majority of this literature was written by white people. What did the slaves themselves think? How did they express their feelings about the peculiar institution of slavery?

BACKGROUND

By the time of the American Revolution, what had begun in 1619 as a trickle of Africans intended to supplement the farm labor of indentured servants from England had swelled to a slave population of approximately 500,000 people, the majority concentrated on tobacco, rice, and cotton plantations in the South. Moreover, as the African American population grew, what apparently had been a fairly loose and unregimented labor system gradually evolved into an increasingly harsh, rigid, and complete system of chattel slavery that tried to control nearly every aspect of the slaves' lives. By 1775, African American slavery had become a significant (some would have said indispensable) part of southern life.

The American Revolution did not reverse those trends. Although northern states in which African American slavery was not so deeply rooted began instituting gradual emancipation, after the Revolution, the slave system—as well as its harshness—increased in the South. The invention of the cotton gin, which enabled seeds to be removed

1. Charles Dickens, *American Notes and Pictures from Italy* (London: Oxford University Press, 1957), p. 137.
2. Fredrika Bremer, *America of the Fifties: Letters of Fredrika Bremer,* ed. Adolph B. Benson (New York: American Scandinavian Foundation, 1924), p. 96.
3. Ibid., p. 100.

from the easily grown short staple cotton, permitted southerners to cultivate cotton on the uplands, thereby spurring the westward movement of the plantation system and slavery. As a result, slavery expanded along with settlement into nearly every area of the South: the Gulf region, Tennessee, Kentucky, and ultimately Texas. Simultaneously, the slave population burgeoned, roughly doubling every 30 years (from approximately 700,000 in 1790 to 1.5 million in 1820 to more than 3.2 million in 1850). Because importation of slaves from Africa was banned in 1808 (although there was some illegal slave smuggling), most further gains in the slave population were from natural increase.

But as the slave population grew, the fears and anxieties of southern whites grew correspondingly. In 1793, a slave rebellion in the Caribbean caused tremendous consternation in the white South. Rumors of uprisings plotted by slaves were numerous. And the actual rebellion of Nat Turner in Virginia in 1831 (in which fifty-five whites were killed, many of them while asleep) only increased white insecurities and dread. In response, southern states passed a series of laws that made the system of slavery even more restrictive. Toward the end of his life, Thomas Jefferson (who did not live to see Nat Turner's uprising) agonized:

> But as it is, we have the wolf by the ears, and we can neither hold him, nor safely let him go. Justice is in one scale, and self-preservation in the other. . . . I regret that I am now to die in the belief, that the useless sacrifice of themselves by the generation of

1776, to acquire self-government and happiness to their country, is to be thrown away by the unwise and unworthy passions of their sons. . . .

By this time, however, Jefferson was nearly alone among white southerners. Most did not question the assertions that slavery was a necessity, that it was good for both the slave and the owner, and that it must be preserved at any cost.

It often has been pointed out that the majority of white southerners did not own slaves. In fact, the proportion of white southern families who did own slaves was actually declining in the nineteenth century, from one-third in 1830 to roughly one-fourth by 1860. Moreover, nearly three-fourths of these slaveholders owned fewer than ten slaves. Slaveholders, then, were a distinct minority of the white southern population, and those slaveholders with large plantations and hundreds of slaves were an exceedingly small group.

How, then, did the peculiar institution of slavery, as one southerner called it, become so imbedded in the Old South? First, even though only a minority of southern whites owned slaves, nearly all southern whites were somehow touched by the institution of slavery. Fear of black uprisings prompted many nonslaveholders to support an increasingly rigid slave system that included night patrols, written passes for slaves away from plantations, supervised religious services for slaves, a law prohibiting teaching slaves to read or write, and other measures to keep slaves ignorant, dependent, and always under the eyes of whites. Too, many nonslave-

CHAPTER 8

THE "PECULIAR
INSTITUTION":
SLAVES TELL
THEIR OWN
STORY

owners were afraid that emancipation would bring them into direct economic competition with blacks, who, it was assumed, would drive down wages. Finally, although large planters represented only a fraction of the white population, they virtually controlled the economic, social, and political institutions and were not about to injure either themselves or their status by eliminating the slave system that essentially supported them.

To defend their peculiar institution, white southerners constructed a remarkably complete and diverse set of arguments. Slavery, they maintained, was actually a far more humane system than northern capitalism. After all, slaves were fed, clothed, sheltered, cared for when they were ill, and supported in their old age, whereas northern factory workers were paid pitifully low wages, used, and then discarded when no longer useful. Furthermore, many white southerners maintained that slavery was a positive good because it had introduced the "barbarous" Africans to civilized American ways and, more importantly, to Christianity. Other southern whites stressed what they believed was the childlike, dependent nature of African Americans, insisting that they could never cope with life outside the paternalistic and "benevolent" institution of slavery. In such an atmosphere, in which many of the white southern intellectual efforts went into the defense of slavery, dissent and freedom of thought were not welcome. Hence those white southerners who disagreed and might have challenged the South's dependence on slavery remained silent, were hushed up, or decided to leave the section. In many

ways, then, the enslavement of African Americans partly rested on the limitation of rights and freedoms for southern whites as well.

But how did the slaves react to an economic and social system that meant that neither they nor their children would ever experience freedom? Most white southerners assumed that slaves were happy and content. Northern abolitionists (a minority of the white population) believed that slaves continually yearned for freedom. Both groups used oceans of ink to justify and support their claims. But evidence of how the slaves felt and thought is woefully sparse. And, given the restrictive nature of the slave system (which included enforced illiteracy among slaves), this pitiful lack of evidence is hardly surprising.

How then can we learn how slaves felt and thought about the peculiar institution? Slave uprisings were almost nonexistent, but does that mean most slaves were happy with their lot? Runaways were common, and some, such as Frederick Douglass and Harriet Jacobs, actually reached the North and wrote about their experiences as slaves. Yet how typical were their experiences? Most slaves were born and then lived and died in servitude, did not participate in organized revolts, and did not run away. How did they feel about the system of slavery?

Although most slaves did not read or write, did not participate in organized revolts, and did not attempt to run away, they did leave a remarkable amount of evidence that can help us understand their thoughts and feelings. Yet we must be imaginative in how we approach and use that evidence.

In an earlier chapter, you discovered that statistical information (about births, deaths, age at marriage, farm size, inheritance, tax rolls, and so forth) can reveal a great deal about ordinary people, such as the New Englanders on the eve of the American Revolution. Such demographic evidence can help the historian form a picture of who these people were and the socioeconomic trends of the time, even if the people themselves were not aware of those trends. In this exercise, you will be using another kind of evidence and asking different questions. Your evidence will not come from white southerners (whose stake in maintaining slavery was enormous), foreign travelers (whose own cultural biases often influenced what they reported), or even white abolitionists in the North (whose urgent need to eradicate the "sin" of slavery sometimes led them to gross exaggerations for propaganda purposes). You will be using anecdotes, stories, and songs from the rich oral tradition of African American slaves, supplemented by the narratives of two runaway slaves, to investigate the human dimensions of the peculiar institution.

Some of the oral evidence was collected and transcribed by people soon after emancipation. However, much of the evidence did not come to light until many years later, when the former slaves who were still alive were very old men and women. In fact, not until the 1920s did concerted efforts to preserve the reminiscences of these people begin. In the 1920s, Fisk University collected a good deal of evidence. In the 1930s, the government-financed Federal Writers' Project accumulated more than two thousand narratives from ex-slaves in every southern state except Louisiana and deposited them in the Library of Congress in Washington, D.C.

Much of the evidence, however, is in the form of slave songs and stories that slaves created and told to one another. Like the narratives of former slaves, these sources also must be used with imagination and care.

The central question you are to answer is: how did the slaves themselves view the peculiar institution? How did they endure under a labor system that, at its very best, was still based on the total ownership of one human being by another?

THE METHOD

Historians must always try to be aware of the limitations of their evidence. In the Federal Writers' Project, most of the former slaves were in their eighties or nineties (quite a few were older than a hundred) at the time they were interviewed. In other words,

most of the interviewees had been children or young people in 1860. It is also important to know that although some of the interviewers were black, the overwhelming majority were white. Lastly, although many of the former slaves had moved to another location

[185]

CHAPTER 8

THE "PECULIAR
INSTITUTION":
SLAVES TELL
THEIR OWN
STORY

or a different state after the Civil War, many others were still living in the same county (sometimes even on the same land) where they had been slaves. In what ways might the age of the former slave, the race of the interviewer, or the place where the former slave was living affect the narratives?

These narratives reveal much about these people's thoughts and feelings about slavery. What direct reactions did the ex-slaves give? Why did many of them choose to be indirect? Some chose to answer questions by telling stories. Why? And remember, although some of the stories or anecdotes may not actually be true, they can be taken as representative of what the former slaves wished had actually happened or what they really thought about an incident. Therefore, often you must pull the true meaning from a narrative, inferring what the interviewee meant as well as what he or she said.

As to slaves' songs and other contemporary evidence, most slaves could never have spoken their thoughts or vented their feelings directly; instead they often hid their true meanings through the use of symbols, metaphors, and allegories. Here again, you must be able to read between the lines, extracting thoughts, attitudes, and feelings that were purposely hidden or concealed from all but other slaves.

Included in the evidence are two accounts of runaway slaves who escaped to the North before the Civil War. Frederick Bailey (who later changed his name to Douglass) ran away when he was about nineteen years old, but he was captured and returned. Two years later, he was able to escape, and he moved to Massachusetts, where he worked as a laborer. After joining an antislavery society and becoming a successful speaker, he published his autobiography (1845) and edited his own abolitionist newspaper, the *North Star*. Harriet Jacobs (who used the pen name Linda Brent) was twenty-seven years old when she ran away in 1845, but her narrative was not published until the beginning of the Civil War. Throughout her story, Jacobs used fictitious names and places to protect those who had helped her and to conceal the escape route she had used. Both Douglass and Jacobs were self-educated people who wrote their own books, although the abolitionist writer Lydia Maria Child made minor editorial revisions in Jacobs's manuscript.

As you examine each piece of evidence, jot down enough notes to allow you to recall that piece of evidence later. But also (perhaps in a separate column) write down what you consider the *attitude* each piece of evidence communicates about the peculiar institution of slavery. What is the hidden message?

After you have examined each piece of evidence, look back over the notes you made. What attitudes about slavery stand out? What did the slaves think about the slave system?

THE EVIDENCE

Sources 1 through 16 from B. A. Botkin, Federal Writers' Project, *Lay My Burden Down: A Folk History of Slavery* (Chicago: University of Chicago Press, 1945).

1. Hog-Killing Time.

. . . I remember Mammy told me about one master who almost starved his slaves. Mighty stingy, I reckon he was.

Some of them slaves was so poorly thin they ribs would kinda rustle against each other like corn stalks a-drying in the hot winds. But they gets even one hog-killing time, and it was funny, too, Mammy said.

They was seven hogs, fat and ready for fall hog-killing time. Just the day before Old Master told off they was to be killed, something happened to all them porkers. One of the field boys found them and come a-telling the master: "The hogs is all died, now they won't be any meats for the winter."

When the master gets to where at the hogs is laying, they's a lot of Negroes standing round looking sorrow-eyed at the wasted meat. The master asks: "What's the illness with 'em?"

"Malitis," they tells him, and they acts like they don't want to touch the hogs. Master says to dress them anyway for they ain't no more meat on the place.

He says to keep all the meat for the slave families, but that's because he's afraid to eat it hisself account of the hogs' got malitis.

"Don't you all know what is malitis?" Mammy would ask the children when she was telling of the seven fat hogs and seventy lean slaves. And she would laugh, remembering how they fooled Old Master so's to get all them good meats.

"One of the strongest Negroes got up early in the morning," Mammy would explain, "long 'fore the rising horn called the slaves from their cabins. He skitted to the hog pen with a heavy mallet in his hand. When he tapped Mister Hog 'tween the eyes with the mallet, 'malitis' set in mighty quick, but it was a uncommon 'disease,' even with hungry Negroes around all the time."

2. The Old Parrot.

The mistress had an old parrot, and one day I was in the kitchen making cookies, and I decided I wanted some of them, so I tooks me out some and put them on a chair; and when I did this the mistress entered the door. I

CHAPTER 8

THE "PECULIAR
INSTITUTION":
SLAVES TELL
THEIR OWN
STORY

picks up a cushion and throws [it] over the pile of cookies on the chair, and Mistress came near the chair and the old parrot cries out, "Mistress burn, Mistress burn." Then the mistress looks under the cushion, and she had me whupped, but the next day I killed the parrot, and she often wondered who or what killed the bird.

3. The Coon and the Dog.

Every time I think of slavery and if it done the race any good, I think of the story of the coon and dog who met. The coon said to the dog, "Why is it you're so fat and I am so poor, and we is both animals?" The dog said: "I lay round Master's house and let him kick me and he gives me a piece of bread right on." Said the coon to the dog: "Better, then, that I stay poor." Them's my sentiment. I'm like the coon, I don't believe in 'buse.

4. The Partridge and the Fox.

. . . A partridge and a fox 'greed to kill a beef. They kilt and skinned it. Before they divide it, the fox said, "My wife says send her some beef for soup." So he took a piece of it and carried it down the hill, then come back and said, "My wife wants more beef for soup." He kept this up till all the beef was gone 'cept the liver. The fox come back, and the partridge says, "Now let's cook this liver and both of us eat it." The partridge cooked the liver, et its parts right quick, and then fell over like it was sick. The fox got scared and said that beef is pizen, and he ran down the hill and started bringing the beef back. And when he brought it all back, he left, and the partridge had all the beef.

5. The Rabbit and the Tortoise.

I want to tell you one story 'bout the rabbit. The rabbit and the tortoise had a race. The tortoise git a lot of tortoises and put 'em 'long the way. Ever' now and then a tortoise crawl 'long the way, and the rabbit say, "How you now, Br'er Tortoise?" And he say, "Slow and sure, but my legs very short." When they git tired, the tortoise win 'cause he there, but he never run the race, 'cause he had tortoises strowed out all 'long the way. The tortoise had other tortoises help him.

6. Same Old Thing.

The niggers didn't go to the church building; the preacher came and preached to them in their quarters. He'd just say, "Serve your masters. Don't steal your master's turkey. Don't steal your master's chickens. Don't steal your master's hogs. Don't steal your master's meat. Do whatsomever your master tells you to do." Same old thing all the time.

7. Freedom.

I been preaching the gospel and farming since slavery time. I jined the church 'most 83 years ago when I was Major Gaud's slave, and they baptizes me in the spring branch close to where I finds the Lord. When I starts preaching I couldn't read or write and had to preach what Master told me, and he say tell them niggers iffen they obeys the master they goes to Heaven; but I knowed there's something better for them, but daren't tell them 'cept on the sly. That I done lots. I tells 'em iffen they keeps praying, the Lord will set 'em free.

8. Prayers.

My master used to ask us children, "Do your folks pray at night?" We said "No," 'cause our folks had told us what to say. But the Lord have mercy, there was plenty of that going on. They'd pray, "Lord, deliver us from under bondage."

9. Hoodoo Doctor.

My wife was sick, down, couldn't do nothing. Someone got to telling her about Cain Robertson. Cain Robertson was a hoodoo doctor in Georgia. They [say] there wasn't nothing Cain couldn't do. She says, "Go and see Cain and have him come up here."

I says, "There ain't no use to send for Cain. Cain ain't coming up here because they say he is a 'two-head' nigger." (They called all them hoodoo men "two-head" niggers; I don't know why they called them two-head). "And you know he knows the white folks will put him in jail if he comes to town."

But she says, "You go and get him."

So I went.

I left him at the house, and when I came back in, he said, "I looked at your wife and she had one of them spells while I was there. I'm afraid to

CHAPTER 8

THE "PECULIAR
INSTITUTION":
SLAVES TELL
THEIR OWN
STORY

tackle this thing because she has been poisoned, and it's been going on a long time. And if she dies, they'll say I killed her, and they already don't like me and looking for an excuse to do something to me."

My wife overheard him and says, "You go on, you got to do something."

So he made me go to town and get a pint of corn whiskey. When I brought it back he drunk a half of it at one gulp, and I started to knock him down. I'd thought he'd get drunk with my wife lying there sick.

Then he said, "I'll have to see your wife's stomach." Then he scratched it, and put three little horns on the place he scratched. Then he took another drink of whiskey and waited about ten minutes. When he took them off her stomach, they were full of blood. He put them in the basin in some water and sprinkled some powder on them, and in about ten minutes more he made me get them and they were full of clear water and there was a lot of little things that looked like wiggle tails swimming around it.

He told me when my wife got well to walk in a certain direction a certain distance, and the woman that caused all the trouble would come to my house and start a fuss with me.

I said, "Can't you put this same thing back on her?"

He said, "Yes, but it would kill my hand. He meant that he had a curing hand and that if he made anybody sick or killed them, all his power to cure would go from him.

I showed the stuff he took out of my wife's stomach to old Doc Matthews, and he said, "You can get anything into a person by putting it in them." He asked me how I found out about it, and how it was taken out, and who did it.

I told him all about it, and he said, "I'm going to see that that nigger practices anywhere in this town he wants to and nobody bothers him." And he did.

10. Buck Brasefield.

They was pretty good to us, but old Mr. Buck Brasefield, what had a plantation 'jining us'n, was so mean to his'n that 'twa'n't nothing for 'em to run away. One nigger, Rich Parker, runned off one time, and whilst he gone he seed a hoodoo man, so when he got back Mr. Brasefield took sick and stayed sick two or three weeks. Some of the darkies told him, "Rich been to the hoodoo doctor." So Mr. Brasefield got up outen that bed and come a-yelling in the field, "You thought you had old Buck, but by God he rose again." Them niggers was so scared they squatted in the field just like partridges, and some of 'em whispered, "I wish to God he had-a died."

11. The White Lady's Quilts.

Now I'll tell you another incident. This was in slave times. My mother was a great hand for nice quilts. There was a white lady had died, and they were going to have a sale. Now this is true stuff. They had the sale, and Mother went and bought two quilts. And let me tell you, we couldn't sleep under 'em. What happened? Well, they'd pinch your toes till you couldn't stand it. I was just a boy and I was sleeping with my mother when it happened. Now that's straight stuff. What do I think was the cause? Well, I think that white lady didn't want no nigger to have them quilts. I don't know what Mother did with 'em, but that white lady just wouldn't let her have 'em.

12. Papa's Death.

My papa was strong. He never had a licking in his life. He helped the master, but one day the master says, "Si, you got to have a whopping," and my poppa says, "I never had a whopping and you can't whop me." And the master says, "But I can kill you," and he shot my papa down. My mama took him in the cabin and put him on a pallet. He died.

13. Forbidden Knowledge.

None of us was 'lowed to see a book or try to learn. They say we git smarter than they was if we learn anything, but we slips around and gits hold of that Webster's old blue-back speller and we hides it till 'way in the night and then we lights a little pine torch, and studies that spelling book. We learn it too. I can read some now and write a little too.

They wasn't no church for the slaves, but we goes to the white folks' arbor on Sunday evening, and a white man he gits up there to preach to the niggers. He say, "Now I takes my text, which is, Nigger obey your master and your mistress, 'cause what you git from them here in this world am all you ever going to git, 'cause you just like the hogs and the other animals—when you dies you ain't no more, after you been throwed in that hole." I guess we believed that for a while 'cause we didn't have no way finding out different. We didn't see no Bibles.

14. Broken Families.

I seen children sold off and the mammy not sold, and sometimes the mammy sold and a little baby kept on the place and give to another woman to raise.

CHAPTER 8

THE "PECULIAR
INSTITUTION":
SLAVES TELL
THEIR OWN
STORY

Them white folks didn't care nothing 'bout how the slaves grieved when they tore up a family.

15. Burning in Hell.

We was scared of Solomon and his whip, though, and he didn't like frolicking. He didn't like for us niggers to pray, either. We never heard of no church, but us have praying in the cabins. We'd set on the floor and pray with our heads down low and sing low, but if Solomon heared he'd come and beat on the wall with the stock of his whip. He'd say, "I'll come in there and tear the hide off you backs." But some the old niggers tell us we got to pray to God that He don't think different of the blacks and the whites. I know that Solomon is burning in hell today, and it pleasures me to know it.

16. Marriage.

After while I taken a notion to marry and Massa and Missy marries us same as all the niggers. They stands inside the house with a broom held crosswise of the door and we stands outside. Missy puts a little wreath on my head they kept there, and we steps over the broom into the house. Now, that's all they was to the marrying. After freedom I gits married and has it put in the book by a preacher.

Sources 17 and 18 from Gilbert Osofsky, compiler, *Puttin' on Ole Massa* (New York: Harper & Row, 1969), p. 22.

17. Pompey.

Pompey, how do I look?
O, massa, mighty.
What do you mean "mighty," Pompey?
Why, massa, you look noble.
What do you mean by "noble"?
Why, sar, you just look like one *lion*.
Why, Pompey, where have you ever seen a lion?
I see one down in yonder field the other day, massa.
Pompey, you foolish fellow, that was a *jackass*.
Was it, massa? Well you look just like him.

18. A Grave for Old Master.

Two slaves were sent out to dig a grave for old master. They dug it very deep. As I passed by I asked Jess and Bob what in the world they dug it so deep for. It was down six or seven feet. I told them there would be a fuss about it, and they had better fill it up some. Jess said it suited him exactly. Bob said he would not fill it up; he wanted to get the old man as near *home* as possible. When we got a stone to put on his grave, we hauled the largest we could find, so as to fasten him down as strong as possible.

Sources of songs 19 through 21 from Lawrence W. Levine, "Slave Songs and Slave Consciousness: An Exploration in Neglected Sources," in *Anonymous Americans: Explorations in Nineteenth Century Social History,* ed. Tamara K. Hareven (Englewood Cliffs, N.J.: Prentice-Hall, 1971).

19.

We raise de wheat,
Dey gib us de corn;
We bake de bread,
Dey gib us de crust;
We sif de meal,
Dey gib us de huss;
We [peel] de meat,
Dey gib us de skin;
And dat's de way
Dey take us in;
We skim de pot,
Dey gib us de liquor,
And say dat's good enough for nigger.

20.

My ole Mistiss promise me,
W'en she died, she'd set me free,
She lived so long dat 'er head got bal',
An' she give out'n de notion a dyin' at all.

CHAPTER 8

THE "PECULIAR
INSTITUTION":
SLAVES TELL
THEIR OWN
STORY

21.

He delivered Daniel from the lion's den,
Jonah from de belly ob de whale,
And de Hebrew children from de fiery furnace,
And why not every man?

Sources of songs 22 and 23 from Sterling Stuckey, "Through the Prism of Folklore: The Black Ethos in Slavery," *Massachusetts Review,* 1968.

22.

When I get to heaven, gwine be at ease,
Me and my God gonna do as we please.
Gonna chatter with the Father, argue with the Son,
Tell um 'bout the world I just come from.

23.

[a song about Samson and Deliah]

He said, 'An' if I had-'n my way,'
He said, 'An' if I had-'n my way,'
He said, 'An' if I had-'n my way,
I'd tear the build-in' down!'

Source 24 from Frederick Douglass, *Narrative of the Life of Frederick Douglass* (New York: Anchor Books, Doubleday, 1963), pp. 1–3, 13–15, 36–37, 40–41, 44–46, 74–75.

24. Autobiography of Frederick Douglass.

I was born in Tuckahoe, near Hillsborough, and about twelve miles from Easton, in Talbot county, Maryland. I have no accurate knowledge of my age, never having seen any authentic record containing it. By far the larger part of the slaves know as little of their ages as horses know of theirs, and it is the wish of most masters within my knowledge to keep their slaves thus ignorant. I do not remember to have ever met a slave who could tell of his birthday. They seldom come nearer to it than planting-time, harvesting time, cherry-time, spring-time, or fall-time. A want of information concerning my own was a source of unhappiness to me even during childhood. The white children could tell their ages. I could not tell why I ought to be deprived of the same privilege. I was not allowed to make any inquiries of my master concerning it. He deemed all such inquiries on the part of a slave improper and impertinent, and evidence of a restless spirit. The nearest estimate I can give makes me now between twenty-seven and twenty-eight years of age. I come to this, from hearing my master say, some time during 1835, I was about seventeen years old.

My mother was named Harriet Bailey. She was the daughter of Isaac and Betsey Bailey, both colored, and quite dark. My mother was of a darker complexion than either my grandmother or grandfather.

My father was a white man. He was admitted to be such by all I ever heard speak of my parentage. The opinion was also whispered that my master was my father; but of the correctness of this opinion, I know nothing; the means of knowing was withheld from me. My mother and I were separated when I was but an infant—before I knew her as my mother. It is a common custom, in the part of Maryland from which I ran away, to part children from their mothers at a very early age. . . .

I never saw my mother, to know her as such, more than four or five times in my life; and each of these times was very short in duration, and at night. She was hired by a Mr. Stewart, who lived about twelve miles from my home. She made her journeys to see me in the night, travelling the whole distance on foot, after the performance of her day's work. She was a field hand, and a whipping is the penalty of not being in the field at sunrise, unless a slave has special permission from his or her master to the contrary—a permission which they seldom get, and one that gives to him that gives it the proud name of being a kind master. I do not recollect of ever seeing my mother by the light of day. She was with me in the night. She would lie down with me, and get me to sleep, but long before I waked she was gone. Very little communication ever took place between us. Death soon ended what little we could have while she lived, and with it her hardships and suffering. She died when I was about seven years old, on one of my master's farms, near Lee's Mill. I was not allowed to be present during her illness, at her death, or burial. She was gone long before I knew any thing about it. Never having enjoyed, to any considerable extent, her soothing presence, her tender and watchful care, I received the tidings of her death with much the same emotions I should have probably felt at the death of a stranger. . . .

The slaves selected to go to the Great House Farm,[4] for the monthly allowance for themselves and their fellow-slaves, were peculiarly enthusiastic.

4. Great House Farm was the huge "home plantation" that belonged to Douglass's owner.

CHAPTER 8

THE "PECULIAR
INSTITUTION":
SLAVES TELL
THEIR OWN
STORY

While on their way, they would make the dense old woods, for miles around, reverberate with their wild songs, revealing at once the highest joy and the deepest sadness. They would compose and sing as they went along, consulting neither time nor tune. The thought that came up, came out—if not in the word, in the sound;—and as frequently in the one as in the other. . . .

I did not, when a slave, understand the deep meaning of those rude and apparently incoherent songs. I was myself within the circle; so that I neither saw nor heard as those without might see and hear. They told a tale of woe which was then altogether beyond my feeble comprehension; they were tones loud, long, and deep; they breathed the prayer and complaint of souls boiling over with the bitterest anguish. Every tone was a testimony against slavery, and a prayer to God for deliverance from chains.

I have often been utterly astonished, since I came to the north, to find persons who could speak of the singing, among slaves, as evidence of their contentment and happiness. It is impossible to conceive of a greater mistake. Slaves sing most when they are most unhappy. The songs of the slave represent the sorrows of his heart; and he is relieved by them, only as an aching heart is relieved by its tears. At least, such is my experience. I have often sung to drown my sorrow, but seldom to express my happiness. Crying for joy, and singing for joy, were alike uncommon to me while in the jaws of slavery. . . .

[Douglass was hired out as a young boy and went to live in the city of Baltimore.]

Very soon after I went to live with Mr. and Mrs. Auld, she very kindly commenced to teach me the A, B, C. After I had learned this, she assisted me in learning to spell words of three or four letters. Just at this point of my progress, Mr. Auld found out what was going on, and at once forbade Mrs. Auld to instruct me further, telling her, among other things, that it was unlawful, as well as unsafe, to teach a slave to read. To use his own words, further, he said, "If you give a nigger an inch, he will take an ell.[5] A nigger should know nothing but to obey his master—to do as he is told to do. Learning would *spoil* the best nigger in the world. Now," said he, "if you teach that nigger (speaking of myself) how to read, there would be no keeping him. It would forever unfit him to be a slave. He would at once become unmanageable, and of no value to his master. As to himself, it could do him no good, but a great deal of harm. It would make him discontented and unhappy." These words sank deep into my heart, stirred up sentiments within that lay slumbering, and called into existence an entirely new train

5. An ell was an English unit of measure for cloth, approximately forty-five inches.

of thought. It was a new and special revelation, explaining dark and mysterious things, with which my youthful understanding had struggled, but struggled in vain. I now understood what had been to me a most perplexing difficulty—to wit, the white man's power to enslave the black man. It was a grand achievement, and I prized it highly. From that moment, I understood the pathway from slavery to freedom. It was just what I wanted, and I got it at a time when I the least expected it. Whilst I was saddened by the thought of losing the aid of my kind mistress, I was gladdened by the invaluable instruction which, by the merest accident, I had gained from my master. Though conscious of the difficulty of learning without a teacher, I set out with high hope, and a fixed purpose, at whatever cost of trouble, to learn how to read. The very decided manner with which he spoke, and strove to impress his wife with the evil consequences of giving me instruction, served to convince me that he was deeply sensible of the truths he was uttering. It gave me the best assurance that I might rely with the utmost confidence on the results which, he said, would flow from teaching me to read. . . .

The plan which I adopted, and the one by which I was most successful, was that of making friends of all the little white boys whom I met in the street. As many of these as I could, I converted into teachers. With their kindly aid, obtained at different times and in different places, I finally succeeded in learning to read. When I was sent of errands, I always took my book with me, and by going one part of my errand quickly, I found time to get a lesson before my return. I used also to carry bread with me, enough of which was always in the house, and to which I was always welcome; for I was much better off in this regard than many of the poor white children in our neighborhood. This bread I used to bestow upon hungry little urchins, who, in return, would give me that more valuable bread of knowledge. I am strongly tempted to give the names of two or three of those little boys, as a testimonial of the gratitude and affection I bear them; but prudence forbids;—not that it would injure me, but it might embarrass them; for it is almost an unpardonable offence to teach slaves to read in this Christian country. . . .

I was now about twelve years old, and the thought of being a *slave for life* began to bear heavily upon my heart. . . . After a patient waiting, I got one of our city papers, containing an account of the number of petitions from the north, praying for the abolition of slavery in the District of Columbia, and of the slave trade between the States. From this time I understood the words *abolition* and *abolitionist,* and always drew near when that word was spoken, expecting to hear something of importance to myself and fellow-slaves.

CHAPTER 8

THE "PECULIAR
INSTITUTION":
SLAVES TELL
THEIR OWN
STORY

The light broke in upon me by degrees. I went one day down on the wharf of Mr. Waters; and seeing two Irishmen unloading a scow of stone, I went, unasked, and helped them. When we had finished, one of them came to me and asked me if I were a slave. I told him I was. He asked, "Are ye a slave for life?" I told him that I was. The good Irishman seemed to be deeply affected by the statement. He said to the other that it was a pity so fine a little fellow as myself should be a slave for life. He said it was a shame to hold me. They both advised me to run away to the north; that I should find friends there, and that I should be free. I pretended not to be interested in what they said, and treated them as if I did not understand them; for I feared they might be treacherous. White men have been known to encourage slaves to escape, and then, to get the reward, catch them and return them to their masters. I was afraid that these seemingly good men might use me so; but I nevertheless remembered their advice, and from that time I resolved to run away. I looked forward to a time at which it would be safe for me to escape. I was too young to think of doing so immediately; besides, I wished to learn how to write, as I might have occasion to write my own pass.[6] I consoled myself with the hope that I should one day find a good chance. Meanwhile, I would learn to write.

The idea as to how I might learn to write was suggested to me by being in Durgin and Bailey's ship-yard, and frequently seeing the ship carpenters, after hewing, and getting a piece of timber ready for use, write on the timber the name of that part of the ship for which it was intended. When a piece of timber was intended for the larboard side, it would be marked thus—"L." When a piece was for the starboard side, it would be marked thus—"S." A piece for the larboard side forward, would be marked thus—"L. F." When a piece was for starboard side forward, it would be marked thus—"S. F." For larboard aft, it would be marked thus—"L. A." For starboard aft, it would be marked thus—"S. A." I soon learned the names of these letters, and for what they were intended when placed upon a piece of timber in the ship-yard. I immediately commenced copying them, and in a short time was able to make the four letters named. After that, when I met with any boy who I knew could write, I would tell him I could write as well as he. The next word would be, "I don't believe you. Let me see you try it." I would then make the letters which I had been so fortunate as to learn, and ask him to beat that. In this way I got a good many lessons in writing, which it is quite possible I should never have gotten in any other way. During this time, my copy-

6. In many areas, slaves were required to carry written passes, stating that they had permission from their owners to travel to a certain place.

book was the board fence, brick wall, and pavement; my pen and ink was a lump of chalk. With these, I learned mainly how to write. I then commenced and continued copying the Italics in Webster's Spelling Book, until I could make them all without looking on the book. By this time, my little Master Thomas had gone to school, and learned how to write, and had written over a number of copy-books. These had been brought home, and shown to some of our near neighbors, and then laid aside. My mistress used to go to class meeting at the Wilk Street meetinghouse every Monday afternoon, and leave me to take care of the house. When left thus, I used to spend the time in writing in the spaces left in Master Thomas's copy-book, copying what he had written. I continued to do this until I could write a hand very similar to that of Master Thomas. Thus, after a long, tedious effort for years, I finally succeeded in learning how to write. . . .

[After the death of his owner, Douglass was recalled to the plantation and put to work as a field hand. Because of his rebellious attitude, he was then sent to work for a notorious "slave-breaker" named Covey. When Covey tried to whip Douglass, who was then about sixteen years old, Douglass fought back.]

We were at it for nearly two hours. Covey at length let me go, puffing and blowing at a great rate, saying that if I had not resisted, he would not have whipped me half so much. The truth was, that he had not whipped me at all. I considered him as getting entirely the worst end of the bargain; for he had drawn no blood from me, but I had from him. The whole six months afterwards, that I spent with Mr. Covey, he never laid the weight of his finger upon me in anger. He would occasionally say, he didn't want to get hold of me again. "No," thought I, "you need not; for you will come off worse than you did before."

This battle with Mr. Covey was the turning point in my career as a slave. It rekindled the few expiring embers of freedom, and revived within me a sense of my own manhood. It recalled the departed self-confidence, and in-spired me again with a determination to be free. The gratification afforded by the triumph was a full compensation for whatever else might follow, even death itself. He only can understand the deep satisfaction which I experi-enced, who has himself repelled by force the bloody arm of slavery. I felt as I never felt before. It was a glorious resurrection, from the tomb of slavery, to the heaven of freedom. My long-crushed spirit rose, cowardice departed, bold defiance took its place; and I now resolved that, however long I might remain a slave in form, the day had passed forever when I could be a slave in fact. I did not hesitate to let it be known of me, that the white man who expected to succeed in whipping, must also succeed in killing me.

CHAPTER 8

THE "PECULIAR
INSTITUTION":
SLAVES TELL
THEIR OWN
STORY

From this time I was never again what might be called fairly whipped, though I remained a slave four years afterwards. I had several fights, but was never whipped.

It was for a long time a matter of surprise to me why Mr. Covey did not immediately have me taken by the constable to the whipping-post, and there regularly whipped for the crime of raising my hand against a white man in defence of myself. And the only explanation I can now think of does not entirely satisfy me; but such as it is, I will give it. Mr. Covey enjoyed the most unbounded reputation for being a first-rate overseer and negro-breaker. It was of considerable importance to him. That reputation was at stake; and had he sent me—a boy about sixteen years old—to the public whipping-post, his reputation would have been lost; so, to save his reputation, he suffered me to go unpunished. . . .

[During the Civil War, Douglass actively recruited African American soldiers for the Union, and he worked steadfastly after the war for African American civil rights. Douglass also held a series of federal jobs that culminated in his appointment as the U.S. minister to Haiti in 1888. He died in 1895 at the age of seventy-eight.]

Source 25 from Linda Brent, *Incidents in the Life of a Slave Girl* (New York: Harcourt Brace Jovanovich, 1973), pp. xiii–xiv, 7, 9–10, 26–28, 48–49, 54–55, 179, 201–203, 207.

25. Autobiography of Linda Brent (Harriet Jacobs).

I wish I were more competent to the task I have undertaken. But I trust my readers will excuse deficiencies in consideration of circumstances. I was born and reared in Slavery; and I remained in a Slave State twenty-seven years. Since I have been at the North, it has been necessary for me to work diligently for my own support, and the education of my children. This has not left me much leisure to make up for the loss of early opportunities to improve myself; and it has compelled me to write these pages at irregular intervals, whenever I could snatch an hour from household duties.

When I first arrived in Philadelphia, Bishop Paine advised me to publish a sketch of my life, but I told him I was altogether incompetent to such an undertaking. Though I have improved my mind somewhat since that time, I still remain of the same opinion; but I trust my motives will excuse what might otherwise seem presumptuous. I have not written my experiences in order to attract attention to myself; on the contrary, it would have been more pleasant to me to have been silent about my own history. Neither do I care to excite sympathy for my own sufferings. But I do earnestly desire to arouse the women of the North to a realizing sense of the condition of two millions of women at the South, still in bondage, suffering what I suffered, and most of them far worse. I want to add my testimony to that of abler pens to convince the people of the Free States what Slavery really is. Only by experience can any one realize how deep, and dark, and foul is that pit of abominations. May the blessing of God rest on this imperfect effort in behalf of my persecuted people!

I was born a slave; but I never knew it till six years of happy childhood had passed away. My father was a carpenter, and considered so intelligent and skilful in his trade, that when buildings out of the common line were to be erected, he was sent for from long distances, to be head workman. On condition of paying his mistress two hundred dollars a year, and supporting himself, he was allowed to work at his trade, and manage his own affairs. His strongest wish was to purchase his children; but, though he several times offered his hard earnings for that purpose, he never succeeded. In complexion my parents were a light shade of brownish yellow, and were termed mulattoes. They lived together in a comfortable home; and, though we were all slaves, I was so fondly shielded that I never dreamed I was a piece of merchandise, trusted to them for safe keeping, and liable to be demanded of them at any moment. I had one brother, William, who was two years younger than myself—a bright, affectionate child. I had also a great treasure in my maternal grandmother, who was a remarkable woman in many respects. . . .

[When Linda Brent was six years old, her mother died, and six years later the kind mistress to whom Brent's family belonged also died. In the will, Linda Brent was bequeathed to the mistress' five-year-old niece, Miss Emily Flint.]

Dr. Flint, a physician in the neighborhood, had married the sister of my mistress, and I was now the property of their little daughter. It was not without murmuring that I prepared for my new home; and what added to my unhappiness, was the fact that my brother William was purchased by the same family. My father, by his nature, as well as by the habit of transacting business as a skilful mechanic, had more of the feelings of a freeman than is common among slaves. My brother was a spirited boy; and being brought up under such influences, he early detested the name of master and mistress. One day, when his father and his mistress both happened to call him at the same time, he hesitated between the two; being perplexed to

CHAPTER 8

THE "PECULIAR
INSTITUTION":
SLAVES TELL
THEIR OWN
STORY

know which had the strongest claim upon his obedience. He finally concluded to go to his mistress. When my father reproved him for it, he said, "You both called me, and I didn't know which I ought to go to first."

"You are *my* child," replied our father, "and when I call you, you should come immediately, if you have to pass through fire and water."

Poor Willie! He was now to learn his first lesson of obedience to a master. Grandmother tried to cheer us with hopeful words, and they found an echo in the credulous hearts of youth. . . .

My grandmother's mistress had always promised her that, at her death, she should be free; and it was said that in her will she made good the promise. But when the estate was settled, Dr. Flint told the faithful old servant that, under existing circumstances, it was necessary she should be sold.

On the appointed day, the customary advertisement was posted up, proclaiming that there would be a "public sale of negroes, horses, &c." Dr. Flint called to tell my grandmother that he was unwilling to wound her feelings by putting her up at auction, and that he would prefer to dispose of her at private sale. My grandmother saw through his hypocrisy; she understood very well that he was ashamed of the job. She was a very spirited woman, and if he was base enough to sell her, when her mistress intended she should be free, she was determined the public should know it. She had for a long time supplied many families with crackers and preserves; consequently, "Aunt Marthy," as she was called, was generally known, and every body who knew her respected her intelligence and good character. Her long and faithful service in the family was also well known, and the intention of her mistress to leave her free. When the day of sale came, she took her place among the chattels, and at the first call she sprang upon the auction-block. Many voices called out, "Shame! Shame! Who is going to sell *you,* aunt Marthy? Don't stand there! That is no place for *you.*" Without saying a word, she quietly awaited her fate. No one bid for her. At last, a feeble voice said, "Fifty dollars." It came from a maiden lady, seventy years old, the sister of my grandmother's deceased mistress. She had lived forty years under the same roof with my grandmother; she knew how faithfully she had served her owners, and how cruelly she had been defrauded of her rights; and she resolved to protect her. The auctioneer waited for a higher bid; but her wishes were respected; no one bid above her. She could neither read nor write; and when the bill of sale was made out, she signed it with a cross. But what consequence was that, when she had a big heart overflowing with human kindness? She gave the old servant her freedom. . . .

During the first years of my service in Dr. Flint's family, I was accustomed to share some indulgences with the children of my mistress. Though this seemed to me no more than right, I was grateful for it, and tried to merit the kindness by the faithful discharge of my duties. But I now entered on my fifteenth year—a sad epoch in the life of a slave girl. My master began to whisper foul words in my ear. Young as I was, I could not remain ignorant of their import. I tried to treat them with indifference or contempt. The master's age, my extreme youth, and the fear that his conduct would be reported to my grandmother, made him bear this treatment for many months. He was a crafty man, and resorted to many means to accomplish his purposes. . . . The mistress, who ought to protect the helpless victim, has no other feelings towards her but those of jealousy and rage. . . . Even the little child, who is accustomed to wait on her mistress and her children, will learn, before she is twelve years old, why it is that her mistress hates such and such a one among the slaves. . . . She listens to violent outbreaks of jealous passion, and cannot help understanding what is the cause. She will become prematurely knowing in evil things. Soon she will learn to tremble when she hears her master's footfall. She will be compelled to realize that she is no longer a child. If God has bestowed beauty upon her, it will prove her greatest curse. That which commands admiration in the white woman only hastens the degradation of the female slave. . . .

I longed for some one to confide in. I would have given the world to have laid my head on my grandmother's faithful bosom, and told her all my troubles. But Dr. Flint swore he would kill me, if I was not as silent as the grave. Then, although my grandmother was all in all to me, I feared her as well as loved her. I had been accustomed to look up to her with a respect bordering upon awe. I was very young, and felt shamefaced about telling her such impure things, especially as I knew her to be very strict on such subjects. Moreover, she was a woman of a high spirit. She was usually very quiet in her demeanor; but if her indignation was once roused, it was not very easily quelled. . . . I dreaded the consequences of a violent outbreak; and both pride and fear kept me silent. . . . It was lucky for me that I did not live on a distant plantation, but in a town not so large that the inhabitants were ignorant of each other's affairs. Bad as are the laws and customs in a slave-holding community, the doctor, as a professional man, deemed it prudent to keep up some outward show of decency. . . .

[Dr. Flint was enraged when he found out that Linda Brent had fallen in love with a young, free, African American carpenter. The doctor redoubled his efforts to seduce Brent, and told her terrible stories about what happened to slaves who ran away. For a long time she was afraid to try to escape because of stories such as the one she recounts here.]

In my childhood I knew a valuable slave, named Charity, and loved her, as all children did. Her young mistress married, and took her to Louisiana.

CHAPTER 8

THE "PECULIAR
INSTITUTION":
SLAVES TELL
THEIR OWN
STORY

Her little boy, James, was sold to a good sort of master. He became involved in debt, and James was sold again to a wealthy slaveholder, noted for his cruelty. With this man he grew up to manhood, receiving the treatment of a dog. After a severe whipping, to save himself from further infliction of the lash, with which he was threatened, he took to the woods. He was in a most miserable condition—cut by the cowskin, half naked, half starved, and without the means of procuring a crust of bread.

Some weeks after his escape, he was captured, tied, and carried back to his master's plantation. This man considered punishment in his jail, on bread and water, after receiving hundreds of lashes, too mild for the poor slave's offence. Therefore he decided, after the overseer should have whipped him to his satisfaction, to have him placed between the screws of the cotton gin, to stay as long as he had been in the woods. This wretched creature was cut with the whip from his head to his feet, then washed with strong brine, to prevent the flesh from mortifying. . . . He was then put into the cotton gin, which was screwed down, only allowing him room to turn on his side when he could not lie on his back. Every morning a slave was sent with a piece of bread and bowl of water, which were placed within reach of the poor fellow. The slave was charged, under penalty of severe punishment, not to speak to him.

Four days passed, and the slave continued to carry the bread and water. On the second morning, he found the bread gone, but the water untouched. When he had been in the press four days and five nights, the slave informed his master that the water had not been used for four mornings, and that a horrible stench came from the gin house. The overseer was sent to examine into it. When the press was unscrewed, the dead body was found partly eaten by rats and vermin. . . .

[Dr. Flint's jealous wife watched his behavior very closely, so Flint decided to build a small cabin out in the woods for Linda Brent, who was now sixteen years old. Still afraid to run away, she became desperate.]

And now, reader, I come to a period in my unhappy life, which I would gladly forget if I could. The remembrance fills me with sorrow and shame. It pains me to tell you of it; but I have promised to tell you the truth, and I will do it honestly, let it cost me what it may. I will not try to screen myself behind the plea of compulsion from a master; for it was not so. Neither can I plead ignorance or thoughtlessness. For years, my master had done his utmost to pollute my mind with foul images, and to destroy the pure principles inculcated by my grandmother, and the good mistress of my childhood. The influences of slavery had had the same effect on me that they had on other young girls; they had made me prematurely knowing, concerning the evil ways of the world. I knew what I did, and I did it with deliberate calculation. . . .

I have told you that Dr. Flint's persecutions and his wife's jealousy had given rise to some gossip in the neighborhood. Among others, it chanced that a white unmarried gentleman had obtained some knowledge of the circumstances in which I was placed. He knew my grandmother, and often spoke to me in the street. He became interested for me, and asked questions about my master, which I answered in part. He expressed a great deal of sympathy, and a wish to aid me. He constantly sought opportunities to see me, and wrote to me frequently. I was a poor slave girl, only fifteen years old.

So much attention from a superior person was, of course, flattering; for human nature is the same in all. I also felt grateful for his sympathy, and encouraged by his kind words. It seemed to me a great thing to have such a friend. By degrees, a more tender feeling crept into my heart. He was an educated and eloquent gentleman; too eloquent, alas, for the poor slave girl who trusted in him. Of course I saw whither all this was tending. I knew the impassable gulf between us; but to be an object of interest to a man who is not married, and who is not her master, is agreeable to the pride and feelings of a slave, if her miserable situation has left her any pride or sentiment. It seems less degrading to give one's self, than to submit to compulsion. There is something akin to freedom in having a lover who has no control over you, except that which he gains by kindness and attachment. A master may treat you as rudely as he pleases, and you dare not speak; moreover, the wrong does not seem so great with an unmarried man, as with one who has a wife to be made unhappy. There may be sophistry in all this; but the condition of a slave confuses all principles of morality, and, in fact, renders the practice of them impossible.

[Linda Brent had two children, Benjy and Ellen, as a result of her relationship with Mr. Sands, the white "gentleman." Sands and Linda's grandmother tried to buy Linda Brent, but Dr. Flint rejected all their offers. However, Sands was able (through a trick) to buy his two children and Linda's brother William. After he was elected to Congress, Sands married a white woman. William escaped to the North, and Linda spent seven years hiding in the tiny attic of a shed attached to her grandmother's house. Finally, Linda Brent and a friend escaped via ship to Philadelphia. She then went to New York City, where she found work as a nursemaid for a kind family, the Bruces, and was reunited with her two children. However, as a fugitive slave she was not really safe, and she used to read the newspapers every day to see whether Dr. Flint or any of his relatives were visiting New York.]

CHAPTER 8

THE "PECULIAR
INSTITUTION":
SLAVES TELL
THEIR OWN
STORY

But when summer came, the old feeling of insecurity haunted me. It was necessary for me to take little Mary[7] out daily, for exercise and fresh air, and the city was swarming with Southerners, some of whom might recognize me. Hot weather brings out snakes and slaveholders, and I like one class of the venomous creatures as little as I do the other. What a comfort it is, to be free to *say* so! . . . .

I kept close watch of the newspapers for arrivals; but one Saturday night, being much occupied, I forgot to examine the Evening Express as usual. I went down into the parlor for it, early in the morning, and found the boy about to kindle a fire with it. I took it from him and examined the list of arrivals. Reader, if you have never been a slave, you cannot imagine the acute sensation of suffering at my heart, when I read the names of Mr. and Mrs. Dodge,[8] at a hotel in Courtland Street. It was a third-rate hotel, and that circumstance convinced me of the truth of what I had heard, that they were short of funds and had need of my value, as *they* valued me; and that was by dollar and cents. I hastened with the paper to Mrs. Bruce. Her heart and hand were always open to every one in distress, and she always warmly sympathized with mine. It was impossible to tell how near the enemy was. He might have passed and repassed the house while we were sleeping. He might at that moment be waiting to pounce upon me if I ventured out of doors. I had never seen the husband of my young mistress, and therefore I could not distinguish him from any other stranger. A carriage was hastily ordered; and, closely veiled, I followed Mrs. Bruce, taking the baby again with me into exile. After various turnings and crossings, and returnings, the carriage stopped at the house of one of Mrs. Bruce's friends, where I was kindly received. Mrs. Bruce returned immediately, to instruct the domestics what to say if any one came to inquire for me.

It was lucky for me that the evening paper was not burned up before I had a chance to examine the list of arrivals. It was not long after Mrs. Bruce's return to her house, before several people came to inquire for me. One inquired for me, another asked for my daughter Ellen, and another said he had a letter from my grandmother, which he was requested to deliver in person.

They were told, "She *has* lived here, but she has left."

"How long ago?"

"I don't know, sir."

"Do you know where she went?"

"I do not, sir." And the door was closed. . . .

7. Mary was the Bruces' baby.
8. Emily Flint and her husband.

[Mrs. Bruce was finally able to buy Linda Brent from Mr. Dodge, and she immediately gave Linda her freedom.]

Reader, my story ends with freedom; not in the usual way, with marriage. I and my children are now free! We are as free from the power of slaveholders as are the white people of the north; and though that, according to my ideas, is not saying a great deal, it is a vast improvement in *my* condition. The dream of my life is not yet realized. I do not sit with my children in a home of my own. I still long for a hearthstone of my own, however humble. I wish it for my children's sake far more than for my own. But God so orders circumstances as to keep me with my friend Mrs. Bruce. Love, duty, gratitude, also bind me to her side. It is a privilege to serve her who pities my oppressed people, and who has bestowed the inestimable boon of freedom on me and my children. . . .

[Harriet Jacobs's story was published in 1861, and during the Civil War she did relief work with the newly freed slaves behind the Union Army lines. For several years after the war ended, she worked tirelessly in Georgia to organize orphanages, schools, and nursing homes. Finally, she returned to the North, where she died in 1897 at the age of eighty-four.]

QUESTIONS TO CONSIDER

The evidence in this chapter falls into three categories: reminiscences from former slaves, culled from interviews conducted in the 1930s (Sources 1 through 18); songs transcribed soon after the Civil War, recalled by runaway slaves, or remembered years after (Sources 19 through 23); and the autobiographies of two slaves who escaped to the North: Frederick Douglass and Harriet Jacobs (Sources 24 and 25).

These categories are artificial at best, and you might want to rearrange the evidence in a way that may suit your purpose better.

But how best to rearrange the evidence? The evidence contains a number of subtopics, and arrangement into those subtopics may be profitable. For example:

1. How did slaves feel about their masters and/or mistresses?
2. How did slaves feel about their work? Their families? Their religion?
3. How did they feel about freedom?
4. How did slaves feel about themselves?

By regrouping the evidence into subtopics and then using each piece of evi-

CHAPTER 8

THE "PECULIAR
INSTITUTION":
SLAVES TELL
THEIR OWN
STORY

dence to answer the question for that subtopic, you should be able to answer the central question: what did slaves (or former slaves) think and feel about the peculiar institution of slavery?

As mentioned, some of the slaves and former slaves chose to be direct in their messages (see, for example, (Source 19), but many more chose to communicate their thoughts and feelings more indirectly or obliquely. Several of the symbols and metaphors used are easy to figure out (see Source 23), but others will take considerably more care. The messages are there, however.

Frederick Douglass and Harriet Jacobs wrote their autobiographies for northern readers. Furthermore, both these runaway slaves were active in abolitionist work. Do these facts mean that this evidence is worthless? Not at all, but the historian must be very careful when analyzing such obviously biased sources. Which parts of Douglass' and Jacobs's stories seem to be exaggerated or unlikely to be true? What do these writers say about such topics as their work, religious beliefs, and families? Does any other evidence from the interviews, tales, or songs corroborate what Douglass and Jacobs wrote?

One last point you might want to consider: why have historians neglected this kind of evidence for so long?

EPILOGUE

Even before the Civil War formally ended, thousands of African Americans began casting off the shackles of slavery. Some ran away to meet the advancing Union armies (who often treated them no better than their former masters and mistresses). Others drifted into cities, where they hoped to find work and opportunities for themselves and their families. Still others stayed on the land, perhaps hoping to become free farmers. At the end of the war, African Americans were quick to establish their own churches and enrolled in schools established by the Freedmen's Bureau. For most former slaves, the impulse seems to have been to look forward and not backward into the agonizing past of slavery.

Yet memories of slavery were not forgotten and often were passed down orally, from generation to generation. In 1976, Alex Haley's book *Roots* and the twelve-part television miniseries based on it stunned an American public that had assumed that blacks' memories of their origins and of slavery had been for the most part either forgotten or obliterated.[9] Although much of Haley's work contains the author's artistic license, the skeleton of the book was the oral tradition transmitted by his family since the capture of his ancestor Kunta Kinte in West Africa in the late eighteenth century. Not only had Haley's family remembered its African origins, but stories about slavery had not been lost—they had

9. A condensed version of *Roots* appeared in 1974 in *Reader's Digest*.

been passed down through the generations.

While Haley was engaged in his twelve years of research and writing, historian Henry Irving Tragle proposed to compile a documentary history of the Nat Turner Rebellion of 1831. Talking to black people in 1968 and 1969 in Southampton County, where the rebellion occurred, Tragle discovered that in spite of numerous attempts to obliterate Turner from the area's historical memory, Turner's action had become part of the oral history of the region. As the surprised Tragle wrote, "I believe it possible to say with certainty that Nat Turner did exist as a folk-hero to several generations of black men and women who have lived and died in Southampton County since 1831."[10] Again, oral his-

tory had persisted and triumphed over time, and professional historians began looking with a new eye on what in the past many had dismissed as unworthy of their attention.

Folk music, customs, religious practices, stories, and artifacts also gained attention. Increasingly, students of history have been able to reconstruct the lives, thoughts, and feelings of people once considered inarticulate. Of course, they were not, but it took imagination to let their evidence speak.

Many people have argued about the impact of slavery on blacks and whites alike, and that question may never be answered fully. What we *do* know is that an enormous amount of historical evidence about slavery exists, from the perspectives of both African Americans and whites. And the memory of that institution lingers. It is part of what one southern white professional historian calls the "burden of southern history," a burden to be overcome but never completely forgotten.

10. Henry Irving Tragle, *The Southampton Slave Revolt of 1831: A Compilation of Source Material* (Amherst: University of Massachusetts Press, 1971), p. 12.

WAR AND MANIFEST DESTINY:
A PROBLEM IN CAUSATION

For days the city of Washington had been abuzz with rumors that the long-expected hostilities had broken out between United States and Mexican troops stationed along the Texas border. On Friday, May 9, 1846, news finally arrived that fighting actually had taken place, and with the aid of several of his cabinet members, President James K. Polk began rapidly drafting a war message.[1] On Monday, May 11, the president's message requesting a declaration of war against the Republic of Mexico was delivered to Congress and read to both Houses. That same day the House of Representatives, by a vote of 174 to 14, approved the war message, and the Sen-

ate, by a vote of 40 to 2, concurred the next day. On Wednesday, May 13, 1846, Polk signed the war bill, and the Mexican War officially began.

Polk's war message (reproduced in the "Evidence" section) summarized his justifications for declaring war against Mexico—a war he thought was both just and necessary. The president listed two principal causes of the war: (1) Mexico had refused to receive United States envoy John Slidell, who had been sent to Mexico City "to adjust every existing difference" between the two nations; and (2) Mexican soldiers "have at last invaded our territory and shed the blood of our fellow-citizens on our own soil." Although the United States, Polk asserted, had made every effort to reach a peaceful agreement with the Republic of Mexico, at last the "cup of forbearance had been exhausted," and war was the only alternative.

1. Polk had talked about drafting a war message *prior to* his learning of the outbreak of hostilities, but there is no evidence that he actually had done so. See entry in Polk's diary for May 8, 1846, in the "Evidence" section of this chapter.

Polk's war message, however, poses an intriguing problem. Were the causes of the war as simple as those Polk addressed? History has proven that the causes of wars, as of other important events in history, are considerably more complex than those seen by casual observers or claimed by the combatants. In almost all cases, one must also look for long-range and underlying causes, some of which might stretch back for years prior to the outbreak of the war. Furthermore, secret decisions or moves may have been made, helping precipitate hostilities. Indeed, assessing what caused the Mexican War can be considerably more difficult than the task at first appears.

In this chapter, you will be examining and analyzing the evidence in order to answer the following questions: What were the principal causes of the Mexican War (1846–1848)? What was President James Polk's role in the coming of that conflict? Finally, on the basis of your analysis of the evidence, do you think the United States's declaration of war on Mexico was justified?

BACKGROUND

Ever since colonial times, Americans had viewed the West as the key to both their individual and collective futures. To land companies and investors, the West held out the promise of great riches, fortunes made in either land speculation or trade. To southern planters who often exhausted the soil growing cash crops like tobacco, it offered the chance to repeat their successes on rich, virgin land. To European immigrants and people from the overpopulated northeastern farming communities, the West was seen as a Garden of Eden where they could make a new start. To Thomas Jefferson, it represented an "Empire of Liberty" that would prevent the rise of unwholesome cities and social conflict in the young republic. Hence it is easy to see why most Americans came to equate national progress with westward expansion. In this atmosphere, the ceding of western lands by the new states to the national government in the 1780s and the Louisiana Purchase of 1803 were seen as the insurers of national greatness. And in a society in which private property was venerated and the acquisition of land had become for many almost a cultural imperative, expansion westward was very nearly inevitable.

Although there were a number of obstacles to westward expansion, at most they proved temporary. The Indian nations offered brisk opposition, but they could fight only a holding action against the more numerous and technologically superior Caucasians. When the United States put its mind to it, the Indians were quickly, and sometimes mercilessly, eradicated or gathered onto reservations, where they were forced to become dependent on the United States government for their existence. For their part, the Spanish (in

CHAPTER 9

WAR AND
MANIFEST
DESTINY: A
PROBLEM IN
CAUSATION

the Floridas), French (in the Louisiana Territory), and British (in the Northwest) could not bring sufficient military power to bear so far from home and ultimately preferred to either sell or give up through treaty their territorial claims. Even the Republic of Mexico, which did choose to fight, was no match for its expansion-minded neighbor.

The demographic, economic, and social imperatives to expand and the absence of powerful opposition gradually convinced many Americans that westward expansion was both a right and a duty, approved by God for "His people." As one editor explained, it was America's "manifest destiny to overspread the continent allotted by Providence for the free development of our yearly multiplying millions." Another contemporary envisaged a time when the American eagle would have its beak in Canada, its talons in Mexico, and its wings flapping in the two oceans. Although in both statements there is more than a trace of arrogance and feelings of superiority, it is important to note that a vast number of American Caucasians sincerely believed in those claims, much as many white southerners in the same era sincerely believed that most slaves were happy with their collective lot.

By the 1830s, the westward expansion of Americans had gone beyond the Louisiana Territory into Texas (owned by the Republic of Mexico) and Oregon (jointly occupied by the United States and Great Britain since 1818). In Texas, settlers from the United States regularly ignored Mexican laws and officials. For example, Mexico's prohibition of slavery did not stop settlers from bringing slaves into Texas. Mexican law, which required that all settlers convert to Roman Catholicism, was scoffed at and almost universally broken. When the Mexican government attempted to enforce these and other laws in 1836, American migrants to Texas (numbering approximately 30,000) rebelled.

Mexico attempted to crush the rebellion. At the Alamo, Mexican general Santa Anna killed all the defenders (he spared women and children and, according to legend, at least one male native Mexican) and then stacked their bodies like cordwood and burned them. Later, Mexicans shot every defender at Goliad, even though a formal surrender had been arranged with an agreement that survivors would be spared. Still, the Texans under General Sam Houston prevailed, and by the end of 1836, Texas was an independent nation. Most Texans, however, did not want Texas to remain independent; they wanted to become a part of the United States.

Whether to annex Texas to the United States was an issue that divided Americans for the next eight years. Some people in the North and Midwest opposed the annexation of Texas, fearing that it would tip the political balance in Congress in favor of the slave states and (prophetically, as it turned out) that annexation would precipitate a war with Mexico. That nation had never relinquished its claim to her lost province. Moreover, Texans maintained that the southern boundary of the Lone Star Republic[2] was the Rio

2. This was the nickname for the Republic of Texas, derived from its flag with one star.

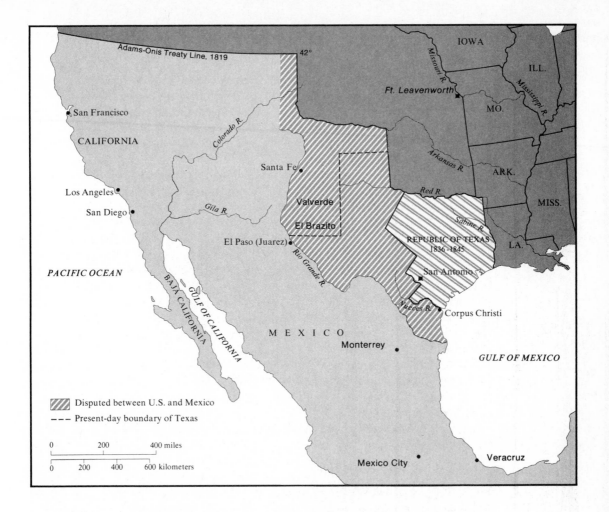

Grande River[3], whereas Mexico continued to insist that the border was the
Nueces River (see the accompanying
map). Border clashes in the disputed
territory between Texans and Mexicans
were common. Meanwhile, the non-In-
dian population of Texas swelled, from

approximately 38,000 in 1836 to about
142,000 ten years later.[4]

In the United States, Presidents
Jackson and Van Buren cautiously
avoided the annexation issue (Jackson
did not even recognize the Republic of
Texas until after the 1836 presidential

3. As you will see in the "Evidence" section,
the river was known by various names: the
Rio Grande del Norte (often shortened to
either the "Rio Grande" or the "del Norte")
and the Rio Bravo.

4. In 1835, United States citizens who
had emigrated to Texas numbered approximately 30,000, whereas the population of
Mexican origin was around 7,800.

CHAPTER 9

WAR AND
MANIFEST
DESTINY: A
PROBLEM IN
CAUSATION

election), whereas Tyler (1841–1845) was rebuffed by the United States Senate when he proposed annexation in 1844. Finally, on March 1, 1845, three days before Polk's inauguration as president, a joint congressional resolution approved the inclusion of Texas in the United States. Mexico promptly broke off diplomatic relations.

There is little doubt that Polk sided with the expansionists. During the presidential campaign of 1844, he had made it clear that he approved of his party's pro-expansion platform and that he would move aggressively to fulfill it. Indeed, it is likely that Polk's and the Democrats' stand on westward expansion was in part responsible for their 1844 victory. The presidential election was a surprisingly close one, with Polk winning 50 percent of the popular vote and 170 electoral votes to Henry Clay's 48 percent of the popular vote and 105 electoral votes. Expansionism could well have made the difference.

In spite of his party's pro-expansion platform and its rather bellicose rhetoric, once in office Polk worked diligently to acquire territory by negotiation rather than war. On the Oregon question, the president privately informed the British ambassador that he would accept a compromise that would set the Oregon-Canadian boundary at the forty-ninth parallel.[5] Troubled by

difficulties at home, Great Britain also was eager to compromise, and an agreement was reached between the two nations in 1846.

Polk's efforts to acquire California and New Mexico from Mexico did not end so amicably. Even before his inauguration, Polk had his eyes on California. Unstable political conditions in Mexico City had prevented Mexico from exercising much power in the area, and by 1841 most semblances of Mexican authority in California had vanished. Such a power vacuum made it likely that another nation would try to acquire California. Many Americans—including Polk—believed that both England and France were anxious to establish footholds in the region. If either nation were to acquire California (which in 1845 contained only a few hundred United States citizens), the United States's "manifest destiny" would be thwarted. With European nations showing increasing interest and Mexico so internally unstable, Polk was determined to move swiftly.

As with the Oregon question, Polk would have preferred to acquire California by negotiation. Yet war with Mexico broke out in May 1846. In this chapter, by assessing the role of long-range and underlying causes and analyzing the below-the-surface events and decisions and combining this information with Polk's announced causes, you will be able to emerge with a more complete understanding of the causes of the Mexican War.

5. The original American claim was considerably north of the forty-ninth parallel, at 54°40′, thus leading to the popular Democratic party slogan in the 1844 presidential race of "Fifty-four forty or fight!"

Your supplementary reading and the introduction to this chapter should help you in determining the long-range causes of the Mexican War (the drive for westward expansion, the Texas war for independence, and so forth). Be sure to note the political considerations (such as the presidential election of 1844), the instability in Mexico, Mexico's feelings about the United States, and the situations in Oregon and California. Also remember the long-held attitudes of United States citizens on the subject of expansion.

The evidence in this chapter begins with President Polk's war message to Congress on May 11, 1846; it will give you a good idea of what Polk believed—or said he believed—were the causes of the Mexican War. As you examine Polk's message, list what he gave as the causes of the war with Mexico.

Subsequent evidence (drawn from official and private correspondence, diplomatic dispatches, diaries and personal recollections, and congressional proceedings), however, leaves the distinct impression that President Polk did not tell the whole story. In other words, the causes of the Mexican War may have been considerably more complicated—and different—than those that Polk gave Congress. As you analyze the evidence, keep asking yourself the extent to which that evidence agrees or disagrees with Polk's explanation.

Your work in previous chapters has taught you that certain pieces of evidence should be weighted more than others. For example, lawyers prefer eyewitnesses to people who have only heard about an event (indeed, "hearsay evidence" is usually inadmissible in American courts). In this exercise, are there pieces of evidence that are more important than others? What are they? Are there pieces of evidence that are more likely to be true? (False evidence is always a problem.) Weigh each piece of evidence carefully. In the chain of explanation, some links are stronger than others.

Except for Polk's war message, the evidence is arranged in chronological order, yet you will see almost immediately that several factors that might have contributed to the advent of war were occurring simultaneously in different places. To get the most out of the evidence, you must divide the evidence into segments, thus partly rearranging it. For example, arrange together in chronological order all the evidence regarding Commodore Robert Stockton. What was Stockton trying to do? Who was aware of Stockton's actions? Was Secretary of the Navy George Bancroft aware of Stockton's actions? Did Polk know what Stockton was doing? How could you prove this? If you rearrange the evidence into segments (around, perhaps, Frémont, Slidell, Taylor, etc.), the evidence will become more understandable. Keep in mind that you have some evidence from the Mexican point of view as well.

Once you have arranged the evidence into segments and then examined each segment for what it can tell you about the coming of the Mexican

CHAPTER 9

WAR AND
MANIFEST
DESTINY: A
PROBLEM IN
CAUSATION

War, link the segments together so that you can offer a general *thesis* (statement of opinion supported by the evidence) about the advent of that conflict. Obviously, the most efficient way of linking the segments together is through Polk himself. What was his role in each segment? How does that role "fit" (or not fit) with Polk's own explanation in his war message?

The problem of causation is a primary concern of historians. Yet unlike the natural sciences, where an experiment in causation can be observed and reproduced (for example, allowing for altitude, water *always* boils at a certain temperature), the study of people—especially people in the past—is not an exact discipline. For instance, although wars have been an almost constant feature throughout history, they have been caused by a variety of factors; knowing what caused one war cannot really explain what caused another. Too, although psychologists, sociologists, and cultural anthropologists have discovered certain patterns of human behavior, few if any of these patterns are valid for all times and all cultures. Therefore historians and social scientists cannot approach the problem of causation in the same way that natural scientists (such as biologists, physicists, chemists, and geologists) can.

What historians can do, however, is look for *probable* cause, an explanation of the evidence that is likely and reasonable. It is not scientific, nor is it verifiable by laboratory experiment. But by closely examining and analyzing the evidence and by knowing something of the background and people involved, the historian can offer a cause that is reasonable, supported by evidence (and not strongly contradicted by other evidence), and possibly the best explanation available.

CHARACTERS

James Knox Polk, president of the United States 1845–1849

George Bancroft, secretary of the navy, 1846

John Slidell, minister to Mexico, 1845–1846

Robert Field Stockton, commodore, U.S. Navy

Anson Jones, president of the Republic of Texas

John C. Frémont, captain, U.S. Army

Charles Elliot, British minister to Texas

Charles Bankhead, British minister to Mexico

Zachary Taylor, general, U.S. Army

William L. Marcy, secretary of war, 1845–1849

José Joaquín Herrera, president of Mexico, 1844–1845

Don Mariano Paredes y Arrillaga, overthrew Herrera and became president of Mexico, December 1845

Source 1 from James D. Richardson, ed., *Messages and Papers of the Presidents,* Vol. IV (Washington, D.C.: U.S. Government Printing Office, 1897), pp. 437–442.

1. May 11, 1846—Polk's War Message

The strong desire to establish peace with Mexico on liberal and honorable terms, and the readiness of this Government to regulate and adjust our boundary and other causes of difference with that power on such fair and equitable principles as would lead to permanent relations of the most friendly nature, induced me in September last to seek the reopening of diplomatic relations between the two countries. Every measure adopted on our part had for its object the furtherance of these desired results. In communicating to Congress a succinct statement of the injuries which we had suffered from Mexico, and which have been accumulating during a period of more than twenty years, every expression that could tend to inflame the people of Mexico or defeat or delay a pacific result was carefully avoided. An envoy of the United States repaired to Mexico with full powers to adjust every existing difference. But though present on the Mexican soil by agreement between the two Governments, invested with full powers, and bearing evidence of the most friendly dispositions, his mission has been unavailing.

CHAPTER 9

WAR AND
MANIFEST
DESTINY: A
PROBLEM IN
CAUSATION

The Mexican Government not only refused to receive him or listen to his propositions, but after a long-continued series of menaces have at last invaded our territory and shed the blood of our fellow-citizens on our own soil.

It now becomes my duty to state more in detail the origin, progress, and failure of that mission. In pursuance of the instructions given in September last, an inquiry was made on the 13th of October, 1845, in the most friendly terms, through our consul in Mexico, of the minister for foreign affairs, whether the Mexican Government "would receive an envoy from the United States intrusted with full powers to adjust all the questions in dispute between the two Governments," with the assurance that "should the answer be in the affirmative such an envoy would be immediately dispatched to Mexico." The Mexican minister on the 15th of October gave an affirmative answer to this inquiry, requesting at the same time that our naval force at Vera Cruz might be withdrawn, lest its continued presence might assume the appearance of menace and coercion pending the negotiations. This force was immediately withdrawn. On the 10th of November, 1845, Mr. John Slidell, of Louisiana, was commissioned by me as envoy extraordinary and minister plenipotentiary of the United States to Mexico, and was intrusted with full powers to adjust both the questions of the Texas boundary and of indemnification to our citizens. The redress of the wrongs of our citizens naturally and inseparably blended itself with the question of boundary. The settlement of the one question in any correct view of the subject involves that of the other. I could not for a moment entertain the idea that the claims of our much-injured and long-suffering citizens, many of which had existed for more than twenty years, should be postponed or separated from the settlement of the boundary question.

Mr. Slidell arrived at Vera Cruz on the 30th of November, and was courteously received by the authorities of that city. But the Government of General Herrera was then tottering to its fall. The revolutionary party had seized upon the Texas question to effect or hasten its overthrow. Its determination to restore friendly relations with the United States, and to receive our minister to negotiate for the settlement of this question, was violently assailed, and was made the great theme of denunciation against it. The Government of General Herrera, there is good reason to believe, was sincerely desirous to receive our minister; but it yielded to the storm raised by its enemies, and on the 21st of December refused to accredit Mr. Slidell upon the most frivolous pretexts. These are so fully and ably exposed in the note of Mr. Slidell of the 24th of December last to the Mexican minister of foreign relations, herewith transmitted, that I deem it unnecessary to enter into further detail on this portion of the subject.

Five days after the date of Mr. Slidell's note General Herrera yielded the Government to General Paredes without a struggle, and on the 30th of December resigned the Presidency. This revolution was accomplished solely by the army, the people having taken little part in the contest; and thus the supreme power in Mexico passed into the hands of a military leader.

Determined to leave no effort untried to effect an amicable adjustment with Mexico, I directed Mr. Slidell to present his credentials to the Government of General Paredes and ask to be officially received by him. . . .

Under these circumstances, Mr. Slidell, in obedience to my direction, addressed a note to the Mexican minister of foreign relations, under date of the 1st of March last, asking to be received by that Government in the diplomatic character to which he had been appointed. This minister in his reply, under date of the 12th of March, reiterated the arguments of his predecessor, and in terms that may be considered as giving just grounds of offense to the Government and people of the United States denied the application of Mr. Slidell. Nothing therefore remained for our envoy but to demand his passports and return to his own country.

Thus the Government of Mexico, though solemnly pledged by official acts in October last to receive and accredit an American envoy, violated their plighted faith and refused the offer of a peaceful adjustment of our difficulties. Not only was the offer rejected, but the indignity of its rejection was enhanced by the manifest breach of faith in refusing to admit the envoy who came because they had bound themselves to receive him. . . .

In my message at the commencement of the present session I informed you that upon the earnest appeal both of the Congress and convention of Texas I had ordered an efficient military force to take a position "between the Nueces and the Del Norte." This had become necessary to meet a threatened invasion of Texas by the Mexican forces, for which extensive military preparations had been made. The invasion was threatened solely because Texas had determined, in accordance with a solemn resolution of the Congress of the United States, to annex herself to our Union, and under these circumstances it was plainly our duty to extend our protection over her citizens and soil. . . .

Meantime Texas, by the final action of our Congress, had become an integral part of our Union. The Congress of Texas, by its act of December 19, 1836, had declared the Rio del Norte to be the boundary of that Republic. Its jurisdiction had been extended and exercised beyond the Nueces. The country between that river and the Del Norte had been represented in the Congress and in the convention of Texas, had thus taken part in the act of annexation itself, and is now included within one of our Congressional dis-

CHAPTER 9

WAR AND
MANIFEST
DESTINY: A
PROBLEM IN
CAUSATION

tricts. Our own Congress had, moreover, with great unanimity, by the act approved December 31, 1845, recognized the country beyond the Nueces as a part of our territory by including it within our own revenue system, and a revenue officer to reside within that district has been appointed by and with the advice and consent of the Senate. It became, therefore, of urgent necessity to provide for the defense of that portion of our country. Accordingly, on the 13th of January last instructions were issued to the general in command of these troops to occupy the left bank of the Del Norte. This river, which is the southwestern boundary of the State of Texas, is an exposed frontier. From this quarter invasion was threatened; upon it and in its immediate vicinity, in the judgment of high military experience, are the proper stations for the protecting forces of the Government. . . .

The movement of the troops to the Del Norte was made by the commanding general under positive instructions to abstain from all aggressive acts toward Mexico or Mexican citizens and to regard the relations between that Republic and the United States as peaceful unless she should declare war or commit acts of hostility indicative of a state of war. He was specially directed to protect private property and respect personal rights.

The Army moved from Corpus Christi on the 11th of March, and on the 28th of that month arrived on the left bank of the Del Norte opposite to Matamoras, where it encamped on a commanding position, which has since been strengthened by the erection of fieldworks. A depot has also been established at Point Isabel, near the Brazos Santiago, 30 miles in rear of the encampment. The selection of his position was necessarily confided to the judgment of the general in command.

The Mexican forces at Matamoras assumed a belligerent attitude, and on the 12th of April General Ampudia, then in command, notified General Taylor to break up his camp within twenty-four hours and to retire beyond the Nueces River, and in the event of his failure to comply with these demands announced that arms, and arms alone, must decide the question. But no open act of hostility was committed until the 24th of April. On that day General Arista, who had succeeded to the command of the Mexican forces, communicated to General Taylor that "he considered hostilities commenced and should prosecute them." A party of dragoons of 63 men and officers were on the same day dispatched from the American camp on the Rio del Norte, on its left bank, to ascertain whether the Mexican troops had crossed or were preparing to cross the river, "became engaged with a large body of these troops, and after a short affair, in which some 16 were killed and wounded, appear to have been surrounded and compelled to surrender."

The grievous wrongs perpetrated by Mexico upon our citizens throughout a long period of years remain unredressed, and solemn treaties pledging her public faith for this redress have been disregarded. A government either unable or unwilling to enforce the execution of such treaties fails to perform one of its plainest duties.

Our commerce with Mexico has been almost annihilated. It was formerly highly beneficial to both nations, but our merchants have been deterred from prosecuting it by the system of outrage and extortion which the Mexican authorities have pursued against them, whilst their appeals through their own Government for indemnity have been made in vain. Our forbearance has gone to such an extreme as to be mistaken in its character. Had we acted with vigor in repelling the insults and redressing the injuries inflicted by Mexico at the commencement, we should doubtless have escaped all the difficulties in which we are now involved.

Instead of this, however, we have been exerting our best efforts to propitiate her good will. Upon the pretext that Texas, a nation as independent as herself, thought proper to unite its destinies with our own, she has affected to believe that we have severed her rightful territory, and in official proclamations and manifestoes has repeatedly threatened to make war upon us for the purpose of reconquering Texas. In the meantime we have tried every effort at reconciliation. The cup of forebearance had been exhausted even before the recent information from the frontier of the Del Norte. But now, after reiterated menaces, Mexico has passed the boundary of the United States, has invaded our territory and shed American blood upon the American soil. She has proclaimed that hostilities have commenced, and that the two nations are now at war.

As war exists, and, notwithstanding all our efforts to avoid it, exists by the act of Mexico herself, we are called upon by every consideration of duty and patriotism to vindicate with decision the honor, the rights, and the interests of our country. . . .

Source 2 from N. C. Brooks, *A Complete History of the Mexican War: Its Causes, Conduct, and Consequences* (Philadelphia: Grigg, Elliot and Co., 1849), p. 54.

2. March 1, 1845—Joint Congressional Resolution Offering Annexation to Texas.

Resolved by the Senate and House of Representatives of the United States of America in Congress assembled: That Congress doth consent that the territory properly included within and rightfully belonging to the Republic of Texas, may be erected into a new state, to be called the State of Texas, with

CHAPTER 9

WAR AND
MANIFEST
DESTINY: A
PROBLEM IN
CAUSATION

a republican form of government to be adopted by the people of said republic
by deputies in convention assembled, with the consent of the existing government, in order that the same may be admitted as one of the states of this
Union. . . .

3. March 4, 1845.

Polk is inaugurated.

Source 4 from James Schouler, *History of the United States Under the Constitution*,
Vol. IV (New York: Dodd, Mead & Co., 1889), p. 498. This conversation was recalled
by Bancroft to historian James Schouler in 1887.

4. Soon after Inauguration—Private Conversation Between Polk and Bancroft.

In a private conversation with one of his chosen cabinet which is still preserved, Polk announced his purpose soon after he had taken the oath of
office. "There are four great measures," said he, with emphasis, striking his
thigh forcibly as he spoke, "which are to be the measures of my administration: one, a reduction of the tariff; another, the independent treasury; a
third, the settlement of the Oregon boundary question; and, lastly, the acquisition of California."

5. March 6, 1845.

Slidell asks for passport.

6. March 23, 1845.

Mexico formally breaks diplomatic relations with the United States in protest over the congressional resolution approving the annexation of Texas
(the formal annexation took place in December 1845).

Sources 7 and 8 from Glenn W. Price, *Origins of the War with Mexico: The Polk-
Stockton Intrigue* (Austin: University of Texas Press, 1967), pp. 48, 11–12.

7. April 22, 1845—Bancroft to Stockton.

You will proceed with the vessels that have been placed under your command to the vicinity of Galveston, Texas, and lay as close to the shore as security will permit. You will take one of the vessels into the port of Galveston, and there display the American flag; or more if the bar will permit.

You will yourself go on shore, and make yourself acquainted with the dispositions of the people of Texas, and their relations with Mexico, of which you will make report to this Department.

After remaining at or off Galveston as long as in your judgment may seem necessary, you will proceed to join the squadron of Commodore Conner, off Vera Cruz.

8. 1859—Anson Jones Memoirs.

In May, 1845, Commodore Stockton, with a fleet of four or five vessels, arrived at Galveston, and with him Hon. C. A. Wickliffe, ex-Postmaster General of the United States. These gentlemen had various interviews with Major Gen. Sherman, the chief officer of the militia of Texas, the character of which is not precisely known to me; but the result of which was active preparations at Galveston for organizing volunteer forces, the ostensible (and no doubt real) object of which was an invasion of Mexico. A party [Jones thus seems to refer to President Polk], it appears, was anxious that the expedition should be set on foot, under the auspices of the Major-General and Com. Stockton; but these gentlemen, it appears, were unwilling to take so great a responsibility: it was therefore resolved that the plan should be submitted to me and my sanction obtained—(quere [sic], forced?)—indeed such, as afterwards became apparent, were the Commodore's instructions; and the organizing, &c, had been gone into for the purpose of forcing my assent to the proposed scheme. On the 28th May, Gen. Sherman for himself and associates in the militia, and Dr. Wright, surgeon of the steamer Princeton, and secretary of the Commodore, (as he informed me) took three days in unfolding to me the object of their visit. Dr. Wright stated that he was sent by Com. Stockton to propose that I should authorize Major Gen. Sherman to raise a force of two thousand men, or as many as might be necessary, and make a descent upon the Mexican town of Matamoras, and capture and hold it; that Com. Stockton would give assistance with the fleet under his command, under the pretext of giving the protection promised by the United States to Texas by Gen. Murphy; that he would undertake to supply the

CHAPTER 9

WAR AND
MANIFEST
DESTINY: A
PROBLEM IN
CAUSATION

necessary provisions, arms and munitions of war for the expedition, would land them at convenient points on our coast, and would agree to pay the men and officers to be engaged; that he had consulted Gen. Sherman, who approved the plan, and was present to say so; and, besides that, the people generally from Galveston to Washington [the city in Texas] had been spoken to about it, that it met their unanimous approval; and all that was now wanting was the sanction of the Government to the scheme. Gen. Sherman confirmed what Dr. Wright stated, said he had had various interviews with Com. Stockton, and hoped I would approve the expedition.

9. May 1845.

Frémont is ordered to take sixty men on expedition to visit both Oregon and California.

Source 10 from Mary Lee Spence and Donald Jackson, eds., *The Expeditions of John Charles Frémont,* Vol. II (Urbana: University of Illinois Press, 1973), pp. 3–4.

10. May 26–August 16, 1845—Frémont Memoirs.

Concurrently with the Report upon the second expedition the plans and scope of a third one had been matured. It was decided that it should be directed to that section of the Rocky Mountains which gives rise to the Arkansas River, the Rio Grande del Norte of the Gulf of Mexico, and the Rio Colorado of the Gulf of California; to complete the examination of the Great Salt Lake and its interesting region; and to extend the survey west and southwest to the examination of the great ranges of the Cascade Mountains and the Sierra Nevada, so as to ascertain the lines of communication through the mountains to the ocean in that latitude. And in arranging this expedition, the eventualities of war were taken into consideration.

Mexico, at war with the United States, would inevitably favor English protection for California. English citizens were claiming payment for loans and indemnity for losses. Our relations with England were already clouded, and in the event of war with Mexico, if not anticipated by us, an English fleet would certainly take possession of the Bay of San Francisco.

For use in such a contingency the only available force was our squadron in the North Pacific, and the measures for carrying out the design of the President fell to the Navy Department. During the year such precautionary measures as were practicable were taken, especially by the vigilant Secretary of the Navy, Mr. [George] Bancroft, whose orders continuously evince comprehending foresight and insistence. Imbued with the philosophy of history, his mind was alive to the bearing of the actual conditions, and he knew how sometimes skill and sometimes bold action determine the advantages of a political situation; and in this his great desire was to secure for the United States the important one that hung in the balance. In the government at Washington he was the active principle [*sic*], having the activity of brain and keen perception that the occasion demanded. With him Mr. Benton[6] had friendly personal relations of long standing.

As affairs resolved themselves, California stood out as the chief subject in the impending war; and with Mr. Benton and other governing men at Washington it became a firm resolve to hold it for the United States. To them it seemed reasonably sure that California would eventually fall to England or to the United States and that the eventuality was near. This was talked over fully during the time of preparation for the third expedition, and the contingencies anticipated and weighed. The relations between the three countries made a chief subject of interest about which our thoughts settled as the probability of war grew into certainty. For me, no distinct course or definite instruction could be laid down, but the probabilities were made known to me as well as what to do when they became facts. The distance was too great for timely communication; but failing this I was given discretion to act.

Sources 11 through 15 from Price, *Origins of the War with Mexico*, pp. 118, 119, 122, 129–130, 131–132.

11. May 21, 1845—Stockton to Bancroft.

War now exists and as any & every man here fights on his "own hook," the Texans ought therefore in my opinion to take possession and drive the Mexicans over the other side of the river before the meeting of Congress.

6. Thomas Hart Benton was senator of Missouri, an influential Democrat, confidant of Polk, and father-in-law of Captain John C. Frémont.

CHAPTER 9

WAR AND
MANIFEST
DESTINY: A
PROBLEM IN
CAUSATION

12. May 22, 1845—Stockton to Bancroft.

I will want more provisions and powder, that [*sic*] I expected when I left the United States. I will send to Pensacola for them, and if not there to New Orleans. Please to send the necessary orders to let me have what I shall deem necessary for the Squadron under my command.

[These were granted by Bancroft on June 2, 1845.]

13. May 27, 1845—Stockton to Bancroft.

My Dear Sir

Since my last letter I have seen Mr. Mayfield late Secretary of State—who says that if the people here did not feel assured that the Boundary line would be the Rio Grande three fourths and himself amongst the number would oppose the annexation—But I need hardly say another word on that subject; its importance is apparent—But it may perhaps be as well for me *in this way* to let you know how I propose to settle the matter without committing the U. States—The Major Genl will call out three thousand men & "R. F. Stockton Esq" will supply them in a private way with provisions & ammunition—

14. June 4, 1845—Stockton to Bancroft.

I am informed that there are seven thousand Mexican troops on the Rio Grande del Norte ready for invasion. No provision has been made to meet such an exigency, but that which I am & have been since my arrival here endeavoring to get the authorities of Texas to adopt.

The Government and people of Texas do most unfortunately entertain the expectation that the Government of the United States can and will protect them from any and all Mexican aggression, from the moment that the Congress of Texas shall accept the resolutions of the congress of the United States. This has caused among the people an apathy on the subject of the necessary defences which ought to be in my judgment alarming.

The Mexicans are ready to inflict a blow on the Territory of Texas as soon as they shall hear the result of Capt. Elliots [*sic*] mission. The United States troops cannot (if it were right to do so) be here to resist them. The Texans must be aroused to a proper sense of their own danger and my advice to this Government has been to call the Texan volunteer army into the field, to defend themselves from aggression, to regulate the Boundary and to be prepared to hand over to the United States and [*sic*] undisturbed and undisputed territory when the U.S. may be (of right) ready to occupy it.

15. June 11, 1845—Charles Elliot to Charles Bankhead.

I should tell you that I learnt as soon as I landed from a source of information entirely to be depended upon that Commodore Stockton was using every effort to induce the President [Anson Jones, President of Texas] to issue a Proclamation calling out Volunteers for the purpose of occupying the Country *to the Rio Grande at once.*

The President frankly admitted to me that such was the case, and told me (I use his own words as nearly as I can remember them) that he said to those parties "I see not one single motive for Annexation if it is not for security and protection, or if we are *to do our own fighting,* and I tell you plainly that I will not be made the scape goat in such an affair as you have proposed to me. The United States Government must take all the responsibility, and all the expense and all the labour of hostile movements upon Mexico. I will issue no Proclamation of the kind you wish, and authorize no movement unless Mexico makes a movement upon us. Somebody else must break up the state of peace. It shall not be me."

Source 16 from Brooks, *A Complete History of the Mexican War*, pp. 60–61.

16. Late July, 1845—John Black[7] to Slidell.

On Saturday evening, the 13th instant, at the request of Mr. Slidell, I called on the Mexican Minister, Señor Pena, at his house, to inquire when an answer would be given to his (Mr. Slidell's) aforesaid note.[8] He replied, that the affair had been submitted to the government council, in a special session of this day, and that it had been referred to a committee, and that as soon as the committee made a report, and the council should decide, he would then advise me . . . when he was ready for the conference to present to me the answer for Mr. Slidell; . . . that the Mexican government understood the

7. John Black was the United States consul in Mexico City.
8. Polk had ordered Slidell to return to Mexico to negotiate for the purchase of California and the Southwest Territory. Slidell had written to the Mexican government to see if he would be received. The Mexican government was willing to receive Slidell *only* to discuss issues relating to Texas, which would have prevented discussions concerning the purchase of California. This restriction was unacceptable to Slidell and he held out, waiting to be received as a full-fledged minister.

CHAPTER 9

WAR AND
MANIFEST
DESTINY: A
PROBLEM IN
CAUSATION

present mission to be a special mission, and confined to the differences in relation to the Texas question, and not as a mission to reside near the Mexican government, as in ordinary cases; that of course would follow when the first question was decided.

I replied, that as I understood it, the Mexican government had not only agreed to receive an envoy intrusted with full powers to settle the question in dispute in relation to the affairs of Texas, but *all* the questions in dispute between the two governments, as proposed by the government of the United States. He replied that the credentials of Mr. Slidell had not reference to any questions in dispute, but merely as a Minister to reside near the Mexican government, without reference to any questions in dispute, just as if the diplomatic and friendly relations between the two governments had not been and were not interrupted; that I knew the critical situation of the Mexican government, and that it had to proceed with great caution and circumspection in this affair; that the government itself was well disposed to arrange all differences.

Source 17 from David M. Pletcher, *The Diplomacy of Annexation: Texas, Oregon, and the Mexican War* (Columbia: University of Missouri, 1973), p. 270.

17. August 9, 1845—Polk to William H. Haywood (U.S. Senator from North Carolina).

Care has been taken—that all our military and naval movements shall be strictly defensive.—We will not be the aggressor upon Mexico;—but if her army shall cross the Del Norte[9] and invade Texas, we will if we can drive her army—to her own territory. Less than this—in good faith to Texas, I think this government could not have done. We invite Texas to unite her destinies with our own. She has accepted the invitation, upon the terms proposed, . . . and if because she has done so, she is invaded by the Mexican Army—surely we are bound to give her our aid in her own defence.

9. Polk always referred to the Rio Grande as the Del Norte. Its full name was the Rio Grande del Norte.

Source 18 from Price, *Origins of the War with Mexico*, p.163.

18. August 12, 1845—T. J. Green (Former Member of Texas Congress) to Robert Walker[10]

. . . that your troops advance west to the Rio Grande. Let one division strike that river at Laredo 140 miles south west from San Antonio, making the latter place head quarters. Let another division strike lower down the river. . . . *These* movements may be strictly defensive as the President please, but they will certainly *provoke offence* from the Mexicans. The bandit soldiery of Mexico will *commence* the game by plundering your commisariat [*sic*], stealing your cavalry horses, and murdering small parties. In such case, even the "National Intelligencer," will say to you "play the game out."[11]

19. August 15, 1845.

Secretary of War William L. Marcy orders General Zachary Taylor to move his 3,900 troops to Texas.

Sources 20 through 24 from Allan Nevins, ed., *Polk: The Diary of a President, 1845–1849* (London and New York: Longmans, Green, 1952), pp. 5–84.

20. August 29, 1845—Polk Diary.

The President called a special meeting of the Cabinet at twelve o'clock, all the members present except Mr. Mason. The President brought up for consideration our relations with Mexico, and the threatened invasion of Texas with that power. He submitted the following propositions which were unanimously agreed to as follows, *viz.*, If Mexico should declare war or actual hostilities should be commenced by that power, orders to be issued to General Taylor to attack and drive her back across the Del Norte. General Taylor shall be instructed that the crossing [of] the Del Norte by a Mexican army in force shall be regarded as an act of war on her part, and in that event General Taylor to be ordered, if he shall deem it advisable, not to wait

10. Robert Walker (1801–1869) was a United States senator from Mississippi from 1836 to 1845, an ardent expansionist, a key figure in the nomination of Polk, and Polk's Secretary of the Treasury. He was considered close to the president.
11. The *National Intelligencer,* published in Washington, was the "official" newspaper of the Whig party and, as such, opposed Polk and his expansionism.

CHAPTER 9

WAR AND
MANIFEST
DESTINY: A
PROBLEM IN
CAUSATION

to be attacked but to attack her army first. General Taylor in case of invasion by Mexico to be ordered not only to drive the invading army back to the west of the Del Norte, but to dislodge and drive back in like manner the Mexican post now stationed at Santiago. General Taylor to be vested with discretionary authority to pursue the Mexican army to the west of the Del Norte, and take Matamoras or any other Spanish post west of that river but not to penetrate any great distance into the interior of the Mexican territory.

21. September 1, 1845—Polk Diary.

Senator Bagby of Alabama called today and held a long conversation with the President. The President asked his opinion as to the necessity or propriety of calling Congress, in the event of a declaration of war or an invasion of Texas by Mexico. Mr. Bagby gave it as his clear opinion that Congress should not be called, and assigned his reasons at some length. . . . Mr. Senator Archer of Virginia called the same day and paid his respects to the President in his office. The subject of the existing relations with Mexico was spoken of. Mr. Archer expressed the opinion that Mexico would neither declare war nor invade Texas. The military and naval preparations which had been made by the Administration were spoken of, and Mr. Archer concurred in an opinion, expressed by the President, that the appearance of our land and naval forces on the borders of Mexico and in the Gulf would probably deter and prevent Mexico from either declaring war or invading Texas.

22. September 16, 1845—Polk Diary.

The Cabinet met today, all the members present. Despatches were read from Dr. Parrott, the confidential agent of the United States in Mexico, giving an account of another threatened revolution, etc., and of the refusal of Paredes to march his army to Texas. Dr. Parrott's latest despatch was of date 29th August, 1845. He gives it as his opinion that there will be no declaration of war against the United States and no invasion of Texas; that the government will be kept employed to keep down another revolution which was threatened. He is also of opinion that the government is desirous to reestablish diplomatic relations with the United States, and that a Minister from the United States would be received. In these opinions Mr. Black, the United States consul at Mexico, of date 23d August, and Mr. Dimond, United States consul at Vera Cruz, of date 30th August, concurred. After much consultation it was agreed unanimously that it was expedient to re-open diplomatic relations with Mexico; but that it was to be kept a profound secret that such a step was contemplated, for the reason mainly that if it was known in advance in the United States that a Minister had been sent to Mexico, it would, of course, be known to the British, French, and other foreign Ministers at Washington, who might take measures to thwart or defeat the objects of the mission. The President, in consultation with the Cabinet, agreed that the Hon. John Slidell of New Orleans, who spoke the Spanish language and was otherwise well qualified, should be tendered the mission. It was agreed that Mr. Slidell, if he accepted, should leave Pensacola in a national armed vessel and proceed to Vera Cruz, without disclosing or making known his official character. One great object of the mission, as stated by the President, would be to adjust a permanent boundary between Mexico and the United States, and that in doing this the Minister would be instructed to purchase for a pecuniary consideration Upper California and New Mexico. He said that a better boundary would be the Del Norte from its mouth to the Passo, in latitude about 32° north, and thence west to the Pacific Ocean, Mexico ceding to the United States all the country east and north of these lines.[12] The President said that for such a boundary the amount of pecuniary consideration to be paid would be of small importance. He supposed it might be had for fifteen or twenty millions, but he was ready to pay forty millions for it, if it could not be had for less. In these views the Cabinet agreed with the President unanimously.

23. October 24, 1845—Polk Diary.

The conversation then turned on California, on which I remarked that Great Britain had her eye on that country and intended to possess it if she could, but that the people of the United States would not willingly permit California to pass into the possession of any new colony planted by Great Britain or any foreign monarchy, and that in reasserting Mr. Monroe's doctrine I had California and the fine bay of San Francisco as much in view as Oregon. Col. Benton agreed that no foreign power ought to be permitted to colonize California, any more than they would be to colonize Cuba. As long as Cuba remained in the possession of the present government we would not object, but if a powerful foreign power was about to possess it, we would not permit it. On the same footing we would place California. . . .

12. That would be the approximate present boundary of the United States, less the 1853 Gadsden Purchase.

CHAPTER 9

WAR AND
MANIFEST
DESTINY: A
PROBLEM IN
CAUSATION

Some conversation occurred concerning Capt. Frémont's expedition, and his intention to visit California before his return. Col. Benton expressed the opinion that Americans would settle on the Sacramento River and ultimately hold the country.

24. November 10, 1845—Polk Diary.

Saw and had a full conversation with Dr. Parrott, who had been in Mexico as a confidential agent of the United States for some months, and who arrived at Washington last night. He confirmed the opinion I had entertained that Mexico was anxious to settle the pending difficulties between the two countries, including those of boundary. I informed Dr. Parrott that I wished him to return to Mexico as secretary of legation to the Minister whom I intended to appoint this day, and told him the Hon. John Slidell of New Orleans was the person I intended to appoint as Minister. He was not anxious to accept the office of secretary of legation, but agreed to do so, and said he would be ready to leave in about ten days. At ten o'clock P.M., the instructions and all the documents referred to being copied, I signed the commission of the Hon. John Slidell as Envoy Extraordinary and Minister Plenipotentiary to Mexico.

25. Late December, 1845.

A revolution takes place in Mexico in which the government of President José Joaquín Herrera is overthrown by General Don Mariano Paredes y Arrillaga and the Mexican army.

Source 26 from José Fernando Ramírez, *Mexico During the War with the United States,* trans. Elliot B. Scherr, in *University of Missouri Studies,* Vol. XXIII, No. 1 (1950), p. 52.

26. January 2, 1846—Ramírez Memoirs.

Very early today posters were put up on all the street corners. They read as follows: "Announcement to the People. Today His Excellency Don Mariano Paredes y Arrillaga will enter the Capital with the army under his command. The citizens are hereby urged to decorate their houses and in this way demonstrate the dictates of their patriotism." A short time later these posters were either torn to pieces or scribbled on with obscene words. When the rebels saw that patriotism would not succeed in getting even one bit of bunting hung up for decoration, they sent out soldiers a short time before the troops were to enter the city, and these soldiers warned the citizens who lived on the streets along which the troops were to pass that balconies were to be properly hung with bunting. This was done. But it was the only display of bunting that Señor Paredes saw on his passage through the city. There was not a single bit of bunting on the main square, except for the *official* decorations of the City Hall and the President's Palace. . . .

27. January 12, 1846.

Washington learns of Slidell's initial rejection.

Source 28 from N. C. Brooks, *A Complete History of the Mexican War:*, pp. 66–67.

28. January 13, 1846—Marcy orders Taylor into the Disputed Territory Between the Nueces River and the Rio Grande.

Sir: I am directed by the President to instruct you to advance and occupy, with the troops under your command, positions on or near the east bank of the Rio del Norte, as soon as it can be conveniently done with reference to the season and the routes by which your movements must be made. From the views heretofore presented to this department, it is presumed Point Isabel will be considered by you an eligible position. This point, or some one near it, and points opposite Matamoros and Mier, and in the vicinity of Laredo, are suggested for your consideration; but you are left to your better knowledge to determine the post or posts which you are to occupy, as well as the question of dividing your forces with a view to occupying two or more positions.

In the positions you may take in carrying out these instructions and other movements that may be made, the use of the Rio del Norte may be very convenient, if not necessary. Should you attempt to exercise the right which the United States have in common with Mexico to the free navigation of this river, it is probable that Mexico would interpose resistance. You will not attempt to enforce this right without further instructions.

You are requested to report to this department, without delay, what means you may require, if any, beyond those you now possess, to enforce and

CHAPTER 9

WAR AND
MANIFEST
DESTINY: A
PROBLEM IN
CAUSATION

maintain our common right to navigate this river, as well as your views of the importance of this right in the defence and protection of the State of Texas.

It is not designed, in our present relations with Mexico, that you should treat her as an enemy; but, should she assume that character by a declaration of war, or any open act of hostility towards us, you will not act merely on the defensive, if your relative means enable you to do otherwise. . . .

Source 29 from Spence and Jackson, eds., *The Expeditions of John Charles Frémont*, Vol. II , p. 75.

29. March 5, 1846—Manuel de Jesus Castro to Frémont (Castro was in Monterey, California).

I have learnt with surprise that you against the laws of the authorities of Mexico have introduced yourself into the towns of this Departmental district under my charge with an armed force under a commission which must have been given you by your government only to survey its own proper lands.

In consequence this Prefectura now orders that you will immediately on receipt of this without any pretext return with your people out of the limits of this territory. If not this office will take the necessary measures to cause respect to this determination.

I have the honor to transcribe this to you for your intelligence that you may act in the case as belongs to your office and that he may comply with the expressed order. God & Liberty. Monterey March 5, 1846.

(Signed)   MANUEL CASTRO

Sources 30 and 31 from Brooks, *A Complete History of the Mexican War*, pp. 84–86, 82–83.

30. March 18, 1846—Proclamation of General Francisco Mejia (Mexican Commander at Matamoros).

Fellow-citizens:—The annexation of the department of Texas to the United States, projected and consummated by the tortuous policy of the cabinet of the Union, does not yet satisfy the ambitious desires of the degenerate sons of Washington. The civilized world has already recognised in that act all the marks of injustice, iniquity, and the most scandalous violation of the rights of nations. Indelible is the stain which will for ever darken the character for virtue falsely attributed to the people of the United States; and posterity will regard with horror their perfidious conduct, and the immorality of the means employed by them to carry into effect that most degrading depredation. The right of conquest has always been a crime against humanity; but nations jealous of their dignity and reputation have endeavoured at least to cover it by the splendour of arms and the prestige of victory. To the United States it has been reserved to put in practice dissimulation, fraud, and the basest treachery, in order to obtain possession, in the midst of peace, of the territory of a friendly nation, which generously relied upon the faith of promises and the solemnity of treaties.

The cabinet of the United States does not, however, stop in its career of usurpation. Not only does it aspire to the possession of the department of Texas, but it covets also the regions on the left bank of the Rio Bravo.[13] Its army, hitherto for some time stationed at Corpus Christi, is now advancing to take possession of a large part of Tamaulipas; and its vanguard has arrived at the Arroya Colorado, distant eighteen leagues from this place. What expectations, therefore, can the Mexican government have of treating with an enemy, who, whilst endeavouring to lull us into security, by opening diplomatic negotiations, proceeds to occupy a territory which never could have been the object of the pending discussion? The limits of Texas are certain and recognised; never have they extended beyond the river Neuces; notwithstanding which, the American army has crossed the line separating Tamaulipas from that department. . . .

Fellow-countrymen: With an enemy which respects not its own laws, which shamelessly derides the very principles invoked by it previously, in order to excuse its ambitious views, we have no other resource than arms. We are fortunately always prepared to take them up with glory, in defence of our country; little do we regard the blood in our veins, when we are called on to shed it in vindication of our honour, to assure our nationality and independence. If to the torrent of devastation which threatens us it be necessary to oppose a dike of steel, our swords will form it; and on their sharp points will the enemy receive the fruits of his anticipated conquest. . . .

13. The Rio Grande.

CHAPTER 9

WAR AND
MANIFEST
DESTINY: A
PROBLEM IN
CAUSATION

31. March 21, 1846—Taylor to the War Department.

Sir:—I respectfully report that my forces are now concentrated at this point, the Third Brigade having joined me to-day. We are nearly north of Matamoros, and about thirty miles distant.

The Arroya Colorado is a salt river, or rather lagoon, nearly one hundred yards broad, and so deep as barely to be fordable. It would have formed a serious obstruction to our march had the enemy chosen to occupy its right bank, even with a small force. On the 19th, the advanced corps encamped within three miles of the ford, and a reconnoissance was pushed forward to the river. A party of irregular cavalry (rancheros) was discovered on the opposite bank, but threw no obstacle in the way of examining the ford. They, however, signified to the officer charged with the reconnoissance that it would be considered an act of hostility if we attempted to pass the river, and that we should, in that case, be treated as enemies. . . . While these dispositions were in progress, the party that had shown themselves the day before again made their appearance. I sent Captain Mansfield to communicate with the officer in command, who said that he had positive orders to fire upon us if we attempted to cross the river. Another party then made its appearance, and passed the river to communicate with me. One of them (who was represented as the adjutant-general of the Mexican troops) repeated substantially what had been sent before, viz.: that they had peremptory orders to fire upon us, and that it would be considered a declaration of war if we passed the river. He placed in my hands, at the same time, a proclamation of General Mejia, issued at Matamoros, a day or two previous, which I enclose. I informed the officer that I should immediately cross the river, and if any of his party showed themselves on the other bank after the passage commenced, they would receive the fire of our artillery. In the mean time, the Second Brigade (which had encamped some miles in my rear) came up and formed on the extreme right. The crossing was then commenced and executed in the order prescribed. Not a shot was fired; and a reconnoissance of cavalry, sent immediately forward, discovered the party which had occupied the bank retreating in the direction of Matamoros. Agreeably to my orders, they were not molested. The Cavalry and First and Second Brigades of Infantry, with a train of two hundred wagons, crossed over and encamped at this point, three miles distant, at an early hour in the afternoon.

I have thought proper to make a detailed report of this operation, as being the first occasion on which the Mexicans have shown themselves in an attitude decidedly hostile. It has also furnished an excellent opportunity for the instruction of the troops, and for displaying their discipline and spirit, which, I am gratified to be able to say, were everything that could be desired. . . .

Source 32 from Nevins, ed., *Polk: The Diary of a President, 1845–1849,* pp. 5–84.

32. March 28, 1846—Polk Diary.

The government of General Paredes, having recently overthrown that of President Herrera, was a military government and depended for its continuance in power upon the allegiance of the army under his command, and by which he had been enabled to effect the late revolution. It was known that the government of Paredes was in great need of money, and that in consequence of the deficiencies in the treasury and the deranged state of the finances, the army upon whose support General Paredes depended to uphold him in power, being badly fed and clothed and without pay, might and probably would soon desert him, unless money could be obtained to supply their wants. I stated that if our Minister could be authorized upon the *signing* of the treaty to pay down a half a million or a million of dollars, it would enable General Paredes to pay, feed, and clothe the army, and maintain himself in power until the treaty could be ratified by the United States and the subsequent instalments which might be stipulated in the treaty be paid. Indeed, I thought that the prompt payment of such a sum might induce him to make a treaty, which he would not otherwise venture to make. In these views there seemed to be a concurrence. The question followed how an appropriation could be obtained from Congress without exposing to the public and to foreign governments its object.

Sources 33 through 35 from Brooks, *A Complete History of the Mexican War,* pp. 93–94, 95, 99.

33. April 12, 1846—General Pedro de Ampudia to Taylor.

God and Liberty!

  To explain to you the many grounds for the just grievances felt by the Mexican nation, caused by the United States government, would be a loss of time, and an insult to your good sense; I, therefore, pass at once to such explanation as I consider of absolute necessity.

CHAPTER 9

WAR AND
MANIFEST
DESTINY: A
PROBLEM IN
CAUSATION

Your government, in an incredible manner—you will even permit me to say an extravagant one, if the usages, or general rules established and received among all civilized nations are regarded—has not only insulted, but has exasperated the Mexican nation, bearing its conquering banner to the left bank of the Rio Bravo del Norte; and in this case, by explicit and definitive orders of my government, which neither can, will, nor should receive new outrages, I require you in all form, and at latest in the peremptory term of twenty-four hours, to break up your camp and retire to the other bank of the Neuces river, while our governments are regulating the pending question in relation to Texas. If you insist on remaining upon the soil of the department of Tamaulipas, it will clearly result that arms, and arms alone, must decide the question; and, in that case, I advise you that we accept the war to which, with so much injustice on your part, you provoke us, and that, on our part, this war shall be conducted conformably to the principles established by the most civilized nations; that is to say, that the law of nations and of war shall be the guide of my operations; trusting that on your part the same will be observed.

34. April 12, 1846—Taylor's Reply to Ampudia.

Senor: I have had the honour to receive your note of this date, in which you summon me to withdraw the forces under my command from their present position, and beyond the river Nueces, until the pending question between our governments, relative to the limits of Texas, shall be settled. . . .

The instructions under which I am acting will not permit me to retrograde from the position I now occupy. In view of the relations between our respective governments, and the individual suffering which may result, I regret the alternative which you offer; but, at the same time, wish it understood that I shall by no means avoid such alternative, leaving the responsibility with those who rashly commence hostilities. In conclusion, you will permit me to give the assurance that on my part the laws and customs of war among civilized nations shall be carefully observed. . . .

35. April 23, 1846[14]—Proclamation of President Paredes.

. . . At the time Mr. Slidell presented himself, the troops of the United States occupied our territory, their squadrons threatened our ports, and they pre-

14. On April 19, a clash between United States and Mexican troops occurred. Paredes knew about this incident when he issued this proclamation, but, as we shall see, Polk did not learn of the event until about 6:00 P.M. on May 9.

pared to occupy the peninsula of the Californias, of which the question of the Oregon with England is only a preliminary. Mr. Slidell was not received, because the dignity of the nation repelled this new insult. Meanwhile the army of the United States encamped at Corpus Christi, and occupied the *Isla del Padre;* following this, they then moved to the point *Santo Isabel,* and their standard of the stars and stripes waved on the right bank of the Rio Bravo del Norte, opposite the city of Matamoros, blockading that river with their vessels of war. The village of Laredo was surprised by a party of their troops, and a small party of our men, reconnoitring there, were disarmed. Hostilities, then, have been commenced, by the United States of North America, beginning new conquests upon the frontier territories of the departments of Tamaulipas and New Leon, and progressing at such a rate, that troops of the same United States threaten Monterey in Upper California. No one can doubt which of the two republics is responsible for this war: a war which any sense of equity and justice, and respect for the rights and laws of civilized nations, might have avoided. . . .

Sources 36 and 37 from Nevins, ed., *Polk: The Diary of a President, 1845–1849*, pp. 5–84.

36. May 8, 1846—Polk Diary.

Saw company until twelve o'clock today. Among others the Hon. John Slidell, late United States Minister to Mexico, called in company with the Secretary of State. Mr. Buchanan[15] retired after a few minutes, and Mr. Slidell remained about an hour in conversation concerning his mission and the state of our relations with Mexico. Mr. Slidell's opinion was that but one course towards Mexico was left to the United States, and that was to take the redress of the wrongs and injuries which we had so long borne from Mexico into our own hands, and to act with promptness and energy. In this I agreed with him, and told him it was only a matter of time when I would make a communication to Congress on the subject, and that I had made up my mind to do so very soon.

15. James Buchanan (1791–1868) was Polk's secretary of state. Entering politics in 1814 as a Federalist, he became a Democrat in 1824, and served as congressman, minister to Russia, and U.S. senator prior to 1844. He was a firm expansionist and helped carry his native Pennsylvania for Polk in 1844. He was president of the United States from 1857 to 1861, in the midst of the sectional crisis that, ironically, his expansionist policies helped fuel.

CHAPTER 9

WAR AND
MANIFEST
DESTINY: A
PROBLEM IN
CAUSATION

37. May 9, 1846—Polk Diary.

The Cabinet held a regular meeting today; all the members present. I brought up the Mexican question, and the question of what was the duty of the administration in the present state of our relations with that country. The subject was very fully discussed. All agreed that if the Mexican forces at Matamoras committed any act of hostility on General Taylor's forces I should immediately send a message to Congress recommending an immediate declaration of war. I stated to the Cabinet that up to this time, as we knew, we had heard of no open act of aggression by the Mexican army, but that the danger was imminent that such acts would be committed. I said that in my opinion we had ample cause of war, and that it was impossible that we could stand in *status quo,* or that I could remain silent much longer; that I thought it was my duty to send a message to Congress very soon and recommend definite measures. I told them that I thought I ought to make such a message by Tuesday next, that the country was excited and impatient on the subject, and if I failed to do so I would not be doing my duty. I then propounded the distinct question to the Cabinet, and took their opinions individually, whether I should make a message to Congress on Tuesday, and whether in that message I should recommend a declaration of war against Mexico. All except the Secretary of the Navy gave their advice in the affirmative. Mr. Bancroft dissented but said if any act of hostility should be committed by the Mexican forces he was then in favour of immediate war. Mr. Buchanan said he would feel better satisfied in his course if the Mexican forces had or should commit any act of hostility, but that as matters stood we had ample cause of war against Mexico, and he gave his assent to the measure. It was agreed that the message should be prepared and submitted to the Cabinet in their meeting on Tuesday. A history of our causes of complaint against Mexico had been at my request previously drawn up by Mr. Buchanan. I stated that what was said in my annual message in December gave that history as succinctly and satisfactorily as Mr. Buchanan's statement, that in truth it was the same history in both, expressed in different language, and that if I repeated that history in a message to Congress now I had better employ the precise language used in my message of December last. Without deciding this point the Cabinet passed to the consideration of some other subjects of minor importance. . . .

About six o'clock P.M. General R. Jones, the Adjutant-General of the army, called and handed to me despatches received from General Taylor by the Southern mail which had just arrived, giving information that a part of the Mexican army had crossed the Del Norte and attacked and killed and captured two companies of dragoons of General Taylor's army consisting of 63 officers and men. The despatch also stated that he had on that day (26th April) made a requisition on the Governors of Texas and Louisiana for four regiments each, to be sent to his relief at the earliest practicable period. Before I had finished reading the despatch, the Secretary of War called. I immediately summoned the Cabinet to meet at half past seven o'clock this evening. The Cabinet accordingly assembled at that hour; all the members present. The subject of the despatch received this evening from General Taylor, as well as the state of our relations with Mexico, were fully considered. The Cabinet were unanimously of opinion, and it was so agreed, that a message should be sent to Congress on Monday laying all the information in my possession before them and recommending vigorous and prompt measures to enable the executive to prosecute the war. The Secretary of War and Secretary of State agreed to put their clerks to work to copy the correspondence between Mr. Slidell and the Mexican Government and Secretary of State and the correspondence between the War Department and General Taylor, to the end that these documents should be transmitted to Congress with my message on Monday. The other members of the Cabinet tendered the services of their clerks to aid in preparing these copies.

Mr. Senator Houston, Hon. Barclay Martin, and several other members of Congress called in the course of the evening, and were greatly excited at the news brought by the Southern mail from the army. They all approved the steps which had been taken by the administration, and were all of opinion that war with Mexico should now be prosecuted with vigor.

The Cabinet adjourned about ten o'clock and I commenced my message; Mr. Bancroft and Mr. Buchanan, the latter of whom had prepared a history of our causes of complaint against Mexico, agreed to assist me in preparing the message.

CHAPTER 9

WAR AND
MANIFEST
DESTINY: A
PROBLEM IN
CAUSATION

QUESTIONS TO CONSIDER

The evidence begins with President Polk's war message to Congress on May 11, 1846 (Source 1). What does Polk claim were the causes of the war with Mexico that he was asking Congress to declare? How does Polk portray the United States? How does he portray Mexico? As you examine the remainder of the evidence, recall the things that Polk did *not* mention in his war message. How important are these omissions?

At first glance, the remainder of the evidence appears to be too large and complicated to be analyzed adequately. As noted in the "Method" section of this chapter, however, the evidence can be divided into manageable segments. The first segment might include the evidence from Polk's inauguration to August 15, 1845, in which Commodore Robert Field Stockton plays a major role (Sources 3 through 8, 11 through 19). Use that evidence to answer the following questions:

1. What was the diplomatic situation between the United States and Mexico at the time of Polk's inauguration?
2. What did Polk see as the goals of his presidency?
3. What was Stockton's mission? What did Jones think Stockton's mission was? Is there evidence to corroborate Jones? What is the significance of "R. F. Stockton Esq" in the May 27 letter?
4. What was Frémont's mission? What do his memoirs reveal?
5. What did Stockton want the Texans to do? Why Texans and not United States troops?
6. How can Polk's letter of August 9, 1845, to Haywood be interpreted? Does other evidence help with this interpretation?
7. Why was Taylor ordered to Texas on August 15, 1845?

Now put together all the evidence from the first segment. What does it tell you? How much of this did Polk mention in his war message?

The second segment might deal with the evidence from August 1845 until January 13, 1846 (Sources 20 through 28), in which special minister John Slidell is a central figure. Ask the following questions of the evidence:

1. Bagby and Archer had one explanation for why United States troops were sent to Texas (Source 21). What was it? How does this explanation fit with the other pieces of evidence?
2. Why was Slidell sent to Mexico? What were his chances of success (remember Stockton and Frémont)?
3. Why did Mexico seem unwilling to receive Slidell? What did Mexico claim? How justified was this claim?
4. Who was Dr. Parrott? What was his role?
5. What was the general feeling in Polk's cabinet about California? What about Benton's opinion?
6. In late 1845, Mexico was in the throes of a revolution. How did Polk attempt to use this event? How likely were his chances of success?

7. On January 13, 1846, Secretary of War William Marcy ordered Taylor into the disputed territory. How does the timing of that order fit with Slidell's mission? How would you interpret the timing of Marcy's order?

Now repeat the process you used for the first segment. What does the evidence collectively tell you? Are there pieces of evidence that do not seem to fit? How can you explain them? How much of this segment's material did Polk mention in his war message?

The last segment deals with the period from mid-January to May 9, 1846 (Sources 28 through 37). As you examine the evidence, ask yourself the following questions:

1. Manuel de Jesus Castro was a Mexican official. What is the gist of his letter to Frémont? Was he justified in writing to Frémont?
2. The proclamation of General Mejia is intended to give the Mexican point of view. How do the Mexicans interpret the actions of the United States? Slidell's mission? Taylor's actions? How justified is this interpretation? How do Mejia's views compare with those of Ampudia? Paredes?
3. How would you compare Mexican words and actions [see Taylor's March 21 report (Source 31)]?
4. What was Polk's frame of mind May 8 to May 9, 1846?
5. The May 9 cabinet meetings (remember there were two of them on the same day) are crucial. In the first meeting, what had Polk made up his mind to do?

Repeat the procedure you followed in the first and second segments. What does the evidence in the third segment tell you? How much of this did Polk mention in his war message?

Now you are ready to put the three groups together. But first read the introduction to this exercise to review the long-range causal factors. Then form a thesis as to the causes of the Mexican War and Polk's role in the coming of that conflict. Are there pieces of evidence that do not fit your thesis? If so, explain them. When most of the evidence does fit, however, and you can explain the pieces that do not fit (your instructor can be very helpful here), you will be ready to offer your explanation for the causes of the Mexican War.

As to whether the United States's declaration of war against Mexico was justified, you will have to compare Polk's justifications in his war message with other reasons for the war that you found in the rest of the evidence. Is Polk's case a strong one? Are there significant omissions from his war message? To what extent do those omissions weaken Polk's justifications?

CHAPTER 9

WAR AND
MANIFEST
DESTINY: A
PROBLEM IN
CAUSATION

EPILOGUE

From the point of view of the United States, the Mexican War was won with a minimum of effort because Mexico was badly overmatched. Troops under General Zachary Taylor moved across the Rio Grande, winning important battles at Monterrey and Buena Vista. Simultaneously, General Winfield Scott landed at Vera Cruz and marched inland to Mexico City. In California, a combined force of army and navy easily scattered the weak Mexican resistance. In all, the war lasted less than twenty-one months and cost the United States only thirteen thousand men.

Several people benefited from the war. Taylor and Scott became war heroes. Indeed, Taylor won the presidency in 1848 almost on the sole basis of being a military hero. He had never even voted, and it has been said that he refused to accept the notification of his nomination for the presidency because the letter had postage due. Many younger men also made their military reputations during the Mexican War and gained valuable combat experience. For example, most of the generals on both sides of the Civil War (including Ulysses S. Grant and Robert E. Lee) saw action in that conflict.

Another person whose reputation benefited from the Mexican War was John C. Frémont. When war broke out, Frémont was in California (disobeying Castro's order: he had never actually left California) where he aided armed civilians in overthrowing the Mexicans and proclaiming California an independent republic (the "Bear Flag Re-

public," because of the flag). When General Stephen Kearny arrived in California with a large American force, he put an end to the Bear Flag Republic, proclaimed California a territory of the United States, and charged a resisting Frémont with insubordination (for which Frémont was subsequently court-martialed). In his struggle for power, Frémont had been aided by none other than Commodore Robert Stockton. Despite the court-martial, however, Frémont's actions made him such a popular figure that he went into politics and was nominated by the new Republican party in 1856 to oppose Buchanan.

In some parts of the United States, however, the Mexican War was the subject of bitter debate. Some northeasterners charged that it was a "slaveholders' war," designed to add slave territory to the United States. Henry David Thoreau refused to pay taxes to support the conflict (he spent one night in jail) and wrote his famous essay "On Civil Disobedience," which posed the timeless question of what people should do when their own moral convictions clash with the will and laws of their government. Writing from far-off Europe, American author, journalist, and feminist Margaret Fuller mourned her country's involvement in what she called an "unjust war." Under this strain, the unity of America's political parties was noticeably weakened.

The extent to which the issue of slavery had intruded itself into American life can be seen in the debate over the future of the territory taken from Mexico. How these territories were to be organized and whether slavery would be permitted in them were subjects of intense discussion that the Compromise of 1850 only partially alleviated. As Americans would come to realize, the linking of the issues of slavery and territorial expansion proved tragic. Ultimately, only the Civil War— and the loss of over 600,000 lives— would settle the question.

The Mexican War also left a residue of bad feelings between the United States and Mexico which has never really been overcome. The southwesterners' treatment of Mexicans as inferiors was not much different from the white southerners' treatment of African Americans and the far westerners' of orientals. President Woodrow Wilson's brief invasion of Mexico hardly furthered better relations, and President Jimmy Carter's offhand comment about the purity of Mexican water was at the very least an unfortunate quip that many Mexicans viewed as offensive. Equally offensive to many is the habit people of the United States have (and, if

you look back in this text, you will see that we have been guilty too) of referring to themselves as "Americans," as if no one else in the Western Hemisphere deserves the title. In all, the relationship between the two nations has been less than harmonious.

Perhaps most important from our point of view, however, is that the Mexican War added significantly (over 529,000 square miles) to the size of the United States, thus further ensuring United States power and world influence. Untold billions of dollars of natural resources, beginning with the discovery of gold in California one month before the end of the Mexican War, have been tapped. In search of gold or land or opportunity, millions of Americans migrated to the areas gained in the war, until by the latter part of the twentieth century, the state of California (which in 1912 had a population smaller than that of Georgia) had become the most populous state in the Union. If, as the editorialist suggested, this was the United States's "manifest destiny," it was one that Americans themselves took a most active part in achieving.

THE PRICE FOR VICTORY:
THE DECISION
TO USE BLACK TROOPS

With the outbreak of war at Fort Sumter in April 1861, many northern African Americans volunteered for service in the Union army. President Abraham Lincoln, however, initially rejected black petitions to become soldiers. On April 29, Secretary of War Simon Cameron wrote one of many letters to African American volunteers; it curtly stated that "this Department has no intention at present to call into the service of the Government any colored soldiers."[1] Later, in July 1862, when Congress passed the Confiscation Act (part of which authorized the president to use escaped slaves for the suppression of the rebellion "in such

1. The letter was addressed to "Jacob Dodson (colored)" and is in *The War of the Rebellion: A Compilation of the Official Records of the Union and Confederate Armies,* Series III, Vol. I (Washington, D.C.: U.S. Government Printing Office, 1899), p. 133.

manner as he may judge best") and the Militia Act (which authorized him to enroll African Americans for military service), Lincoln virtually ignored both laws by using the somewhat dubious logic that the two acts *authorized* him to recruit blacks but did not *require* him to do so.

Curiously, in the South too, free blacks and some slaves petitioned to be included in the newly formed Confederate army, perhaps hoping that such service might improve their conditions or even win them freedom. Like Lincoln, Confederate president Jefferson Davis rejected African American volunteers for military service and consistently opposed their use. Yet ultimately both chief executives changed their minds and accepted African Americans into the armed forces, although in Davis's case the policy reversal came too late for black units to see action on the

Confederate side. And although the recruitment of African American soldiers by the South might have prolonged the conflict, it probably would not have altered the ultimate outcome. In this chapter you will examine the evidence so as to answer the following questions:

1. What were the arguments in the North and in the South against arming African Americans and using them as regular soldiers? What were the arguments in favor of this move? How did the reasons in the North and in the South differ? How were they similar?
2. What do you think were the principal reasons why both the United States and the Confederate States of America changed their policies? How did the reasons in the North and in the South differ? How were they similar?

BACKGROUND

Although many leaders in both the North and South denied it at the time, the institution of slavery unquestionably played a major role in bringing on the American Civil War. As slavery intruded into the important issues and events of the day (such as westward expansion, the Mexican War, the admission of new states to the Union, the course charted for the proposed transcontinental railroad, and the right of citizens to petition Congress) as well as into all the major institutions (churches and schools, for example), an increasing number of northerners and southerners came to feel that the question of slavery must be settled, and settled on the battlefield. Therefore, when news arrived of the firing on Fort Sumter, many greeted the announcement with relief. Lincoln's call for 75,000 volunteers was answered with an enormous response. A wave of patriotic fervor swept across the northern states, as crowds greeted Union soldiers marching south to "lick the rebels." In the South, too, the outbreak of war was greeted with great enthusiasm. In Charleston, South Carolina, a day of celebration was followed by a night of parades and fireworks. Many southerners compared the upcoming war to the American Revolution, when, so the thinking went, an outnumbered but superior people had been victorious over the tyrant.

Yet, for a number of reasons, most northern and southern leaders carefully avoided the slavery issue even after war had begun. To Abraham Lincoln, the debate over the abolition of slavery threatened to divert northerners from what he considered the war's central aim: preserving the Union and denying the South's right to secede. In addition, Lincoln realized that a great number of northern whites, including himself, did not view African Americans as equals and might well oppose a war designed to liberate slaves from bondage. Finally, in large parts of Virginia, North Carolina, Kentucky, and Tennes-

[247]

CHAPTER 10

THE PRICE FOR
VICTORY: THE
DECISION TO
USE BLACK
TROOPS

see and in other pockets in the South, Union sentiment was strong, largely because of the antiplanter bias in these states. But anti-Negro sentiment was also strong in these same areas. With the border states so crucial to the Union both politically and militarily (as points of invasion into the South), it is not surprising that Lincoln purposely discouraged any notion that the war was for the purpose of emancipating slaves. Therefore, when influential editor Horace Greeley publicly called on Lincoln in August 1862 to make the Civil War a war for the emancipation of slaves, the president replied that the primary purpose of the war was to preserve the Union. "My paramount object in this struggle," Lincoln wrote, "is *not* either to save or destroy slavery" (italics added).

> If I could save the Union without freeing *any* slave I would do it, and if I could save it by freeing *all* the slaves I would do it; and if I could save it by freeing some and leaving others alone I would also do that. What I do about slavery, . . . I do because I believe it helps to save the Union; and what I forbear, I forbear because I do *not* believe it would help to save the Union[2] (italics added).

Hence President Lincoln, in spite of his "*personal* wish that all men every where could be free" (italics added), strongly resisted all efforts to turn the Civil War into a moral crusade to, in his words, "destroy slavery."

On the Confederate side, President Jefferson Davis also had reasons to avoid making slavery (in this case its preservation) a primary war aim. Davis feared, correctly, that foreign governments would be unwilling to recognize or aid the Confederacy if the preservation of slavery was the most important southern reason for fighting. Too, the majority of white southerners did not own slaves, often disliked people who did, and, Davis feared, might not fight if the principal war aim was to defend the peculiar institution. Therefore, while Lincoln was explaining to northerners that the war was being fought to preserve the Union, Davis was trying to convince southerners that the struggle was for independence and the defense of constitutional rights.

Yet as it became increasingly clear that the Civil War was going to be a long and costly conflict, issues concerning slavery and the use of African Americans in the war effort continually came to the surface. In the North, reports of battle casualties in 1862 caused widespread shock and outrage, and some feared that the United States would be exhausted before the Confederacy was finally subdued—if it was to be subdued at all.[3] Also, many northerners came to feel that emancipation could be used as both a political and diplomatic weapon. Those European nations (especially England, which had ended slavery throughout its own empire in 1833) that had been technically neu-

2. Lincoln to Greeley, Aug. 22, 1862, in Roy P. Basler, ed., *The Collected Works of Abraham Lincoln*, Vol. V (New Brunswick, N.J.: Rutgers University Press, 1953), pp. 388–389.

3. The following is an estimate of Union casualties (the sum of those killed, wounded, and missing) for the principal engagements of 1862: Shiloh (April, 13,000 casualties), Seven Pines (May, 6,000), Seven Days (June, 16,000), Antietam (September, 12,400), Fredericksburg (December, 12,000).

tral but were leaning toward the Confederacy might, northerners reasoned, be afraid to oppose a government committed to such a worthy cause as emancipation. Too, some northerners hoped that a proclamation of emancipation would incite widespread slave rebellions in the South that would cripple the Confederacy. Not to be overlooked, however, are those northerners (a minority) who sincerely viewed slavery as a stain on American society and whose eradication was a moral imperative.

Gradually President Lincoln came to favor the emancipation of slaves, although never to the extent that the abolitionists wanted. In early 1862, the president proposed the gradual emancipation of slaves by the states, with compensation for the slave owners and colonization of the former slaves outside the boundaries of the United States. When Congress mandated that Lincoln go further than that, by passing the Confiscation Act of 1862, which explicitly called for the permanent emancipation of all slaves in the Confederacy, the president simply ignored the law, choosing not to enforce it.[4] But political and diplomatic considerations prompted Lincoln to alter his course and support the issuing of the Emancipation Proclamation. So that his action would not be interpreted as one of desperation, the president waited until after the Union "victory" at the Battle of Antietam. Although the proclamation actually freed slaves only in areas still under Confederate control (hence immedi-

4. It was this action of Lincoln that prompted the exchange between Greeley and the president in August 1862.

ately freeing no one), the act was a significant one regarding a shift in war aims.

The second important issue that Lincoln and other northern leaders had to face was whether or not to arm African Americans and make them regular soldiers in the Union Army. Blacks had seen service in the American Revolution and the War of 1812, prompting abolitionist Frederick Douglass, a former slave, to criticize the United States's initial policy of excluding African Americans from the army in the Civil War, saying in February 1862,

Colored men were good enough to fight under Washington. They are not good enough to fight under McClellan. They were good enough to fight under Andrew Jackson. They are not good enough to fight under Gen. Halleck. They were good enough to help win American Independence, but they are not good enough to help preserve that independence against treason and rebellion.

Emancipation of slaves in the South was one thing, but making blacks United States soldiers was another.

Such a decision would imply that white northerners recognized African Americans as equals. Although most abolitionists preached the dual message of emancipation and racial equality, most northern whites did not look on African Americans as equals, a belief that they shared with their president. Would whites fight alongside blacks even in racially separated units? Were blacks, many northern whites asked, courageous enough to stand and hold their positions under fire? What would African Americans want as a price for their aid? Throughout

CHAPTER 10

THE PRICE FOR
VICTORY: THE
DECISION TO
USE BLACK
TROOPS

1862, northern leaders carried on an almost continual debate over whether to accept African Americans into the Union army, an issue that had a number of social, ideological, and moral implications.

In the Confederacy, the issue of arming African Americans for the southern war effort was also a divisive one. The northern superiority in population, supplemented by continued immigration from Europe, put the South at a terrific numerical disadvantage, a disadvantage that could be lessened by the enlistment of at least a portion of the approximately four million slaves. Southern battle casualties also had been fearfully high, in some battles higher than those of the Union.[5] How long could the Confederacy hold out as its numbers continually eroded? If the main goal of the war was southern independence, shouldn't Confederate leaders use all available means to secure that objective? It was known that some northern whites, shocked by Union casualty figures, were calling on Lincoln to let the South go in peace.

If the Confederacy could hold out, many southerners hoped, northern peace sentiments might grow enough to force the Union to give up. If slaves could help in that effort, some reasoned, why not arm them? Yet, as in the North, the question of whether or not to arm African Americans had significance far beyond military considerations. Except for the promise of freedom, what would motivate the slaves to fight for their masters? If freedom was to be offered, then what, many surely would argue, was the war being fought over in the first place? Would southern whites fight with blacks? Would some African Americans, once armed, then turn against their masters? And finally, if southern whites were correct in their insistence that African Americans were essentially docile, childlike creatures, then what conceivable support could they give to the war effort? Interestingly, there were some remarkable similarities in the points debated by the northern and southern policymakers and citizens.

THE METHOD

In this chapter you are confronted with two series of speeches, private and official correspondence, reports, newspaper articles and editorials, and

5. The following are estimates of Confederate casualties for the principal engagements of 1862–1863: Seven Days (June 1862, 20,000), Antietam (September 1862, 13,700). Fredericksburg (December 1862, 5,000), Gettysburg (July 1863, 28,000).

laws and proclamations. One series concerns the argument in the North over whether to arm blacks and the other series deals with the same question in the South. Read and analyze each series separately. Take notes as you go along, always being careful not to lose track of your central objectives.

By now you should be able to easily identify and list the major points, pro and con, in a debate. Jotting down notes as you read the evidence is extremely helpful. Be careful, however, because some reports, articles, and letters contain more than one argument.

Several earlier chapters required that you read between the lines, that is, identify themes and issues that are felt or implied although never directly stated. What emotional factors can you identify on both sides of the question? How important would you say these factors were in the final decision? For example, you will see from the evidence that at no time in the debate being carried on in the North are battle casualties mentioned. Were casualties therefore of no importance in the debate? How would you go about answering this question?

In some cases, the identity of the author of a particular piece (if known) can give you several clues as to that person's emotions, fears, anxieties, and needs. In other cases, where the identity of the author is not known, you may have to exercise a little historical imagination. What might this person really mean when he or she says (or fails to say) something? Can you infer from the context of the argument any emotions that are not explicitly stated?

THE EVIDENCE

NORTH

Source 1 from James M. McPherson, *The Negro's Civil War: How American Negroes Felt and Acted During the War for the Union* (New York: Vintage Books, 1967), p. 33.

1. Petition of Some Northern Blacks to President Lincoln, October 1861.

We, the undersigned, respectfully represent to Your Excellency that we are native citizens of the United States, and that, notwithstanding much injustice and oppression which our race have suffered, we cherish a strong attachment for the land of our birth and for our Republican Government. We are filled with alarm at the formidable conspiracy for its overthrow, and lament the vast expense of blood and treasure which the present war involves. . . . We are anxious to use our power to give peace to our country and permanence to our Government.

We are strong in numbers, in courage, and in patriotism, and in behalf of our fellow countrymen of the colored race, we offer to you and to the nation a power and a will sufficient to conquer rebellion, and establish peace on a permanent basis. We pledge ourselves, upon receiving the sanction of Your

CHAPTER 10

THE PRICE FOR
VICTORY: THE
DECISION TO
USE BLACK
TROOPS

Excellency, that we will immediately proceed to raise an efficient number of regiments, and so fast as arms and equipments shall be furnished, we will bring them into the field in good discipline, and ready for action.

Source 2 from Bell Irvin Wiley, *The Life of Billy Yank: The Common Soldier of the Union* (Baton Rouge: Louisiana State University Press, 1971), p. 109.

2. A. Davenport (a Union Soldier from New York) to His Homefolk, June 19, 1861.

I think that the best way to settle the question of what to do with the darkies would be to shoot them.

Source 3 from McPherson, *The Negro's Civil War*, p. 162.

3. Newspaper Editorial by Frederick Douglass, *Douglass' Monthly*, September 1861.

Our Presidents, Governors, Generals and Secretaries are calling, with almost frantic vehemence, for men—"Men! men! send us men!" they scream, or the cause of the Union is gone; . . . and yet these very officers, representing the people and Government, steadily and persistently refuse to receive the very class of men which have a deeper interest in the defeat and humiliation of the rebels, than all others. . . . What a spectacle of blind, unreasoning prejudice and pusillanimity is this! The national edifice is on fire. Every man who can carry a bucket of water, or remove a brick, is wanted; but those who have the care of the building, having a profound respect for the feeling of the national burglars who set the building on fire, are determined that the flames shall only be extinguished by Indo-Caucasian hands, and to have the building burnt rather than save it by means of any other. Such is the pride, the stupid prejudice and folly that rules the hour.

Why does the Government reject the negro? Is he not a man? Can he not wield a sword, fire a gun, march and countermarch, and obey orders like any other? . . . If persons so humble as we can be allowed to speak to the President of the United States, we should ask him if this dark and terrible hour of the nation's extremity is a time for consulting a mere vulgar and unnatural prejudice? . . . We would tell him that this is not time to fight with one hand, when both are needed; that this is no time to fight only with your white hand, and allow your black hand to remain tied. . . . While the Government continues to refuse the aid of colored men, thus alienating them from the national cause, and giving the rebels the advantage of them, it will not deserve better fortunes than it has thus far experienced.—Men in earnest don't fight with one hand, when they might fight with two, and a man drowning would not refuse to be saved even by a colored hand.

Source 4 from Roy P. Basler, ed., *The Collected Works of Abraham Lincoln,* Vol. V (New Brunswick, N.J.: Rutgers University Press, 1953), p. 222.

4. Proclamation Revoking General Hunter's Order of Military Emancipation of May 9, 1862[6].

May 19, 1862

I, Abraham Lincoln, president of the United States, proclaim and declare, that the government of the United States, had no knowledge, information, or belief, of an intention on the part of General Hunter to issue such a proclamation; nor has it yet, any authentic information that the document is genuine. And further, that neither General Hunter, nor any other commander, or person, has been authorized by the Government of the United States, to make proclamations declaring the slaves of any State free; and that the supposed proclamation, now in question, whether genuine or false, is altogether void, so far as respects such declaration.

Sources 5 and 6 from *Diary and Correspondence of Salmon P. Chase,*[7] in Vol. 2 of *Annual Report of the American Historical Association for the Year 1902* (Washington, D.C.: U.S. Government Printing Office, 1903), pp. 45–46, 48–49.

5. Diary of Salmon P. Chase, Entry for July 21, 1862.

. . . I went at the appointed hour, and found that the President had been profoundly concerned at the present aspect of affairs, and had determined

6. On April 12, 1862, General David Hunter organized the first official regiment of African American soldiers. On May 9, Hunter then proclaimed that slaves in Georgia, Florida, and South Carolina were free. Lincoln overruled both proclamations,and the regiment was disbanded without pay. Observers reported that the regiment, composed of former slaves, was of poor quality. Do you think those reports influenced Lincoln's thinking? Lincoln also overruled similar proclamations by General John C. Frémont in Missouri.
7. Chase was Lincoln's Secretary of the Treasury from 1861 until 1864.

CHAPTER 10

THE PRICE FOR
VICTORY: THE
DECISION TO
USE BLACK
TROOPS

to take some definitive steps in respect to military action and slavery. He had prepared several Orders, the first of which contemplated authority to Commanders to subsist their troups in the hostile territory—the second, authority to employ negroes as laborers—the third requiring that both in the case of property taken and of negroes employed, accounts should be kept with such degrees of certainty as would enable compensation to be made in proper cases—another provided for the colonization of negroes in some tropical country.

A good deal of discussion took place upon these points. The first Order was universally approved. The second was approved entirely; and the third, by all except myself. I doubted the expediency of attempting to keep accounts for the benefit of the inhabitants of rebel States. The Colonization project was not much discussed.

The Secretary of War presented some letters from Genl. Hunter in which he advised the Department that the withdrawal of a large proportion of his troups to reinforce Genl. McClellan, rendered it highly important that he should be immediately authorized to enlist all loyal persons without reference to complexion. Messrs. Stanton, Seward and myself, expressed ourselves in favor of this plan, and no one expressed himself against it. (Mr. Blair was not present.) The President was not prepared to decide the question but expressed himself as averse to arming negroes. The whole matter was postponed until tomorrow. . . .

6. Diary of Salmon P. Chase, Entry for July 22, 1862.

. . . The question of arming slaves was then brought up and I advocated it warmly. The President was unwilling to adopt this measure, but proposed to issue a proclamation, on the basis of the Confiscation Bill, calling upon the States to return to their allegiance—warning the rebels the provisions of the Act would have full force at the expiration of sixty days adding on his own part, a declaration of his intention to renew, at the next session of Congress, his recommendation of compensation to States adopting the gradual abolishment of slavery and proclaiming the emancipation of all slaves within States remaining in insurrection on the first of January, 1863.

I said that I should give to such a measure my cordial support: but I should prefer that no new expression on the subject of compensation should be made, and I thought that the measure of Emancipation could be much better and more quietly accomplished by allowing Generals to organize and arm the slaves (thus avoiding depredation and massacre on the one hand, and support to the insurrection on the other) and by directing the Commanders of Departments to proclaim emancipation within their Districts as soon as practicable; but I regarded this as so much better than inaction on the subject, that I should give it my entire support.

The President determined to publish the first three Orders forthwith, and to leave the other for some further consideration. The impression left upon my mind by the whole discussion was, that while the President thought that the organization, equipment and arming of negroes, like other soldiers, would be productive of more evil than good, he was not willing that Commanders should, at their discretion, arm, for purely defensive purposes, slaves coming within their lines.

Mr. Stanton brought forward a proposition to draft 50,000 men. Mr. Seward proposed that the number should be 100,000. The President directed that, whatever number were drafted, should be a part of the 3,000,000 already called for. No decision was reached, however.

Source 7 from Basler, ed., *The Collected Works of Abraham Lincoln,* Vol. 5, p. 338.

7. Memorandum on Recruiting Negroes.

[July 22, 1862?]

To recruiting free negroes, no objection.
To recruiting slaves of disloyal owners, no objection.
To recruiting slaves of loyal owners, *with their consent,* no objection.
To recruiting slaves of loyal owners *without* consent, objection, *unless the necessity is urgent.*
To conducting offensively, while recruiting, and to carrying away slaves not suitable for recruits, objection.

Source 8 from *Diary and Correspondence of Salmon P. Chase,* pp. 53–54.

8. Diary of Salmon P. Chase, Entry for August 3, 1862.

. . . There was a good deal of conversation on the connection of the Slavery question with the rebellion. I expressed my conviction for the tenth or twentieth time, that the time for the suppression of the rebellion without interference with slavery had passed; that it was possible, probably, at the outset, by striking the insurrectionists wherever found, strongly and decisively; but

CHAPTER 10

THE PRICE FOR
VICTORY: THE
DECISION TO
USE BLACK
TROOPS

we had elected to act on the principles of a civil war, in which the whole population of every seceding state was engaged against the Federal Government, instead of treating the active secessionists as insurgents and exerting our utmost energies for their arrest and punishment;—that the bitternesses of the conflict had now substantially united the white population of the rebel states against us; that the loyal whites remaining, if they would not prefer the Union without Slavery, certainly would not prefer Slavery to the Union; that the blacks were really the only loyal population worth counting; and that, in the Gulf States at least, their right to Freedom ought to be at once recognized, while, in the Border States, the President's plan of Emancipation might be made the basis of the necessary measures for their ultimate enfranchisement;—that the practical mode of effecting this seemed to me quite simple;—that the President had already spoken of the importance of making of the freed blacks on the Mississippi, below Tennessee, a safeguard to the navigation of the river;—that Mitchell, with a few thousand soldiers, could take Vicksburgh;—assure the blacks freedom on condition of loyalty; organize the best of them in companies, regiments etc. and provide, as far as practicable for the cultivation of the plantations by the rest:—that Butler should signify to the slaveholders of Louisiana that they must recognize the freedom of their workpeople by paying them wages;—and that Hunter should do the same thing in South-Carolina.

Mr. Seward expressed himself as in favor of any measures likely to accomplish the results I contemplated, which could be carried into effect without Proclamations; and the President said he was pretty well cured of objections to any measure except want of adaptedness to put down the rebellion; but did not seem satisfied that the time had come for the adoption of such a plan as I proposed. . . .

Source 9 from Basler, ed., *The Collected Works of Abraham Lincoln*, Vol. 5, pp. 356–357.

9. President Lincoln, "Remarks to Deputation of Western Gentlemen," August 4, 1862.

A deputation of Western gentlemen waited upon the President this morning to offer two colored regiments from the State of Indiana. Two members of Congress were of the party. The President received them courteously, but stated to them that he was not prepared to go the length of enlisting negroes as soldiers. He would employ all colored men offered as laborers, but would not promise to make soldiers of them.

The deputation came away satisfied that it is the determination of the Government not to arm negroes unless some new and more pressing emergency arises. The President argued that the nation could not afford to lose Kentucky at this crisis, and gave it as his opinion that to arm the negroes would turn 50,000 bayonets from the loyal Border States against us that were for us. . . .

Source 10 from McPherson, *The Negro's Civil War*, pp. 163–164.

10. New York Tribune, August 16, 1862.[8]

I am quite sure there is not one man in ten but would feel himself degraded as a volunteer if negro equality is to be the order in the field of battle. . . . I take the liberty of warning the abettors of fraternizing with the blacks, that one negro regiment, in the present temper of things, put on equality with those who have the past year fought and suffered, will withdraw an amount of life and energy in our army equal to disbanding ten of the best regiments we can now raise.

Source 11 from William Wells Brown,[9] *The Negro in the American Rebellion: His Heroism and His Fidelity* (Boston: Lee & Shepard, 1867), pp. 101–104.

11. Reminiscence of a Black Man of the Threat to Cincinnati, September 1862.[10]

The mayor's proclamation, under ordinary circumstances, would be explicit enough. "Every man, of every age, be he citizen or alien," surely meant the colored people. . . . Seeking to test the matter, a policeman was approached, as he strutted in his new dignity of provostguard. To the question, humbly, almost tremblingly, put, "Does the mayor desire colored men to report for service in the city's defence?" he replied, "You know d---d well he doesn't mean you. Niggers ain't citizens."—"But he calls on all, citizens and aliens.

8. This was a letter to the editor and did not reflect the opinion of Horace Greeley, editor of the *Tribune* and supporter of racial equality for African Americans.
9. Brown was an African American man who ultimately served in the Union army and recorded his experiences.
10. In early September 1862, the citizens of Cincinnati, Ohio, feared a raid on the city by Confederates. Mayor George Hatch issued a proclamation calling on "every man of every age" to take part in the defense of the city.

CHAPTER 10

THE PRICE FOR
VICTORY: THE
DECISION TO
USE BLACK
TROOPS

If he does not mean all, he should not say so."—"The mayor knows as well as you do what to write, and all he wants is for you niggers to keep quiet." This was at nine o'clock on the morning of the second. The military authorities had determined, however, to impress the colored men for work upon the fortifications. The privilege of volunteering, extended to others, was to be denied to them. Permission to volunteer would imply some freedom, some dignity, some independent manhood. . . .

If the guard appointed to the duty of collecting the colored people had gone to their houses, and notified them to report for duty on the fortifications, the order would have been cheerfully obeyed. But the brutal ruffians who composed the regular and special police took every opportunity to inflict abuse and insult upon the men whom they arrested. . . .

The captain of these conscripting squads was one William Homer, and in him organized ruffianism had its fitting head. He exhibited the brutal malignity of his nature in a continued series of petty tyrannies. Among the first squads marched into the yard was one which had to wait several hours before being ordered across the river. Seeking to make themselves as comfortable as possible, they had collected blocks of wood, and piled up bricks, upon which they seated themselves on the shaded side of the yard. Coming into the yard, he ordered all to rise, marched them to another part, then issued the order, "D--n you, squat." Turning to the guard, he added, "Shoot the first one who rises." Reaching the opposite side of the river, the same squad were marched from the sidewalk into the middle of the dusty road, and again the order, "D--n you, squat," and the command to shoot the first one who should rise. . . .

Calling up his men, he would address them thus: "Now, you fellows, hold up your heads. Pat, hold your musket straight; don't put your tongue out so far; keep your eyes open: I believe you are drunk. Now, then, I want you fellows to go out of this pen, and bring all the niggers you can catch. Don't come back here without niggers: if you do, you shall not have a bit of grog. Now be off, you shabby cusses, and come back in forty minutes, and bring me niggers; that's what I want." This barbarous and inhuman treatment of the colored citizens of Cincinnati continued for four days, without a single word of remonstrance, except from the "Gazette."

Source 12 from John G. Nicolay and John Hay, eds., *Abraham Lincoln—Complete Works* (New York: The Century Co., 1894), Vol. 2, pp. 234–235, 242–243.

12. Reply to a Committee From the Religious Denominations of Chicago, Asking the President to Issue a Proclamation of Emancipation. September 13, 1862.

The subject presented in the memorial is one upon which I have thought much for weeks past, and I may even say for months. I am approached with the most opposite opinions and advice, and that by religious men who are equally certain that they represent the divine will. I am sure that either the one or the other class is mistaken in that belief, and perhaps in some respects both. I hope it will not be irreverent for me to say that if it is probable that God would reveal his will to others on a point so connected with my duty, it might be supposed he would reveal it directly to me; for, unless I am more deceived in myself than I often am, it is my earnest desire to know the will of Providence in this matter. And if I can learn what it is, I will do it. These are not, however, the days of miracles, and I suppose it will be granted that I am not to expect a direct revelation. I must study the plain physical facts of the case, ascertain what is possible, and learn what appears to be wise and right. . . .

I admit that slavery is the root of the rebellion, or at least its *sine qua non*. The ambition of politicians may have instigated them to act, but they would have been impotent without slavery as their instrument. I will also concede that emancipation would help us in Europe, and convince them that we are incited by something more than ambition. I grant, further, that it would help somewhat at the North, though not so much, I fear, as you and those you represent imagine. Still, some additional strength would be added in that way to the war, and then, unquestionably, it would weaken the rebels by drawing off their laborers, which is of great importance; but I am not so sure we could do much with the blacks. If we were to arm them, I fear that in a few weeks the arms would be in the hands of the rebels; and, indeed, thus far we have not had arms enough to equip our white troops. I will mention another thing, though it meet only your scorn and contempt. There are fifty thousand bayonets in the Union armies from the border slave States. It would be a serious matter if, in consequence of a proclamation such as you desire, they should go over to the rebels. I do not think they all would—not so many, indeed, as a year ago, or as six months ago—not so many to-day as yesterday. Every day increases their Union feeling. They are also getting their pride enlisted, and want to beat the rebels.

CHAPTER 10

THE PRICE FOR
VICTORY: THE
DECISION TO
USE BLACK
TROOPS

Sources 13 through 15 from Basler, ed., *The Collected Works of Abraham Lincoln,*
Vol. 5, pp. 444, 509, 28–30.

13. Lincoln to Vice President Hannibal Hamlin.

(Strictly private.)   Executive Mansion,
Washington, September 28, 1862.

My Dear Sir:

Your kind letter of the 25th is just received. It is known to some that while
I hope something from the proclamation,[11] my expectations are not as san-
guine as are those of some friends. The time for its effect southward has not
come; but northward the effect should be instantaneous.

It is six days old, and while commendation in newspapers and by distinguished individuals is all that a vain man could wish, the stocks have declined, and troops came forward more slowly than ever. This, looked soberly
in the face, is not very satisfactory. We have fewer troops in the field at the
end of six days than we had at the beginning—the attrition among the old
outnumbering the addition of the new. The North responds to the proclamation sufficiently in breath; but breath alone kills no rebels.

I wish I could write more cheerfully; nor do I thank you the less for the
kindness of your letter. Yours very truly,

A. LINCOLN

14. Lincoln to Carl Schurz.

Gen. Carl Schurz   Executive Mansion,
Washington, Nov. 24, 1862.

My dear Sir

I have just received, and read, your letter of the 20th. The purport of it is
that we lost the late elections,[12] and the administration is failing, because
the war is unsuccessful; and that I must not flatter myself that I am not
justly to blame for it. I certainly know that if the war fails, the administration fails, and that I *will* be blamed for it, whether I deserve it or not. And
I ought to be blamed, if I could do better. You think I could do better; there-

11. Lincoln was referring to his preliminary Emancipation Proclamation, which he issued
on September 22, 1862.
12. In the congressional elections of 1862, the Republicans lost three seats in the House of
Representatives, although they were still the majority party. Senators were not elected by
the people until the Seventeenth Amendment to the Constitution was ratified in 1913.

fore you blame me already. I think I could not do better; therefore I blame you for blaming me. . . .

15. The Emancipation Proclamation.

January 1, 1863

By the President of the United States of America:

A Proclamation. . . .

Now, therefore I, Abraham Lincoln, President of the United States, by virtue of the power in me vested as Commander-in-Chief, of the Army and Navy of the United States in time of actual armed rebellion against authority and government of the United States, and as a fit and necessary war measure for suppressing said rebellion, do, on this first day of January, in the year of our Lord one thousand eight hundred and sixty three, and in accordance with my purpose so to do publicly proclaimed for the full period of one hundred days, from the day first above mentioned, order and designate as the States and parts of States wherein the people thereof respectively, are this day in rebellion against the United States, the following, towit: . . .

[Here Lincoln identified the geographic areas of the South still under the control of the Confederacy:]

And by virtue of the power, and for the purpose aforesaid, I do order and declare that all persons held as slaves within said designated States, and parts of States, are, and henceforward shall be free; and that the Executive government of the United States, including the military and naval authorities thereof, will recognize and maintain the freedom of said persons.

And I hereby enjoin upon the people so declared to be free to abstain from all violence, unless in necessary self-defence; and I recommend to them that, in all cases when allowed, they labor faithfully for reasonable wages.

And I further declare and make known, that such persons of suitable condition, will be received into the armed services of the United States to garrison forts, positions, stations, and other places, and to man vessels of all sorts in said service.[13]

13. This paragraph was not part of the preliminary proclamation issued by Lincoln on September 22, 1862. See Basler, ed., *The Collected Works of Abraham Lincoln,* Vol. 5, pp. 433–436.

CHAPTER 10

THE PRICE FOR
VICTORY: THE
DECISION TO
USE BLACK
TROOPS

And upon this act, sincerely believed to be an act of justice, warranted by the Constitution, upon military necessity, I invoke the considerate judgment of mankind, and the gracious favor of Almighty God.

In witness whereof, I have hereunto set my hand and caused the seal of the United States to be affixed.

Done at the City of Washington, this first day of January, in the year of our Lord one thousand eight hundred and sixty three, and of the Independence of the United States of America the eighty-seventh.

By the President: ABRAHAM LINCOLN

Source 16 from George Washington Williams, *A History of the Negro Troops in the War of the Rebellion, 1861–65* (New York: Harper and Brothers, 1888), pp. 66–67, 90–91.

16. Reminiscence of a Former Black Soldier in the Union Army.

At first the faintest intimation that Negroes should be employed as soldiers in the Union Army was met with derision. By many it was regarded as a joke. The idea of arming the ex-slaves seemed ridiculous to most civil and military officers. . . .

Most observing and thoughtful people concluded that centuries of servitude had rendered the Negro slave incapable of any civil or military service. . . . Some officers talked of resigning if Negroes were to be called upon to fight the battles of a free republic. The privates in regiments from large cities and border States were bitter and demonstrative in their opposition. The Negro volunteers themselves were subjected to indignities from rebel civilians within the Union lines, and obtained no protection from the white troops. . . .

Source 17 from Lawrence Frederick Kohl and Margaret Cosse Richard, eds., *Irish Green and Union Blue: The Civil War Letters of Peter Welsh, Color Sergeant, 28th Regiment, Massachusetts Volunteers* (New York: Fordham University Press, 1986), p. 62.

17. Fragment of a Letter from a Union Soldier, Early 1863.

I see by late papers that the governor of Massachusetts has been autheured to raise nigar regiments. i hope he may succeed but it doubt it very much if they can raise a few thousand and sent them out here i can assure you that whether they have the grit to go into battle or not if they are placed in front and any brigade of this army behind them they will have to go in or they will meet as hot a reception in their retreat as in their advance The feeling against nigars is intensly strong in this army as is plainly to be seen wherever and whenever they meet them They are looked upon as the principal cause of this war and this feeling is especially strong in the Irish regiments

Source 18 from *The War of the Rebellion,* p. 16.

18. L. Thomas to Governor of Rhode Island, January 15, 1863.

ADJUTANT-GENERAL'S OFFICE,
Washington, D. C., January 15, 1863.

GOVERNOR OF RHODE ISLAND,
     Providence, R. I.:
  SIR: I am directed to say that the President will accept into the service of the United States an infantry regiment of volunteers of African descent, if offered by your State and organized according to the rules and regulations of the service.
  I am, very respectfully,

L. THOMAS,
Adjutant-General.

Source 19 from Glenn W. Sunderland, *Five Days to Glory* (South Brunswick: A. S. Barnes & Co., 1970), pp. 97–98.

19. Letter from Tighlman Jones (a Union Soldier) to Brother Zillman Jones, October 6, 1863.

You have heard of Negroes being enlisted to fight for Uncle Sam. If you would like to know what the soldiers think about that idea I can almost tell you. Why, that is just what they desire. There is some soldiers who curse and blow and make a great noise about it but we set him as a convalescent who is like a man who is afraid of the smallpox who curses the works of a power he can in no way avoid, but will kick and rail and act the part of a fool, but of no avail, nature will have its own course, or to say that this war will free the Negroes and that they will enlist and fight to sustain the Government. I think more of a Negro Union soldier than I do of all the cowardly

CHAPTER 10

THE PRICE FOR
VICTORY: THE
DECISION TO
USE BLACK
TROOPS

Copperhead trash of the north[14] and there is no soldier but what approves of the course of the present administration and will fight till the Rebels unconditionally surrender and return to their allegiance.

Source 20 from Dudley Cornish, *The Sable Arm: Negro Troops in the Union Army, 1861–1865* (New York: W. W. Norton, 1966).

20. Editorial, *New York Times,* March 7, 1864.

There has been no more striking manifestation of the marvelous times that are upon us than the scene in our streets at the departure of the first of our colored regiments. Had any man predicted it last year he would have been thought a fool, even by the wisest and most discerning. History abounds with strange contrasts. It always has been an ever-shifting melo-drama. But never, in this land at least, has it presented a transition so extreme and yet so speedy as what our eyes have just beheld.

Eight months ago the African race in this City were literally hunted down like wild beasts.[15] They fled for their lives. When caught, they were shot down in cold blood, or stoned to death, or hung to the trees or the lamp-posts. Their homes were pillaged; the asylum which Christian charity had provided for their orphaned children was burned; and there was no limit to the persecution but in the physical impossibility of finding further material on which the mob could wreak its ruthless hate. Nor was it solely the raging horde in the streets that visited upon the black man the nefarious wrong. Thousands and tens of thousands of men of higher social grade, of better education, cherished precisely the same spirit. . . .

How astonishingly has all this been changed. The same men who could not have shown themselves in the most obscure street in the City without peril of instant death, even though in the most suppliant attitude, now march in solid platoons, with shouldered muskets, slung knapsacks, and buckled cartridge boxes down through our gayest avenues and our busiest thoroughfares to the pealing strains of martial music and are everywhere saluted with waving handkerchiefs, with descending flowers, and with the acclamations and plaudits of countless beholders. They are halted at our

14. Copperheads were northerners who opposed the war and advocated "peace at any price."
15. In mid-1863, demonstrations against conscription in New York City turned into an ugly mob action against African Americans, partly because of their connection, through the Emancipation Proclamation of January 1, 1863, to the war and partly because of economic competition with the poorer whites who constituted most of the rioters.

most beautiful square, and amid an admiring crowd, in the presence of many of our most prominent citizens, are addressed in an eloquent and most complimentary speech by the President of our chief literary institution, and are presented with a gorgeous stand of colors in the names of a large number of the first ladies of the City, who attest on parchment, signed by their own fair hands, that they "will anxiously watch your career, glorifying in your heroism, ministering to you when wounded and ill, and honoring your martyrdom with benedictions and with tears."

It is only by such occasions that we can at all realize the prodigious revolution which the public mind everywhere is experiencing. Such developments are infallible tokens of a new epoch.

SOUTH

Sources 21 and 22 from *The War of the Rebellion:*, Series IV, Vol. I, pp. 482, 529.

21. Correspondence Between W. S. Turner and the Confederate War Department, July 17, 1861.

HELENA, ARK., *July 17, 1861.*

Hon. L. P. WALKER:[16]

DEAR SIR: I wrote you a few days since for myself and many others in this district to ascertain if we could get negro regiments received for Confederate service, officered, of course, by white men. All we ask is arms, clothing, and provisions, and usual pay for officers and not one cent pay for negroes. Our negroes are too good to fight Lincoln hirelings, but as they pretend to love negroes so much we want to show them how much the true Southern cotton-patch negro loves them in return. The North cannot complain at this. They proclaim negro equality from the Senate Chamber to the pulpit, teach it in their schools, and are doing all they can to turn the slaves upon master, mistress, and children. And now, sir, if you can receive the negroes that can be raised we will soon give the Northern thieves a gorge of the negroes' love for them that will never be forgotten. As you well know, I have had long experience with negro character. I am satisfied they are easy disciplined and less trouble than whites in camp, and will fight desperately as long as they have a single white officer living. I know one man that will furnish and arm

16. Walker was the Confederate Secretary of War from February to September 1861.

CHAPTER 10

THE PRICE FOR
VICTORY: THE
DECISION TO
USE BLACK
TROOPS

100 of his own and his son for their captain. The sooner we bring a strong
negro force against the hirelings the sooner we shall have peace, in my humble judgment. Let me hear from you.

Your old friend,

W. S. TURNER

22. Correspondence Between W. S. Turner and the Confederate War Department, August 2, 1861.

CONFEDERATE STATES OF AMERICA, WAR DEPARTMENT,

Richmond, August 2, 1861.

W. S. TURNER,

Helena, Ark.:

SIR: In reply to your letter of the 17th of July I am directed by the Secretary of War to say that this Department is not prepared to accept the negro
regiment tendered by you, and yet it is not doubted that almost every slave
would cheerfully aid his master in the work of hurling back the fanatical
invader. Moreover, if the necessity were apparent there is high authority for
the employment of such forces. Washington himself recommended the enlistment of two negro regiments in Georgia, and the Congress sanctioned
the measure. But now there is a superabundance of our own color tendering
their services to the Government in its day of peril and ruthless invasion, a
superabundance of men when we are bound to admit the inadequate supply
of arms at present at the disposal of the Government.

Respectfully,

A. T. BLEDSOE
Chief of Bureau of War.

Sources 23 through 26 from Robert F. Durden, *The Gray and the Black: The
Confederate Debate of Emancipation* (Baton Rouge: Louisiana State University
Press, 1972), pp. 30–31, 54–58, 61, 66–67.

23. *Montgomery* (Ala.) *Weekly Mail,* "Employment of Negroes in the Army," September 9, 1863.

. . . We must either employ the negroes ourselves, or the enemy will employ
them against us. While the enemy retains so much of our territory, they are,
in their present avocation and status, a dangerous element, a source of
weakness. They are no longer negative characters, but subjects of volition
as other people. They must be taught to know that this is peculiarly the

country of the black man—that in no other is the climate and soil so well adapted to his nature and capacity. He must further be taught that it is his duty, as well as the white man's, to defend his home with arms, if need be.

We are aware that there are persons who shudder at the idea of placing arms in the hands of negroes, and who are not willing to trust them under any circumstances. The negro, however, is proverbial for his faithfulness under kind treatment. He is an affectionate, grateful being, and we are persuaded that the fears of such persons are groundless.

There are in the slaveholding States four millions of negroes, and out of this number at least six hundred thousand able-bodied men capable of bearing arms can be found. Lincoln proposes to free and arm them against us. There are already fifty thousand of them in the Federal ranks. Lincoln's scheme has worked well so far, and if no[t] checkmated, will most assuredly be carried out. The Confederate Government must adopt a counter policy. It must thwart the enemy in this gigantic scheme, at all hazards, and if nothing else will do it—if the negroes cannot be made effective and trustworthy to the Southern cause in no other way, we solemnly believe it is the duty of this Government to forestall Lincoln and proceed at once to take steps for the emancipation or liberation of the negroes itself. Let them be declared free, placed in the ranks, and told to fight for their homes and country. . . .

Such action on the part of our Government would place our people in a purer and better light before the world. It would disabuse the European mind of a grave error in regard to the cause of our separation. It would prove to them that there were higher and holier motives which actuated our people than the mere love of property. It would show that, although slavery is one of the principles that we started to fight for, yet it falls far short of being the chief one; that, for the sake of our liberty, we are capable of any personal sacrifice; that we regard the emancipation of slaves, and the consequent loss of property as an evil infinitely less than the subjugation and enslavement of ourselves; that it is not a war exclusively for the privilege of holding negroes in bondage. It would prove to our soldiers, three-fourths of whom never owned a negro, that it is not "the rich man's war and the poor man's fight," but a war for the most sacred of all principles, for the dearest of all rights—the right to govern ourselves. It would show them that the rich man who owned slaves was not willing to jeopardize the precious liberty of the country by his eagerness to hold on to his slaves, but that he was ready to give them up and sacrifice his interest in them whenever the cause demanded it. It would lend a new impetus, a new enthusiasm, a new and powerful strength to the cause, and place our success beyond a peradventure. It would at once remove all the odium which attached to us on account of slavery, and bring us speedy recognition, and, if necessary, intervention.

CHAPTER 10

THE PRICE FOR
VICTORY: THE
DECISION TO
USE BLACK
TROOPS

24. General Patrick Cleburne to General Joseph Johnston, January 2, 1864.

We have now been fighting for nearly three years, have spilled much of our best blood, and lost, consumed, or thrown to the flames an amount of property equal in value to the specie currency of the world. . . . Our soldiers can see no end to this state of affairs except in our own exhaustion; hence, instead of rising to the occasion, they are sinking into a fatal apathy, growing weary of hardships and slaughters which promise no results. In this state of things it is easy to understand why there is a growing belief that some black catastrophe is not far ahead of us, and that unless some extraordinary change is soon made in our condition we must overtake it. . . .

In view of the state of affairs what does our country propose to do? In the words of President Davis "no effort must be spared to add largely to our effective force as promptly as possible. The sources of supply are to be found in restoring to the army all who are improperly absent, putting an end to substitution, modifying the exemption law, restricting details, and placing in the ranks such of the able-bodied men now employed as wagoners, nurses, cooks, and other employees, as are doing service for which the negroes may be found competent." . . . [W]e propose, in addition to a modification of the President's plans, that we retain in service for the war all troops now in service, and that we immediately commence training a large reserve of the most courageous of our slaves, and further that we guarantee freedom within a reasonable time to every slave in the South who shall remain true to the Confederacy in this war. As between the loss of independence and the loss of slavery, we assume that every patriot will freely give up the latter—give up the negro slave rather than be a slave himself. If we are correct in this assumption it only remains to show how this great national sacrifice is, in all human probabilities, to change the current of success and sweep the invader from our country.

Our country has already some friends in England and France, and there are strong motives to induce these nations to recognize and assist us, but they cannot assist us without helping slavery, and to do this would be in conflict with their policy for the last quarter of a century. . . . But this barrier once removed, the sympathy and the interests of these and other nations will accord with their own, and we may expect from them both moral support and material aid. . . .

Will the slaves fight? . . . The negro slaves of Saint Domingo, fighting for freedom, defeated their white masters and the French troops sent against them. The negro slaves of Jamaica revolted, and under the name of Maroons held the mountains against their masters for 150 years; and the experience of this war has been so far that half-trained negroes have fought as bravely as many other half-trained Yankees. If, contrary to the training of a lifetime, they can be made to face and fight bravely against their former masters, how much more probable is it that with the allurement of a higher reward, and led by those masters, they would submit to discipline and face dangers.

25. President Jefferson Davis to General Walker, January 13, 1864—Reaction to Cleburne's Proposal.

I have received your letter, with its inclosure, informing me of the propositions [Cleburne's proposal] submitted to a meeting of the general officers on the 2d instant, and thank you for the information. Deeming it to be injurious to the public service that such a subject should be mooted, or even known to be entertained by persons possessed of the confidence and respect of the people, I have concluded that the best policy under the circumstances will be to avoid all publicity, and the Secretary of War has therefore written to General Johnston requesting him to convey to those concerned my desire that it should be kept private. If it be kept out of public journals its ill effect will be much lessened.

26. General Joseph Johnston to General Hardee et al., January 31, 1864—Reaction to Cleburne's Proposal.

Lieutenant-General Hardee, Major-Generals Cheatham, Hindman, Cleburne, Stewart, Walker, Brigadier-Generals Bate and P. Anderson:
GENERAL:
  I have just received a letter from the Secretary of War in reference to Major-General Cleburne's memoir read in my quarters about the 2d instant. In this letter the Honorable Secretary expresses the earnest conviction of the President "that the dissemination or even promulgation of such opinions under the present circumstances of the Confederacy, whether in the Army or among the people, can be productive only of discouragement, distraction, and dissension." The agitation and controversy which must spring from the presentation of such views by officers high in the public confidence are to be deeply deprecated, and while no doubt or mistrust is for a moment entertained of the patriotic intents of the gallant author of the memorial, and such of his brother officers as may have favored his opinions, it is requested

CHAPTER 10

THE PRICE FOR
VICTORY: THE
DECISION TO
USE BLACK
TROOPS

that you communicate to them, as well as all others present on the occasion, the opinions, as herein expressed, of the President, and urge on them the suppression, not only of the memorial itself, but likewise of all discussion and controversy respecting or growing out of it. . . .

Source 27 from Bell Irvin Wiley, ed., *Letters of Warren Akin, Confederate Congressman* (Athens: University of Georgia Press, 1959), pp. 32–33.

27. Letter from Warren Akin to Nathan Land, October 31, 1864.

As to calling out the negro men and placing them in the army, with the promise that they shall be free at the end of the war, I can only say it is a question of fearful magnitude. Can we prevent subjugation, confiscation, degradation and slavery without it? If not, will our condition or that of the negro, be any worse by calling them into service?

On the other hand: Can we feed our soldiers and their families if the negro men are taken from the plantations? Will our soldiers submit to having our negroes along side them in the ditches, or in line of battle? When the negro is taught the use of arms and the art of war, can we live in safety with them afterwards? Or if it be contemplated to send them off to another country, when peace is made, will it be right to force them to a new, distant and strange land, after they have fought for and won the independence of this? Would they go without having another war? Involving, perhaps a general insurrection of all the negroes? To call forth the negroes into the army, with the promise of freedom, will it not be giving up the great question involved by doing the very thing Lincoln is now doing? The Confederate States may take private property for public use, by paying for it; but can we ever pay for 300,000 negro men at present prices, in addition to our other indebtedness? The Confederate Government may buy the private negro property of the Citizens, but can it set them free among us, to corrupt our slaves, and place in peril our existence? These are some of the thoughts that have passed th[r]ough my mind on the subject. But I can not say that I have a definite and fixed opinion. If I were convinced that we will be subjugated, with the long train of horrors that will follow it, unless the negroes be placed in the army, I would not hesitate to enrol our slaves and put them to fighting. Subjugation will give us free negroes in abundance—enemies at that— while white slaves will be more numerous than free negroes. We and our children will be slaves, while our freed negroes will lord it over us. It is impossible for the evils resulting from placing our slaves in the army to be greater than those that will follow subjugation. We may (if necessary) put our slaves in the army, win our independence, and have liberty and homes for ourselves and children. But subjugation will deprive us of our homes, houses, property, liberty, honor, and every thing worth living for, leaving for us and our posterity only the chains of slavery, tenfold more galling and degrading than that now felt by our negroes. But I will not enlarge, I have made suggestions merely for your reflection.

Source 28 from McPherson, *The Negro's Civil War,* pp. 243–244.

28. Judah P. Benjamin (Secretary of War, Confederacy) to Fred A. Porcher (an Old Friend and Former Classmate), December 21, 1864.

For a year past I have seen that the period was fast approaching when we should be compelled to use every resource at our command for the defense of our liberties. . . . The negroes will certainly be made to fight against us if not armed for our defense. The drain of that source of our strength is steadily fatal, and irreversible by any other expedient than that of arming the slaves as an auxiliary force.

I further agree with you that if they are to fight for our freedom they are entitled to their own. Public opinion is fast ripening on the subject, and ere the close of the winter the conviction on this point will become so widespread that the Government will have no difficulty in inaugurating the policy [of recruiting Negro soldiers].

. . . It is well known that General Lee, who commands so largely the confidence of the people, is strongly in favor of our using the negroes for defense, and emancipating them, if necessary, for that purpose. Can you not yourself write a series of articles in your papers, always urging this point as the true issue, viz, is it better for the negro to fight for us or against us?

Source 29 from Durden, *The Gray and the Black,* pp. 89–91.

29. *Richmond Enquirer,* November 4, 1864, Letter to the Editor in Reply to the Editorial of October 6, 1864.

Can it be possible that you are serious and earnest in proposing such a step to be taken by our Government? Or were you merely discussing the matter as a something which might be done? An element of power which might be used—meaning thereby to intimidate or threaten our enemy with it as a

CHAPTER 10

THE PRICE FOR
VICTORY: THE
DECISION TO
USE BLACK
TROOPS

weapon of offence which they may drive us to use? Can it be possible that a Southern man—editor of a Southern journal—recognizing the right of property in slaves, admitting their inferiority in the scale of being and also their social inferiority, would recommend the passage of a law which at one blow levels all distinctions, deprives the master of a right to his property, and elevates the negro to an equality with the white man?—for, disguise it as you may, those who fight together in a common cause, and by success win the *same* freedom, enjoy equal rights and equal position, and in this case, are distinguished only by color. Are we prepared for this? Is it for this we are contending? Is it for this we would seek the aid for our slaves? . . . When President Davis said: "We are not fighting for slavery, but independence," he meant that the question and subject of slavery was a matter settled amongst ourselves and one that admitted of no dispute—that he intended to be independent of all foreign influences on this as well as on other matters—free to own slaves if he pleased—free to lay our own taxes—free to govern ourselves. He never intended to ignore the question of slavery or to do aught else but express the determination to be *independent* in this as well as in all other matters. What has embittered the feelings of the two sections of the old Union? What has gradually driven them to the final separation? What is it that has made two nationalities of them, if it is not slavery?

The Yankee *steals* my slave, and makes a soldier and freeman of him to *destroy* me. You *take* my slave, and make a soldier and freeman of him to *defend* me. The difference in your intention is very great; but is not the practice of both equally pernicious to the slave and destruction to the country? And at the expiration of ten years after peace what would be the relative difference between my negro *stolen* and freed by the Yankee and my negro taken and freed by you? Would they not be equally worthless and vicious? How would you distinguish between them? How prevent the return of him whose hand is red with his master's blood, and his enjoyment of those privileges which you so lavishly bestow upon the faithful freedman?

Have you thought of the influence to be exerted by these half or quarter million of free negroes in the midst of slaves as you propose to leave them at the end of the war; these men constitute the bone and sinew of our slaves, the able-bodied between 18 and 45. They will be men who know the value and power of combination; they will be well disciplined, trained to the use of arms, with the power and ability of command; at the same time they will be grossly and miserably ignorant, without any fixed principle of life or the ability of acquiring one. . . .

Sources 30 and 31 from McPherson, *The Negro's Civil War,* p. 244.

30. Howell Cobb, Speech in the Confederate Senate, 1864.

. . . if slaves will make good soldiers our whole theory of slavery is wrong. . . . The day you make soldiers of them is the beginning of the end of the revolution.

31. Robert Toombs, Speech in the Confederate Senate, 1864.

. . . the worst calamity that could befall us would be to gain our independence by the valor of our slaves. . . . The day that the army of Virginia allows a negro regiment to enter their lines as soldiers they will be degraded, ruined, and disgraced.

Source 32 from Durden, *The Gray and the Black, pp. 93–94.*

32. *Lynchburg* (Va.) *Republican,* November 2, 1864.

The proposition is so strange—so unconstitutional—so directly in conflict with all of our former practices and teachings—so entirely subversive of our social and political institutions—and so completely destructive of our liberties, that we stand completely appalled [and] dumfounded at its promulgation.

They propose that Congress shall conscribe two hundred and fifty thousand slaves, arm, equip and fight them in the field. As an inducement of them to be faithful, it is proposed that, at the end of the war, they shall have their freedom and live amongst us. "The conscription of negroes," says the *Enquirer,* "should be accompanied with freedom and the privilege of remaining in the States." This is the monstrous proposition. The South went to war to defeat the designs of the abolitionists, and behold! in the midst of the war, we turn abolitionists ourselves! We went to war because the Federal Congress kept eternally meddling with our domestic institutions, with which we contended they had nothing to do, and now we propose to end the war by asking the Confederate Congress to do precisely what Lincoln proposes to do—free our negroes and make them the equals of the white man! We have always been taught to believe that slaves are property, and under the exclusive control of the States and the courts. This new doctrine teaches us that

CHAPTER 10

THE PRICE FOR
VICTORY: THE
DECISION TO
USE BLACK
TROOPS

Congress has a right to free our negroes and make them the equals of their masters. . . .

Source 33 from Wiley, ed., *Letters of Warren Akin,* p. 117.

33. Mary V. Akin to Warren Akin, January 8, 1865.

. . . Every one I talk to is in favor of putting negros in the army and that *immediately.* Major Jones speaks very strongly in favor of it. I think slavery is now gone and what little there is left of it should be rendered as serviceable as possible and for that reason the negro men ought to be put to fighting and where some of them will be killed, if it is not done there will soon be more negroes than whites in the country and they will be the free race. I want to see them *got rid of soon.* . . .

Sources 34 through 36 from Durden, *The Gray and the Black,* pp. 163, 195, 202–203.

34. *Macon* (Ga.) *Telegraph and Confederate,* January 11, 1865.

Mr. Editor:

A lady's opinion may not be worth much in such an hour as this, but I cannot resist the temptation of expressing my approbation of "The crisis—the Remedy," copied from the Mobile Register. Would to God our Government would act upon its suggestions at once. The women of the South are not so in love with their negro property, as to wish to see husbands, fathers, sons, brothers, slain to protect it; nor would they submit to Yankee rule, could it secure to them a thousand waiting maids, whence now they possess one. . . .

35. *Richmond Whig,* February 28, 1865.

Mobile, Feb. 14—One of the largest meetings ever assembled in Mobile was held at the Theatre last night, which was presided over by Hon. Judge Forsyth.

Resolutions were unanimously adopted declaring our unalterable purpose to sustain the civil and military authorities to achieve independence—that our battle-cry henceforth should be—"Victory or Death"—that there is now no middle-ground between treachery and patriotism—that we still have an abiding confidence in our ability to achieve our independence—that the Government should immediately place one hundred thousand negroes in the field—that reconstruction is no longer an open question.

36. Confederate Congress, "An Act to Increase the Military Force of the Confederate States," March 13, 1865.

The Congress of the Confederate States of America do enact, That in order to provide additional forces to repel invasion, maintain the rightful possession of the Confederate States, secure their independence, and preserve their institutions, the President be, and he is hereby, authorized to ask for and accept from the owners of slaves, the services of such number of able-bodied negro men as he may deem expedient, for and during the war, to perform military service in whatever capacity he may direct.

Sec. 2. That the General-in-Chief be authorized to organize the said slaves into companies, battalions, regiments and brigades, under such rules and regulations as the Secretary of War may prescribe, and to be commanded by such officers as the President may appoint.

Sec. 3. That while employed in the service the said troops shall receive the same rations, clothing and compensation as are allowed to other troops in the same branch of the service.

Sec. 4. That if, under the previous sections of this act, the President shall not be able to raise a sufficient number of troops to prosecute the war successfully and maintain the sovereignty of the States and the independence of the Confederate States, then he is hereby authorized to call on each State, whenever he thinks it expedient, for her quota of 300,000 troops, in addition to those subject to military service under existing laws, or so many thereof as the President may deem necessary to be raised from such classes of the population, irrespective of color, in each State, as the proper authorities thereof may determine: *Provided,* that not more than twenty-five per cent of the male slaves between the ages of eighteen and forty-five, in any State, shall be called for under the provisions of this act.

Sec. 5. That nothing in this act shall be construed to authorize a change in the relation which the said slaves shall bear toward their owners, except by consent of the owners and of the States in which they may reside, and in pursuance of the laws thereof.

Approved March 13, 1865.

CHAPTER 10

THE PRICE FOR
VICTORY: THE
DECISION TO
USE BLACK
TROOPS

QUESTIONS TO CONSIDER

Begin by examining the evidence from the North. For each piece of evidence, answer the following questions:

1. Is the writer for or against using African Americans as soldiers?
2. What are the principal reasons for taking this position? (A piece of evidence may have more than one reason, as does Lincoln's September 13, 1862, reply to a delegation of Chicago Christians.)

At this point you will confront your first problem. Some pieces of evidence do not speak directly to the issue of enlisting African Americans as soldiers (two such examples are A. Davenport's letter or William Wells Brown's recollections, Sources 2 and 11). Yet are there implied reasons for or against arming African Americans? Included in these reasons may be unstated racial feelings (look again at Lincoln's September 13, 1862, remarks in Source 12), casualty figures (note when the casualties were suffered and consult the evidence for any shifts in the argument at that time), or political considerations.

The central figure in the decision of whether or not the United States should arm African Americans was Abraham Lincoln. In July 1862, Congress gave the president the authority to do so, yet Lincoln hesitated. How did members of Lincoln's cabinet attempt to influence his opinion in July–August 1862? What was Lincoln's reply?

President Lincoln's memorandum (Source 7) probably written after the July 22 cabinet meeting, appears to show a shift in his opinion. How does this compare with his remarks on August 3, 4 (Sources 8 and 9), and September 13, 1862? How would you explain this shift?

By January 1, 1863, the president had changed his public stance completely and was publicly on record as favoring taking African Americans into the United States Army (Source 15). Because President Lincoln did not live to write his memoirs and kept no diary, we are not sure what arguments or circumstances were responsible for the shift in his position. Yet a close examination of the evidence and some educated guesswork will allow you to come very close to the truth. Do Lincoln's letters to Hamlin and Schurz (Sources 13 and 14) provide any clues?

The remaining evidence from the North deals with northern reactions to Lincoln's decision (Sources 16 through 20). Was the decision a popular one in the army? Among private citizens? Can you detect a shift in northern white public opinion? Can you explain this shift?

Now repeat the same steps for the South (Sources 21 through 36). In what ways was the debate in the South similar to that in the North? In what ways was it different? Which reasons do you think were most influential in the Confederacy's change of mind about arming African Americans? How would you prove this?

EPILOGUE

Even after northern leaders adopted the policy that blacks would be recruited as soldiers in the Union army, many white northerners still doubted whether blacks would volunteer and, if they did, whether they would fight. Yet the evidence overwhelmingly demonstrates that African Americans rushed to the colors and were an effective part of the Union war effort. By the end of the Civil War, approximately 190,000 African American men had served in the United States Army and Navy, a figure that represents roughly 10 percent of all the North's fighting men throughout the entire war. Former slaves who had come within the Union lines during the war made up the majority of African American soldiers, and Louisiana, Kentucky, and Tennessee contributed the most African American soldiers to the Union cause (approximately 37 percent of the total), probably because these states had been occupied the longest by United States troops.

Black soldiers were employed by the Union largely in noncombat roles (to garrison forts, protect supply dumps and wagons, load and unload equipment and supplies, guard prison camps, etc.). Nevertheless, a number of black regiments saw combat, participating in approximately four hundred engagements, including thirty-nine major battles. African American casualties were high: more than one-third of the African American soldiers were killed or wounded, although the majority of deaths, as with white soldiers, came from disease rather than from battle wounds. The percent-age of desertions among African Americans was lower than for the army as a whole. Moreover, twenty-one black soldiers and sailors were awarded congressional medals of honor, the nation's most distinguished award to military personnel.

Yet there is another side to the story of African American service in the Union army and navy. African American volunteers were rigidly segregated, serving in all-black regiments, usually under white officers. At first black troops received less pay than their white counterparts. However, after many petitions and protests by African American soldiers, Congress at last established the principle of equal pay for African American soldiers in June 1864. Unfortunately, racial incidents within the Union army and navy were not uncommon.

Confederate reaction to the Union's recruitment of African American troops was predictably harsh. The Confederate government announced that any blacks taken as prisoners of war would be either shot on the spot or returned to slavery. In retaliation, Lincoln stated that he would order a Confederate prisoner of war executed for every African American prisoner shot by the South and would order a southern prisoner to do hard labor for every African American prisoner returned to slavery. Most Confederates treated black prisoners of war the same way they dealt with whites. Nevertheless, in several instances surrendering African Americans were murdered, the most notable

CHAPTER 10

THE PRICE FOR
VICTORY: THE
DECISION TO
USE BLACK
TROOPS

instance occurring at Fort Pillow, Tennessee, where apparently a number of African American prisoners of war were shot and others returned to slavery. Because it was impossible to obtain accurate information about what actually had occurred, Lincoln did not retaliate, even though a United States Senate investigating committee charged about three hundred African American black Union soldiers had been murdered. The president probably felt that any action on his part would only further inflame Confederates.

Within the Confederacy, the adoption of the policy to recruit African American soldiers came too late, the last gasp of a dying nation that had debated too long between principle and survival. In the month between the approval of the policy and the end of the war at Appomattox Court House, some black companies were organized, but there is no record that they ever saw action. For a conflict that had raged for four agonizingly long years, the end came relatively quickly.

The debate over the use of black troops points out what many abolitionists had maintained for years: although slavery was a moral concern that consumed all who touched it, the institution of slavery was but part of the problem facing black—and white—Americans. More insidious and less easily eradicated was racism, a set of assumptions, feelings, and emotions that survived long after slavery had been destroyed. The debate in both the North and the South over the use of black troops clearly demonstrates that the true problem confronting many people of the Civil War era was their own feelings, anxieties, and fears.

RECONSTRUCTING RECONSTRUCTION:
THE POLITICAL CARTOONIST AND
THE NATIONAL MOOD

THE PROBLEM

The Civil War took a tremendous toll on North and South alike. In the defeated South, more than one-fourth of all men who had borne arms for the Confederacy died, and an additional 15 percent were permanently disabled. Indeed, in 1865 Mississippi spent one-fifth of the state's total revenue on artificial arms and legs for Confederate veterans. Combined with the damage to agriculture, industry, and railroads, the human cost of the Civil War to the South was nearly catastrophic. For its part, the North had suffered frightful human losses as well, although proportionately less than those of the South.

And yet the Civil War, although appalling in its human, physical, and psychological costs, did settle some important issues that had plagued the nation for decades before that bloody conflict. First, the triumph of Union arms had established the United States as "one nation indivisible," from which no state could secede.[1] No less important, the "peculiar institution" of slavery was eradicated, and African Americans at last were free. In truth,

1. In response to President Benjamin Harrison's 1892 appeal for schoolchildren to mark the 400th anniversary of Columbus's discovery with patriotic exercises, Bostonian Francis Bellamy composed the pledge of allegiance to the American flag, from which the phrase "one nation indivisible" comes. In 1942, Congress made it the official pledge to the flag, and in 1954, Congress added the words "under God" in the middle of Bellamy's phrase.

CHAPTER 11

RECON-
STRUCTING
RECON-
STRUCTION: THE
POLITICAL
CARTOONIST
AND THE
NATIONAL MOOD

although the Civil War had been costly, the issues it settled were momentous.

The victory of the United States, however, raised at least as many questions as it settled. There was the question of what should happen to the defeated South. Should the states of the former Confederacy be permitted to take their natural place in the Union as quickly and smoothly as possible, with minimum concessions to their northern conquerors? Or should the North insist on a thorough reconstruction of the South, with new economic and social institutions to replace the old? Tied to this issue was the thorny constitutional question of whether the South actually had left the Union at all in 1861. If so, then the southern states in 1865 were territories, to be governed and administered by Congress. If not, then the Civil War had been an internal insurrection and the president, as Commander in Chief, would administer the South's re-entry into the Union.

Perhaps the most difficult question the Union's victory raised was the status of the former slaves. To be sure, they were no longer in bondage. But should they possess all the rights that whites had? Should they be assisted in becoming landowners; if not, how would they earn a living? Should they be allowed to vote and run for elective office? Indeed, no more complex and difficult issue confronted the country than the "place" of the newly freed slaves in the nation.

In all these questions, public opinion in the victorious North was a critical factor in shaping or altering the policies designed to reconstruct the South. Earlier democratic reforms made it unlikely that either the president or Congress could defy public opinion successfully. Yet public opinion can shift with remarkable speed, and political figures forever must be sensitive to its sometimes fickle winds.

Who shapes or reflects public opinion? In this chapter you will be examining and analyzing the work of one person who attempted to shape and reflect public opinion in the North: editorial cartoonist Thomas Nast (1840–1902). Clearly Thomas Nast was not the *only* person who attempted to influence or reflect public opinion in the North. In this chapter, however, you will be concentrating on his work, principally to see the influence of public opinion on governmental policy.

BACKGROUND

By early 1865, it was evident to most northerners and southerners that the Civil War was nearly over. While Grant was hammering at Lee's depleted forces in Virginia, Union general William Tecumseh Sherman broke the back of the Confederacy with his devastating march through Georgia and then northward into the Carolinas. Atlanta fell to Sherman's troops in September 1864, Savannah in December, and Charleston and Columbia, South Carolina, in February 1865. Two-thirds of Columbia lay in ashes. Meanwhile, General Philip Sheridan had driven the Confederates out of the Shenandoah Valley of Virginia, thus blocking any escape attempts by Lee and further cutting southern supply routes. The Union naval blockade of the South was taking its fearful toll, as parts of the dying Confederacy were facing real privation. Hence, although northern armies had suffered terrible losses, by 1865 they stood poised on the brink of victory.

In the South, all but the extreme die-hards recognized that defeat was inevitable. The Confederacy was suffering in more ways than militarily. The Confederate economy had almost completely collapsed, and Confederate paper money was nearly worthless. Slaves were abandoning their masters and mistresses in great numbers, running away to Union armies or roaming through the South in search of better opportunities. In many areas, civilian morale had almost totally deteriorated, and one Georgian wrote, "The people are soul-sick and heartily tired of the hateful, hopeless strife. . . . We have had enough of want and woe, of cruelty and carnage, enough of cripples and corpses."[2] As the Confederate government made secret plans to evacuate Richmond, most southerners knew that the end was very near.

Yet, even with victory almost in hand, many northerners had given little thought to what should happen after the war was over. Would southerners accept the changes that defeat would almost inevitably force on them (most especially the end of slavery)? What demands should the victors make upon the vanquished? Should the North assist the South in rebuilding after the devastation of war? If so, should the North dictate how that rebuilding, or reconstruction, should take place? What efforts should the North make to ensure that the former slaves were receiving the rights of free men and women? During the war, few northerners had seriously considered these questions. Now that victory was within their grasp, they could not avoid them.

One person who had been wrestling with these questions was Abraham Lincoln. In December 1863, the president announced his own plan for reconstructing the South, a plan in keeping with his later hope, as expressed in his second inaugural address, for "malice toward none; with charity for all; . . . Let us . . . bind up the nation's wounds."[3] In Lincoln's plan, a southern state could resume its normal activities in the Union as soon as 10 percent of the voters of 1860 had taken an oath of loyalty to the United States. High-ranking Confederate leaders would be excluded, and some blacks might gain the right to vote. No mention was made of protecting the civil rights of former slaves; it was presumed that this matter would be left to the slaves' former masters and mistresses.

To many northerners, later known as Radical Republicans, Lincoln's plan was much too lenient. In the opinion of these

2. The letter probably was written by Georgian Herschel V. Walker. See Allan Nevins, *The Organized War to Victory, 1864–1865,* Vol. IV of *The War for the Union* (New York: Charles Scribner's Sons, 1971), p. 221.

3. The full text of Lincoln's second inaugural address, delivered on March 4, 1865, can be found in Roy P. Basler, ed., *The Collected Works of Abraham Lincoln,* Vol. VIII (New Brunswick, NJ: Rutgers University Press, 1953), pp. 332–333.

CHAPTER 11

RECON-
STRUCTING
RECON-
STRUCTION: THE
POLITICAL
CARTOONIST
AND THE
NATIONAL MOOD

people, a number of whom had been abolitionists, the South, when conquered, should not be allowed to return to its former ways. Not only should slavery be eradicated, they claimed, but freed blacks should be assisted in their efforts to attain economic, social, and political equity. Most of the Radical Republicans favored education for African Americans, and some advocated carving the South's plantations into small parcels to be given to the freedmen. To implement these reforms, Radical Republicans wanted detachments of the United States Army to remain in the South and favored the appointment of provisional governors to oversee the transitional governments in the southern states. Lincoln approved plans for the Army to stay and supported the idea of provisional governors. But he opposed the more far-reaching reform notions of the Radical Republicans, and as president he was able to block them.

In addition to having diametrically opposed views of Reconstruction, Lincoln and the Radical Republicans differed over the constitutional question of which branch of the federal government would be responsible for the reconstruction of the South. The Constitution made no mention of secession, reunion, or reconstruction. But Radical Republicans, citing passages in the Constitution giving Congress the power to guarantee each state a republican government, insisted that the reconstruction of the South should be carried out by Congress.[4] For his part,

however, Lincoln maintained that as chief enforcer of the law and as Commander in Chief, the president was the appropriate person to be in charge of Reconstruction. Clearly a stalemate was in the making, with Radical Republicans calling for a more reform-minded Reconstruction policy and Lincoln continuing to block them.

President Lincoln's death on April 15, 1865 (one week after Lee's surrender at Appomattox Court House)[5] brought Vice President Andrew Johnson to the nation's highest office. At first, Radical Republicans had reason to hope that the new president would follow policies more to their liking. A Tennessean, Johnson had risen to political prominence from humble circumstances, had become a spokesperson for the common white men and women of the South, and had opposed the planter aristocracy. Upon becoming president, he excluded from amnesty all former Confederate political and military leaders as well as all southerners who owned taxable property worth more than $20,000 (an obvious slap at his old planter-aristocrat foes). Moreover, Johnson issued a proclamation setting up provisional military governments in the conquered South and told his cabinet he favored black suffrage, although as a states' rightist he insisted that states adopt the measure voluntarily. At the outset, then, Johnson appeared to be all the Radical Republicans wanted, preferable to the more moderate Lincoln.

Yet it did not take Radical Republi-

4. See Article IV, Section 4, of the Constitution. Later Radical Republicans also justified their position using the Thirteenth Amendment, adopted in 1865, which gave Congress the power to enforce the amendment ending slavery in the South.

5. The last Confederate army to give up, commanded by General Joseph Johnston, surrendered to Sherman at Durham Station, North Carolina, on April 18, 1865.

cans long to realize that President Johnson was not one of them. Although he spoke harshly, he pardoned hundreds of former Confederates who quickly captured control of southern state governments and congressional delegations. Many northerners were shocked to see former Confederate generals, officials, and even former Confederate vice president Alexander Stephens returned to Washington. The new southern state legislatures passed a series of laws, known collectively as black codes, that so severely restricted the rights of former slaves that they were all but slaves again. Moreover, Johnson privately told southerners that he opposed the Fourteenth Amendment to the Constitution, which was intended to confer full civil rights on the newly freed slaves. He also used his veto power to block Radical Republican Reconstruction measures in Congress and seemed to do little to combat the general defiance of the former Confederacy (exhibited in many forms, including insults thrown at Union occupation soldiers, the desecration of the United States flag, and the formation of organized resistance groups such as the Ku Klux Klan).

To an increasing number of northerners, the unrepentant spirit of the South and Johnson's acquiescence to it were nothing short of appalling. Had the Civil War been fought for nothing? Had more than 364,000 federal soldiers died in vain? White southerners were openly defiant, African Americans were being subjugated by white southerners and virtually ignored by President Johnson, and former Confederates were returning to positions of power and prominence. Radical Republicans had sufficient power in Con-

gress to pass harsher measures, but Johnson kept vetoing them, and the Radicals lacked the votes to override his vetoes.[6] Indeed, the impasse that had existed before Lincoln's death continued.

In such an atmosphere, the congressional elections of 1866 were bitterly fought campaigns, especially in the northern states. President Johnson traveled throughout the North, defending his moderate plan of Reconstruction and viciously attacking his political enemies. However, the Radical Republicans were even more effective. Stirring up the hostilities of wartime, they "waved the bloody shirt" and excited northern voters by charging that the South had never accepted its defeat and that the 364,000 Union dead and 275,000 wounded would be for nothing if the South was permitted to continue its arrogant and stubborn behavior. Increasingly, Johnson was greeted by hostile audiences as the North underwent a major shift in public opinion.

The Radical Republicans won a stunning victory in the congressional elections of 1866 and thus broke the stalemate between Congress and the president. Armed with enough votes to override Johnson's vetoes almost at will, the new Congress proceeded rapidly to implement the Radical Republican vision of Reconstruction. The South was divided into five military districts to be ruled by martial law. Southern states had to ratify the Fourteenth Amendment and institute black suffrage before being allowed to take their formal places in the Union.

6. Congress was able to override Johnson's vetoes of the Civil Rights Act and a revised Freedmen's Bureau bill.

CHAPTER 11

RECON-
STRUCTING
RECON-
STRUCTION: THE
POLITICAL
CARTOONIST
AND THE
NATIONAL MOOD

The Freedmen's Bureau, founded earlier, was given additional federal support to set up schools for African Americans, negotiate labor contracts, and, with the military, help monitor elections. Only the proposal to give land to blacks was not adopted, being seen as too extreme by even some Radical Republicans. Congressional Reconstruction had begun.

President Johnson, however, had not been left completely powerless. Determined to undercut the Radical Republicans' Reconstruction policies, he issued orders increasing the powers of civil governments in the South and removed military officers who were enforcing Congress' will, replacing them with commanders less determined to protect black voting rights and more willing to turn the other way when disqualified white southerners voted. Opposed most vigorously by his own secretary of war, Edwin Stanton, Johnson tried to discharge Stanton. To an increasing number of Radicals, the president would have to be removed from office.

In 1868, the House of Representatives voted to impeach Andrew Johnson. Charged with violating the Tenure of Office Act and the Command of the Army Act (both of which had been passed over Johnson's vetoes), the president was tried in the Senate, where two-thirds of the senators would have to vote against Johnson for him to be removed.[7] The vast majority of senators disagreed with the president's Reconstruction policies, yet they feared that impeachment had become a politi-

cal tool that, if successful, threatened to destroy the balance of power between the branches of the federal government. The vote on removal fell one short of the necessary two-thirds, and Johnson was spared the indignity of removal. Nevertheless, the Republican nomination of General Ulysses Grant and his subsequent landslide victory (running as a military hero, Grant carried twenty-six out of thirty-four states) gave Radical Republicans a malleable president, one who, although not a Radical himself, could assure the continuation of their vision of Reconstruction.[8]

By 1872, a renewed Democratic party believed it had a chance to oust Grant and the Republicans. The Grant administration had been rocked by a series of scandals, some involving men quite close to the president. Although honest himself, Grant lost a good deal of popularity by defending the culprits and naively aiding in a cover-up of the corruption. These actions, along with some of his other policies, triggered a revolt within the Republican party, in which a group calling themselves Liberal Republicans bolted the party ranks and nominated well-known editor and reformer Horace Greeley to oppose Grant for the presidency.[9] Hoping for a coalition to defeat Grant, the Democrats also nominated the controversial Greeley.

8. Southern states, where the Democratic party had been strong, in 1868 either were not in the Union or were under the control of Radical Reconstruction governments. Grant's victory therefore was not as sweeping as it first appears.

9. See Volume 1, Chapter 10, for a discussion of Greeley's position on the emancipation of slaves in 1862.

7. See Article I, Sections 2 and 3, of the Constitution.

Greeley's platform was designed to attract as many disparate groups of voters as possible to the Liberal Republican–Democratic political fold. Greeley favored civil service reform, the return to a "hard money" fiscal policy, and the reservation of western lands for settlers rather than for large land companies. He vowed an end to corruption in government. But the most dramatic part of Greeley's message was his call for an end to the bitterness of the Civil War, a thinly veiled promise to bring an end to Radical Reconstruction in the South. For their part, Radical Republicans attacked Greeley as the tool of die-hard southerners and labeled him as the candidate of white southern bigots and northern urban Irish immigrants manipulated by political machines. They took one of Greeley's phrases, "Let us shake hands over the bloody chasm" (a phrase with which Greeley intended to state his hope for an end to sectional hostilities), and warped that utterance almost beyond recognition. By contrast, Grant was labeled as a great war hero and a friend of blacks and whites alike. The incumbent Grant won easily, capturing 55 percent of the popular vote and 286 electoral votes. Greeley died soon after the exhausting campaign.

Gradually, however, the zeal of Radical Republicanism began to fade. An increasing number of northerners grew tired of the issue. With their commitment to full civil rights for African Americans never strong, they had voted into office Radical Republicans more out of anger at southern intransigence than out of any lofty notions of black equality. Hence northerners said little when, one by one, southern Dem-

ocrats returned to power in the states of the former Confederacy.[10] As a mark of how little their own attitudes had changed in the years since the Civil War, white southerners labeled these native Democrats "Redeemers." Yet, as long as southern Democrats made no overt moves to subvert the rights of African Americans, most northerners were willing to put the whole agony of Reconstruction behind them. Hence, although much that was fruitful and beneficial was accomplished in the South during the Reconstruction period (most notably black suffrage and public education), some of this was to be temporary, and many opportunities for progress were lost. By the presidential election of 1876, both candidates (Rutherford B. Hayes and Samuel Tilden) promised an end to Reconstruction, and the Radical Republican experiment, to all intents and purposes, was over.

It is clear that northern public opinion from 1865 to 1876 was not static but was almost constantly shifting. This public opinion was influenced by a number of factors, among them speeches, newspapers, and word of mouth. Especially influential were editorial cartoons, which captured the issues visually, often simplifying them so that virtually everyone could understand them. Perhaps the master of this style was Thomas Nast, a political

10. Southerners regained control of the state governments in Tennessee and Virginia in 1869, North Carolina in 1870, Georgia in 1871, Arkansas and Alabama in 1874, and Mississippi in early 1876. By the presidential election of 1876, only South Carolina, Louisiana, and Florida were still controlled by Reconstruction governments.

CHAPTER 11

RECON-
STRUCTING
RECON-
STRUCTION: THE
POLITICAL
CARTOONIST
AND THE
NATIONAL MOOD

cartoonist whose career, principally with *Harper's Weekly,* spanned the tumultuous years of the Civil War and Reconstruction. Throughout his career, Nast produced more than 3,000 cartoons, illustrations for books, and paintings. He is credited with originating the modern depiction of Santa Claus, the Republican elephant, and the Democratic donkey. Congratulating themselves for having hired Nast, the editors of *Harper's Weekly* once exclaimed that each of Nast's drawings was at once "a poem and a speech."

Apparently Thomas Nast developed his talents early in life. Born in the German Palatinate (one of the German states) in 1840, Nast was the son of a musician in the Ninth Regiment Bavarian Band. The family moved to New York City in 1846, at which time young Thomas was enrolled in school. It seems that art was his only interest—one teacher admonished him, "Go finish your picture. You will never learn to read or figure." After unsuccessfully trying to interest their son in music, his parents eventually encouraged the development of his artistic talent. By the age of fifteen, Thomas Nast was drawing illustrations for *Frank Leslie's Illustrated Newspaper.* He joined *Harper's Weekly* in 1862 (at the age of twenty-two), where he developed the cartoon style that was to win him a national reputation, as well as enemies: He received praise from Abraham Lincoln, Ulysses Grant, and Samuel Clemens (also known as Mark Twain, who in 1872 asked Nast to do the illustrations for one of his books so that "then I will have good pictures"). On the other hand, one of Nast's favorite targets, political boss

William Marcy Tweed of New York's Tammany Hall, once shouted, "Let's stop these damn pictures. I don't care so much what the papers say about me—my constituents can't read; but damn it, they can see pictures!"

It is obvious from his work that Thomas Nast was a man of strong feelings and emotions. In his eyes, those people whom he admired possessed no flaws. Conversely, those whom he opposed were, to him, capable of every conceivable villainy. As a result, his characterizations were often terribly unfair, gross distortions of reality, and more than occasionally libelous. In his view, however, his central purpose was not to entertain but to move his audiences, to make them scream out in outrage or anger, to prod them to action. The selection of Nast's cartoons in this chapter therefore is typical of the body of his work for *Harper's Weekly*: artistically inventive and polished, blatantly slanted, and brimming with indignation and emotion.

Your task in this chapter is to analyze Nast's cartoons and read the appropriate material in your textbook to answer the following questions:

1. How did Nast attempt to influence public opinion in the North regarding Reconstruction?
2. Did Nast change his views regarding Reconstruction between 1865 and 1876? Did public opinion change? How (if at all)?
3. How did public opinion in the North, as reflected in the work of Thomas Nast, influence public policy (if at all)?

To complete the assignment, you should do the following:

1. Read the introduction to this chapter and supplementary texts carefully to identify the principal issues of Reconstruction. You should make a list of those issues.
2. Examine closely the cartoons presented to determine where Nast stood on those issues.
3. Compare where public opinion in the North stood on those issues *at different times* during Reconstruction with how Nast stood *at different times*.
4. Compare shifting public opinion with changing government policies

regarding Reconstruction, in an attempt to measure the impact of public opinion on policymakers.

Public opinion is not always easy to measure. But we do have certain clues. Election results, for example, are a good gauge of public opinion, as are audience responses to speakers (recall the audiences that President Johnson faced in 1866). As you read, looking for public opinion, be sensitive to these clues.

THE METHOD

Although Thomas Nast developed the political cartoon into a true art form, cartoons and caricatures had a long tradition both in Europe and America before Nast. English artists helped bring forth the cartoon style that eventually made *Punch* (founded in 1841) one of the liveliest-illustrated periodicals on both sides of the Atlantic. In America, Benjamin Franklin is traditionally credited with publishing the first newspaper cartoon in 1754, the multidivided snake (each part of the snake representing one colony) with the ominous warning "Join or Die." By the time Andrew Jackson sought the presidency, the political cartoon had become a regular and popular feature of American political life. Crude by modern standards, these cartoons influenced some people far more than did the printed word.

As we noted, the political cartoon, like the newspaper editorial, is intended to do more than objectively report events. It is meant to express an opinion, a point of view. Cartoons often praise or ridicule. Those who create them want to move people, anger them, make them laugh, or spur them to action. In short, political cartoons are poor devices for learning what is happening, but they are excellent devices for portraying popular reaction to what is happening.

How, then, can we analyze political cartoons? First, cartoons almost always portray events. As you examine the cartoons in this chapter, try to determine what event is being portrayed. Often a cartoon's caption, dialogue, or other clues will help you discover the event in question. By careful scrutiny, you can discern what the car-

CHAPTER 11

RECON-
STRUCTING
RECON-
STRUCTION: THE
POLITICAL
CARTOONIST
AND THE
NATIONAL MOOD

toonist's opinion of the event is. Is the cartoonist approving or disapproving? How did you reach that conclusion?

Examine the people in each cartoon. Is the cartoonist aiming for a true likeness? Is he or she portraying the people sympathetically or unsympathetically? Nast often placed his characters out of their historical context (in Roman circuses, for example). Why did he do this? What did he intend to show? Sometimes cartoonists accentuate their subjects' physical features. Why do they do this?

After you examine a cartoon in detail, try to determine the message the cartoonist is trying to convey. What reactions does he or she hope those who see the cartoon will have? What do you think people's reactions might have been at the time the cartoon was published?

Before you begin the exercises in this chapter, familiarize yourself with both the method discussed above and Nast by making a "trial run" on one of Nast's cartoons on another subject, that of public subsidy of private schools.

In 1868, the New York state legislature ruled that public funds could be made available to private schools. Most of the schools that benefited from this law were parochial schools of the Roman Catholic Church. Shortly thereafter, Roman Catholics complained about the compulsory use of the King James Version of the Bible in public schools.

The cartoon in Source 1 appeared in *Harper's Weekly* on September 30, 1871. It graphically shows Nast's opinion on the issue. Examine the cartoon carefully. How are Roman Catholic clergymen portrayed? In the upper right, who is the woman being led to the gallows, and who is leading her? To the left of that, who are the adults at the top of the cliff, and what are they doing? In what condition are the public schools? What is Tammany Hall (upper left), and what is the building intended to look like? In the foreground, what is stuck in the largest child's coat? What are the children's reactions? Finally, what was Thomas Nast's opinion of Tammany Hall? The Irish Americans? The New York state legislature? The Roman Catholic Church? What feelings was Nast trying to elicit from those who saw this cartoon?

As you can see, a political cartoon must be analyzed to the most minute detail to get the full meaning the cartoonist is trying to convey. From that analysis, one can discover the creator's full meaning or message and can imagine the emotions the cartoon was likely to evoke.

Now you are ready to begin your analysis of the Reconstruction period through the cartoons of Thomas Nast. As you analyze each cartoon, be aware of the collective message of *all* the cartoons. Most subscribers to *Harper's Weekly* saw all the cartoons. What was their general reaction likely to be?

Sources 1 through 13 from Morton Keller, *The Art and Politics of Thomas Nast* (New York: Oxford University Press, 1968), plates 108; 55 and 56; 22; 17; 27; 32; 47; 50; 38; 196; 197; 155; and 209, respectively. Courtesy of the publisher.

1.

THE AMERICAN RIVER GANGES.

THE PRIESTS AND THE CHILDREN.—[SEE PAGE 913.]

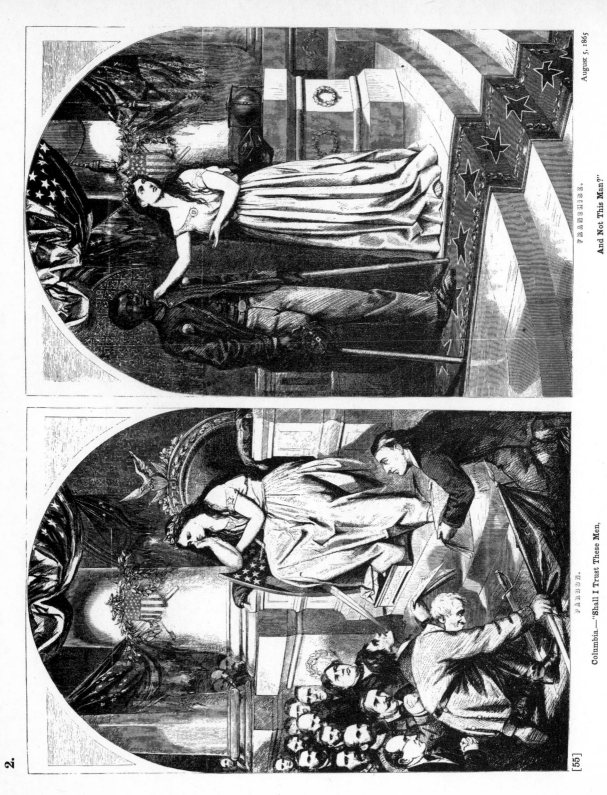

2.

FRANCHISE.

And Not This Man?"

August 5, 1865

PARDON.

Columbia.—"Shall I Trust These Men,

[55]

THE CONTRAST OF SUFFERING ANDERSONVILLE & FORTRESS MONROE.

TREASON MUST   BE MADE ODIOUS.

June 30, 1866

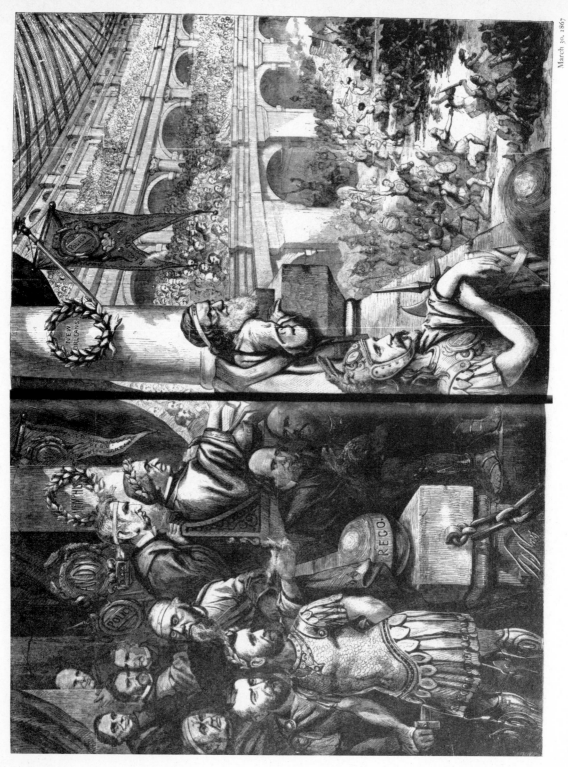

March 30, 1867

Amphitheatrum Johnsonianum—Massacre of the Innocents
At New Orleans, July 30, 1866.

September 5, 1868

"This Is a White Man's Government."

"We regard the Reconstruction Acts (so called) of Congress as usurpations, and unconstitutional, revolutionary, and void."—*Democratic Platform.*

October 3, 1868

The Modern Samson.

August 3, 1872

Baltimore 1861–1872.

"Let Us Clasp Hands over the Bloody Chasm."

CHAPTER 11

RECON-
STRUCTING
RECON-
STRUCTION: THE
POLITICAL
CARTOONIST
AND THE
NATIONAL MOOD

8.

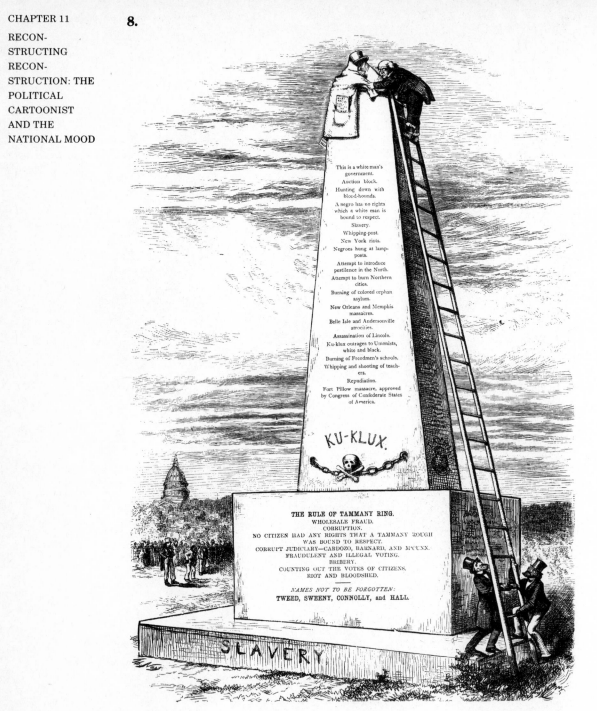

September 7, 1872

The Whited Sepulchre.

Covering the monument of infamy with his white hat and coat.

April 13, 1872

The Republic Is Not Ungrateful.

"It is not what is *charged* but what is *proved* that damages the party defendant. Any one may be accused of the most heinous offenses; the Saviour of mankind was not only arraigned but convicted; but what of it? Facts alone are decisive."—*New York Tribune*, March 13, 1872.

CHAPTER 11

RECON-
STRUCTING
RECON-
STRUCTION: THE
POLITICAL
CARTOONIST
AND THE
NATIONAL MOOD

10.

March 14, 1874

Colored Rule in a Reconstructed (?) State.

(THE MEMBERS CALL EACH OTHER THIEVES, LIARS, RASCALS, AND COWARDS.)

COLUMBIA. "You are aping the lowest whites. If you disgrace your race in this way you had better take back seats."

September 26, 1874

The Commandments in South Carolina.

"We've pretty well smashed that; but I suppose, Massa Moses, you can get another one."

CHAPTER 11
RECON-
STRUCTING
RECON-
STRUCTION: THE
POLITICAL
CARTOONIST
AND THE
NATIONAL MOOD

12.

December 9, 1876

The Ignorant Vote—Honors Are Easy.

13.

October 24, 1874

A Burden He Has To Shoulder.
And they say, "He wants a third term."

Source 14 from J. Chal Vinson, *Thomas Nast, Political Cartoonist* (Athens: University of Georgia Press, 1967).

14.

A review of the process you must use to complete this exercise is helpful. First, identify the principal issues of the Reconstruction period. Second, determine where Nast stood on each issue. Third, determine the extent to which Nast's cartoons reflect a changing public opinion in the North regarding Reconstruction. And fourth, compare shifting public opinion with governmental policy changes in an attempt to measure the impact of public opinion on government policies.

The process readily lends itself to a chart:

Issues:

_____

Nast's Position:

_____

How Northern Public Opinion Changed, As Reflected by Nast's Cartoons:

_____

Impact of Public Opinion on Government:

_____

A close reading of the introduction to this chapter and supplementary texts will provide the data for the first row, and an examination of Nast's cartoons will help you fill in the second row. Then, by comparing the first and second rows, you should be able to answer the question of how Nast's cartoons can be used to gain insight into shifts in northern public opinion regarding Reconstruction. The fourth row will require you to compare public opinion (as reflected in Nast's work) with your reading on shifting Reconstruction policies.

Sources 2 through 4 represent Nast's views of Reconstruction under President Andrew Johnson. Sources 5 and 6 deal with an issue crucial to Radical Republicans. Sources 7 and 8 focus on the presidential election of 1872, and Sources 9 through 13 evaluate Radical Reconstruction in its latter years. You will be examining these cartoons in these four groupings to determine shifts in northern public opinion regarding Reconstruction.

Source 2 must first be examined for its symbolism. Who is Columbia? What emotions do her two different poses suggest? Who are the people asking for pardon in the first frame? Now look carefully at the black man in the second frame. Who does he represent? Can you formulate one sentence that summarizes the message of both parts of Source 2?

Source 3 is more complex: two drawings within two other drawings. If you do not already know what purpose Andersonville and Fortress Monroe served, consult a text on this time period, an encyclopedia, or a good Civil War history book. Then look at the upper left and upper right outside drawings. Contrast the appearance of the man entering with the man leaving. Now examine the lower left and lower right outside drawings the same way. What was Nast trying to tell? The larger inside drawings explain the contrast. What were the conditions like at Andersonville? At Fortress Monroe? What did the cartoonist think were the physical and psychological results?

Source 4 also must be examined for its symbolism. Who is the emperor? What is the amphitheater intended to

CHAPTER 11

RECON-
STRUCTING
RECON-
STRUCTION: THE
POLITICAL
CARTOONIST
AND THE
NATIONAL MOOD

represent? Who is the person in the lower left intended to represent? On July 30, 1866, several blacks attending a Radical Republican convention in New Orleans were shot and killed by white policemen. How did Nast react to this event? What did he think caused it? How is President Andrew Johnson portrayed with regard to what is taking place?

Each of the three people standing in Source 5 represents part of the Democratic Party coalition, and each has something to contribute to the party. Can you identify the groups that the man on the right and the man in the center represent? What do they offer the party? Notice the facial features of the man on the left as well as his dress, particularly the hatband from Five Points (a notorious slum section of New York City). Who is this man supposed to represent, and what does he give the party? Notice what the black man lying on the ground has dropped. What does he represent? What is he reaching for? What is happening in the background of the cartoon?

Source 6 also explores the question of rights for freed blacks, this time within the setting of the well-known story of Samson and Delilah. Who is Nast's Delilah, and what has she done? Who are her supporters at the left? What other things do they advocate? Now look carefully at the figure in the upper right-hand corner. Who is he? What has he promised African Americans? What has he done?

Sources 7 through 9 were published just before the presidential election of 1872. Who is the plump little man with the white beard and glasses who appears in all three cartoons?

What part of this character's campaign did Nast find especially objectionable? Why? What is wrong with what the character is trying to do? (Because these cartoons show many reasons for Nast's disgust, it is helpful to keep a list as you study each cartoon separately.) On the other hand, who is portrayed in Source 9? To whom is he linked?

Sources 10 through 13 reflect Nast's thinking in the latter years of Reconstruction. Sources 10 and 11 portray his opinion of Reconstruction in South Carolina, presided over by Radical Republican Governor Franklin J. Moses (caricatured in Source 11). How are African Americans pictured (compare to Sources 2, 5, and 6)? To whom are African Americans compared in Source 12? What does this say about Nast's opinion on Reconstruction? Source 13 portrays President Ulysses Grant (compare to Sources 4 and 9). How is he pictured?

The last cartoon (Source 14) shows Nast's opinion of the South in 1876, near the end of Reconstruction. What scene was Nast re-creating? What is the significance of this scene? How is the black man depicted? What was Nast trying to show? How would you compare or contrast this cartoon with Sources 10 through 12? What does this tell you about Nast's views?

You should now return to the central questions asked earlier and to your text on Reconstruction. How did Nast attempt to influence public opinion in the North regarding Reconstruction? Did Nast change his views on Reconstruction? Did the general public in the North change its views? How did public opinion in the North influence public policy on Reconstruction?

Undoubtedly Nast's work had an important impact on northern opinion of Reconstruction, the Democratic Party, Horace Greeley, the Irish Americans, and other issues as well. Yet gradually northern ardor began to decline as other issues and concerns eased Reconstruction out of the limelight and as it appeared that the crusade to reconstruct the South would be an endless one. Radical Republicans, who insisted on equality for the freed slaves, received less and less attention, and southern Democrats, who regained control of southern state governments, were essentially allowed a free hand as long as they did not obviously violate the Constitution and federal law. By 1877, the South was once again in the hands of white Democrats.

Yet as long as African Americans did not insist on their rights, white southern leaders allowed them to retain, in principle, all that the Civil War and Reconstruction had won. In other words, as long as black voters did not challenge the Redeemers, they were allowed to retain their political rights. Economically, many African Americans gradually slipped into the status of tenant farmer, sharecropper, or even peon. The political structure, local courts, and law-enforcement agencies tended to support this arrangement. For his part, African American leader Booker T. Washington was praised by white southerners for urging that blacks seek education and economic opportunities but not "rock the boat" politically in the white-controlled South. Finally, in the late 1880s, when white southerners real-

ized that the Reconstruction spirit had waned in the North, southern state legislatures began instituting rigid segregation of schools, public transportation and accommodations, parks, restaurants and theaters, elevators, drinking fountains, and so on. Not until the 1950s did those chains begin to be broken.

As the reform spirit waned in the latter years of Reconstruction, Nast's popularity suffered. The public appeared to tire of his anger, his self-righteousness, his relentless crusades. The new publisher of *Harper's Weekly* sought to make the magazine less political, and in that atmosphere there was no place for Nast. He resigned in 1886.

Nast continued to free-lance for a number of magazines and tried unsuccessfully to start his own periodical, *Nast's Weekly*. Financially struggling, he appealed to friends, who influenced President Theodore Roosevelt to appoint Nast to a minor consular post in Ecuador. He died there of yellow fever in 1902.

Yet Thomas Nast was a pioneer of a tradition and of a political art form. His successors, people such as Herbert Block (Herblock), Bill Mauldin, Oliphant, and even Garry Trudeau ("Doonesbury"), have continued to prick the American conscience, fret and irritate newspaper readers, and assert through their art the proposition that no evildoer can escape the scrutiny and ultimate justice of the popular will. Sometimes these successors are effective, sometimes not.

Acknowledgments continued from page iv.

Source 8: Portuguese oil on panel, 1550. Museu National de Arte Antiga, Lisbon.

Source 9: German engraving, 1590. Library of Congress/Rare Book Division.

Source 10: German engraving, 1591. Library of Congress/Rare Book Division.

Source 11: German engraving, 1591 (Vespucci discovering America). Metropolitan Museum of Art.

Source 14: French engraving, 1579–1600 (America personified). New York Historical Society.

Source 15: English watercolor, 1585. British Museum.

Source 16: English watercolor, 1585. British Museum.

CHAPTER TWO

Source 1: Reprinted by permission of Harvard University Press from *The History of the Colony and Province of Massachusetts Bay*, Vol. II, pp. 11, 366–391. Copyright © 1936 by the President and Fellows of Harvard College.

CHAPTER THREE

Map of Massachusetts: Courtesy of the John Carter Brown Library at Brown University.

Sources 2, 4–6, 12, 15–17: Reprinted from Philip J. Greven, Jr.: *Four Generations: Population, Land, and Family in Colonial Andover, Massachusetts.* Copyright © 1970 by Cornell University. Used by permission of the publisher, Cornell University Press.

Sources 3, 6, 8–10, 14, 17, 19: Excerpts from *The Minutemen and Their World* by Robert A. Gross. Copyright © 1976 by Robert A. Gross. Reprinted by permission of Farrar, Straus & Giroux, Inc.

Sources 7, 11, 13: Data from *The Evolution of American Society, 1700–1815* by James A. Henretta. Copyright © 1973 by D. C. Heath and Company. Reprinted by permission of the publisher.

Sources 18, 20–22: Reprinted from *The Journal of Interdisciplinary History*, VI (1976), 549, 557, 564, with permission of the editors of *The Journal of Interdisciplinary History* and The MIT Press, Cambridge, Massachusetts. © 1976 by the Massachusetts Institute of Technology and the editors of *The Journal of Interdisciplinary History*.

CHAPTER FOUR

Source 3: Reprinted by permission of Harvard University Press from *The Legal Papers of John Adams*, Vol. III, pp. 46–98. The Belknap Press of Harvard University Press. Copyright © 1965 by the President and Fellows of Harvard College.

Source 6: Paul Revere's engraving of the Boston Massacre. American Antiquarian Society.

CHAPTER FIVE

Sources 8–9: Figures from "The Best Poor Man's Country: Living Standards of the 'Lower Sort' in Late Eighteenth Century Philadelphia," calculated in *Working Papers from the Regional Economic History Research Center*, copyright 1979, pp. 57–70. Reprinted by permission of Eleutherian Mills-Hagley Foundation.

Sources 13–14: Excerpts from *Letters of Benjamin Rush*, Vol. II, edited by L. H. Butterfield, American Philosophical Society, 1951, pp. 644–645, 657–658. Reprinted by permission.

ACKNOWL-
EDGMENTS

CHAPTER SEVEN

Sources 3, 5, 12, 15: Museum of American Textile History.

Source 14: Mildred C. Tunis.

CHAPTER EIGHT

Sources 1–16: From *Lay My Burden Down: A Folk History of Slavery* from Federal Writer's Project, by B. A. Botkin. Copyright 1945. Reprinted by permission.

Sources 22–23: Songs from S. Stuckey, "Through the Prism of Folklore," *Massachusetts Review*, 1968, reprinted by permission of the Editors of *Massachusetts Review*.

Source 24: From *Narrative of the Life of Frederick Douglass* by Frederick Douglass, pp. 1–3, 13–15, 36–37, 40–41, 44–46, and 74–75. Copyright 1963 by Doubleday. Reprinted by permission of Doubleday, a division of Bantam, Doubleday, Dell Publishing Group, Inc.

Source 25: Excerpts from *Incidents in the Life of a Slave Girl* by Linda Brent and edited by Walter Magnes Teller, copyright © 1973 by Walter Magnes Teller, reprinted by permission of Harcourt Brace Jovanovich, Inc.

CHAPTER NINE

Sources 7–8, 11–15, 18: From Glenn W. Price, *Origins of the War with Mexico: The Polk-Stockton Intrigue*, pp. 48, 11–12, 118, 119, 122, 129–130, 131–132. Copyright 1967. Reprinted by permission of University of Texas Press.

CHAPTER TEN

Sources 1, 3, 10, 28, 30–31: Excerpts from pages 33, 162, 243–244 from James McPherson, *The Negro's Civil War*, reprinted by courtesy of Pantheon Books, a Division of Random House, Inc.

Sources 4, 7, 9, 13–15: From *The Collected Works of Abraham Lincoln* edited by Roy P. Basler. Copyright © 1953 by the Abraham Lincoln Association. Reprinted by permission of Rutgers University Press.

Source 20: Selections are reprinted from *The Sable Arm: Negro Troops in the Union Army, 1861–1865*, by Dudley Taylor Cornish, by permission of W. W. Norton & Company, Inc. Copyright © 1966 by W. W. Norton & Company, Inc. Copyright © 1956 by Dudley Taylor Cornish.

Sources 23–26, 29, 32, 34–36: From Robert F. Durden, *The Gray and the Black*. Reprinted by permission of the publisher, Louisiana State University Press.

Source 27, 33: Reprinted by permission of the University of Georgia Press from *Letters of Warren Akin, Confederate Congressman*, edited by Bell Irwin Wiley. Copyright 1959 UGA Press.